Praise for Ingrid Newkirk and *Making Kind Choices*

"As this book explores, acts of kindness, even in the simplest ways, are what make our lives meaningful, bringing happiness to ourselves and others."
—The Dalai Lama

"Ingrid Newkirk is not only a thoughtful animal rights and environmental activist, she is an inspirational leader. A heroine. A woman upon whom so many depend, around the world, for information and guidance. In a world where all animals, everywhere, are more threatened than ever, Ingrid Newkirk is their champion."
—Alec Baldwin

"Ingrid Newkirk's wonderful new book is about us—about how in a world so violent and cruel, there is no way to pretend we're kind people unless we extend our kindness to those who are the most innocent and helpless. Animals, be they in our homes or in the wild, are always the canary in the mineshaft as to how we treat one another."
—Bill Maher

"Ingrid Newkirk writes as she lives—with integrity, conviction, courage, and humor. These qualities, along with her innate grace, allow her to operate successfully in a profession that would not only break my heart, but send me to the funny farm. Thank you, God, for this remarkable woman, and thank you, Ingrid, for this remarkable book."
—Rue McClanahan

"Ingrid Newkirk's new book is a must-read, filled with simple and easy-to-follow roads to kindness. Her sensitivity and compassion jump out

from the pages. She is a hero for the animals; she is a cultural hero; she is my hero."
—Russell Simmons

"This powerful book offers easy ways to make your compassionate mark on the world. Parts of the book made me smile and parts made me wistful, but all of it is very useful. I like it!"
—Moby

"Thanks, Ingrid, for being such an animal friend and adviser."
—Bea Arthur

Making Kind Choices

Also by

INGRID NEWKIRK

250 Things You Can Do to Make Your Cat Adore You

The PETA Celebrity Vegan Cookbook

Making Kind Choices

Everyday Ways to Enhance Your Life Through Earth- and Animal-Friendly Living

INGRID NEWKIRK

FOREWORD BY SIR PAUL McCARTNEY

ST. MARTIN'S GRIFFIN NEW YORK

 For information, address St. Martin's Press, 175 Fifth Avenue, New York, N.Y. 10010.

www.stmartins.com

Book design by Jennifer Ann Daddio

Grateful acknowledgment is made to the following for granting permission to reprint previously published material:

Recipe for Mushroom Pâtė from *American Wholefoods Cuisine* by Nikki and David Goldbeck (www.healthyhighways.com). Copyright © Nikki and David Goldbeck.

Excerpt from the poem "Baggage" by Evelyn Colbath. Reprinted by permission of the author.

Recipe for Golden Tofu Strips from *Virtues of Soy: A Practical Health Guide and Cookbook* by Monique N. Gilbert (www.virtuesofsoy.com). Copyright © Monique N. Gilbert. All rights reserved.

Excerpt from "Samson Agonistes" by Ogden Nash. Copyright © 1942 by Ogden Nash, renewed. Reprinted by permission of Curtis Brown, Ltd.

Excerpt from the poem "A Sort of Proof" by Daniel Lusk. Reprinted by permission of the author.

Recipes from *From the Table of Lebanon: Traditional Vegetarian Cuisine* by Dalal A. Holmin and Maher A. Abbas and *From the Traditional Greek Kitchen: Vegetarian Cuisine* by Aphrodite Polemis. Reprinted by permission of Book Publishing Company.

Excerpt from an essay by Dave Barry in *The Miami Herald*, June 4, 1999. Reprinted by permission.

Recipe for Stawberry-Rhubarb Compote from *The Jewish Vegetarian Year Cookbook* by Roberta Kalechofsky and Rosa Rasiel. Reprinted by permission of the authors and Micah Publications.

Recipe for Passover Broccoli Knishes by Naomi Arbit from *The Wisconsin Jewish Chronicle* (www.jewishchronicle.com).

Recipe for "Blissed" French Toast by Tanya Petrovna of Native Foods (www.nativefoods.com).

ISBN 0-312-32993-8
EAN 978-0312-32993-8

First Edition: January 2005

10 9 8 7 6 5 4 3 2 1

The Dalai Lama looked at the moon shining in the night sky and said, "Isn't it beautiful up there!" Everyone sighed and agreed. "Ah, but we don't live on the moon," he said. "Our job is to make it beautiful down here."

This book is dedicated to every person whose kind words and deeds help make life easier for anyone regardless of race, color, species, creed, gender, or ability.

CONTENTS

Part Two: Fashion and Beauty

Part Three: Food and Entertaining

Part Four: Recreation and Vacations

Part Five: Animals in the Home

Part Six: Children and Family

Part Seven: Business and Education

Part Eight: Health

Part Nine: Volunteering and Getting Active

Part Ten: Celebrations

ACKNOWLEDGMENTS

First, my abiding gratitude goes to Mary Ann Naples of the Creative Culture, Inc., for her idea for the book, her diligence, and her constant support.

Many thanks to all the people who have shown how to be role models for compassionate living, including Diana Artemis, a systems analyst who put her savings to work for the earth and animals; Ronald Baumbarten, Ph.D., who remembered what was important when he retired; Janice Blue, who started her own radio show; boat-rocking veterinarian "Dr. Ned" Buyukmihci, his sister, Nermin, the bee protector, and their mother, the late Hope Buyukmihci, whose lessons in kindness live on through her sanctuary for wildlife; Jeannie Daniels and Amy and Brook Dubman, for being compassionate business leaders; Andrea Eastman, horse rescuer; Rachel Freelund, M.D., a medical pioneer for students' rights; James Silver and Lisa Grill, for creating the perfect home; Mike Handley, for thinking and writing about fishing; Marcia Hutter, for sending her furs to Afghanistan's refugee children, and her son, Larry, for letting her know she could; Elaine Keeve-Sloane and Ruth Heidrich, fearless cancer survivors; Ron and Ritchie Laymon, who have an "ethical car"; Anna Lewis, who learned to write for causes; Patty Mark, Australia's "sheep mother"; Jayn and Tom Meinhardt, who are into everything useful; Christian and Dawn Pilosi, whose wedding shone with love; Anita Roddick, founder of the Body Shop; the late Polly Strand, who was one hell of an activist; Robert Tappan, who works to stop religious prejudice; Doris Thompson and Marlene Wedin, advocates of natural menopause therapy; Maru Vigo, who discovered how to use her savings to support good in the world; and Susan Wilkie, who chose a wonderful way to memorialize her husband, Steve.

Thanks, too, to PETA staff and friends who provided assistance and expertise, including Donna Albergotti, Bea Arthur, Alec Baldwin, Carla Bennett, Linda Blair, Stephanie Boyles, Alka Chandna, Debbie Chissell, the Guillermo family, Bob and Loretta Hirsch, Bill Maher, Jennie Taylor Martin, Sir Paul McCartney and his daughter Stella, Rue McClanahan, Heather Moore, Paula Moore, Alisa Mullins, Karen Porreca, Tal Ronnen, Philip and Hannah Schein, Dan Shannon, Russell Simmons, Mary Beth Sweetland, Patricia Trostle, Jane Vaughn, Robyn Wade, Robyn Wesley, Anna West, Corina Wilder, and my executive assistant, Sara Chenoweth, who is always extremely helpful and remarkably technical.

And special thanks to the guiding hands at St. Martin's Press: Barbara Cohen, Julie Mente, Sheila Curry Oakes, Ann Marie Tallberg, and Marian Lizzi, who started the process before going to hang her hat elsewhere.

FOREWORD

I grew up in a society that didn't think much about the food we ate.. We simply took what was offered us and didn't ask too many questions about what it was or where it came from.

Many years later, I was sitting with Linda eating a dinner of roast lamb and watching the sheep that lived in the field outside our window. Seeing the lambs running up and down the field with such joy made us question the wisdom of eating such beautiful creatures. This was to be the start of our inquiries into the vegetarian way of life and our consideration for the welfare of all the beautiful animals that share planet Earth with us.

There are still millions of people who for one reason or another believe that our fellow creatures do not deserve such respect or attention and that they are placed on this planet merely for us to eat them.

During our efforts to persuade others to realize how good it would be for the planet and its inhabitants if we all respected each other's right to a peaceful existence, we met many people who agreed with us and were passionate in the same way that we were.

One of the most passionate, influential, and hardworking people we were lucky to meet was Ingrid, who, with her colleagues, ran PETA, People for the Ethical Treatment of Animals. The simplicity of the idea that we should treat our fellow creatures in an ethical way was very appealing, and we have since joined together, on many occasions, to try to persuade people to make a kinder choice. In the end, it is a more sensible, humane, and compassionate way to live.

Ingrid has been a good friend for many years, and I am proud to say these few words in the foreword of this book, and my family and I wish her the very best now and in the future. Moreover, we wish our quest of enlightening people to the wisdom of making the kind choice the success it deserves.

—Sir Paul McCartney
London
January 2005

INTRODUCTION:

Why Choosing a Compassionate Lifestyle Matters

We are not living in a private world of our own. Everything we say and do and think has its effect on everything around us.

—JOHN GALSWORTHY,
WRITER, PHILOSOPHER, SOCIAL REFORMER

I remember when I was about five or six years old, my great-aunt took me to see her neighbor. I can't recall his name, but I do remember that he belonged to the famous professional magicians' league, the Magic Circle. This elderly gentleman came out of his house wearing a sweeping magician's cloak, just the trick to impress a child. I couldn't wait to see what he'd do.

We stood under a large monkey puzzle tree in his garden and chatted about this and that. Then, suddenly, he pointed up into its branches and said, "Oh, look!" I did. And there, hanging from the branches, were pennies that, I swear, hadn't been there a moment before. "Take one if you like," he said. I reached up and did as I was told. "Now cup it in your hand really tightly." I squeezed that penny hard. The old man took a handkerchief out of his pocket and covered my hand with it and said a few "magic" words. "Now," he whispered, "open your hand." The penny had disappeared.

Isn't time like that penny? It can slip away and you won't know where it has gone.

One way to make the most of the time we have left is to adopt more compassion in our everyday lives. Kind deeds and warm exchanges, conscious friendliness and caring, can so easily be part and parcel of daily living. Life is all about choices. Almost every choice we make, from what to buy and eat, to what to say to our neighbors and what to teach our children, can be a grand opportunity to incorporate compassion, if only we see it that way.

From my earliest days, being taken by my parents to the Taj Mahal—where I stubbornly refused to come inside to see the jeweled walls, and instead ran down to help the little boys wash their cart buffaloes in the river—to the present time, presiding over an organization that deals with every conceivable use and abuse of animals worldwide, I have been drawn to the animal part of the helping equation. Funnily enough, watching out for the animals' interests seems automatically to mean bringing a benefit to human beings. Helping them means helping myself with issues concerning my body, the earth, my relationship with other human beings, and my role in the community. In fact, echoing Chief Seattle's admonition that whatever we do to the earth and the animals, we eventually visit upon ourselves, the animal protection movement uses this slogan: "Animal liberation is human liberation." We are all tied together in the great "web of life."

To take just a few examples: When we oppose large feedlots for cattle and intensive pig farms, we are also tackling pollution of our waterways, something that affects us all. When we fight to end deforestation because up to forty species of animals—from birds to raccoons to frogs—can live in and around one tree, we preserve those woodlands for the enjoyment (and oxygen supply) of all who visit there. If we organize a group to collect trash around a lake, fearing that egrets and swans will become entangled in it, we are helping to preserve an ecosystem for everyone's enjoyment. And when I decide to bring my friend a vegan meal, I am not contributing to his hardening of the arteries or raising his blood pressure.

You will find me mentioning animals a lot in this book! Some of the issues might be as familiar as old socks to you, and others might sound quite strange at first. After all, marketers and manufacturers have not found it in their best interests to mention any issue that could make the would-be consumer walk away from the shelf. So if you find yourself scratching your head at a particular chapter, thinking, "Oh, surely no one could find anything amiss with wool?" or "Why on earth would I bother cooking for my dog?," to take just two examples, wade right in, and prepare to be surprised—perhaps even shocked! I just might shatter an illusion or two, and I guarantee that you will end up armed with the facts that will allow you to make truly informed decisions, whether you are setting out into the marketplace or simply planning a meal. Embrace the adventure of learning what's behind the label and the fabulous options we often don't even think about but that will enhance our lives.

We have a tremendous opportunity every day to fill our hearts and hours with as many positive experiences as we can. For instance, how comforting to know that when we pick up a fallen baby bird from the sidewalk, we can help him gain his strength back and nourish him properly rather than just remember him throughout the day and wonder if he has "made it." How satisfying to switch on a news story and think, "Yes, I know that some face creams contain cow collagen and I have already protected myself from any risk of mad cow disease by picking ones that don't." How good to know that your morning cup of coffee comes from a farm that does not poison deer who might be tempted to chew the leaves and is actually helping a little boy or girl in South America get a better education.

How useful to have information at our fingertips that allows us to join in the effort to stop the use of rabbits to test cosmetics or floor cleaner; and how reassuring to be able to select alternatives to hormone replacement therapy that are good for both woman and beast.

What joy to easily pick out coffees that protect birds, to confidently entertain guests with delicious entrées that protect animals and our health, and to be able to help forests retain their old-growth trees even if we live in the city. Even being able to plan a relaxing or exciting vacation with the animals and ecoconsciousness in mind can be an empowering experience.

Life is full of possibilities to make a positive contribution. We only have to be open to them. As William Blake advises in "Auguries of Innocence," you can start to "see a World in a Grain of Sand / and a Heaven in a Wild Flower / Hold Infinity in the palm of your hand / and Eternity in an hour."

I have been lucky enough to learn so many ways to incorporate positive possibilities into my own work and personal experiences in the almost twenty-five years of my work at PETA that I can barely curb my enthusiasm to share them on paper. And from the letters I receive at my office, I can see there is a great thirst for information on how to make the world a kinder place.

Every day at PETA headquarters we feel the satisfaction of being able to provide a worried parent with simple or sophisticated alternatives to cutting up a frog in class—alternatives that end up teaching the child, the teacher, and often the child's whole class how to be innovative and how to derive more from a positive learning experience. Such a lesson can be as complex as using a new software program to take apart a human brain and put it back together again after witnessing how it works; or as simple as walking into the woods and realizing how clever it is for a field mouse, who has no tools, no supermarket, and no refrigerator and has never had any formal lessons, to dig a home for her young with only her hands, to know what and how to feed them from the sparse vegetation available to them in winter, and to teach them how to cope with life.

Often we are asked to help when someone who has lost a loved one wishes to write a check or take up a collection for a health charity but wants to be sure her funds will be used wisely and humanely. It is wonderful to be able to guide her to a host of choices, pointing out which charities have pledged assurances to use their funds on direct human help, such as treatment, rehabilitation, prevention of disease, and human clinical studies, rather than on animal tests.

We are in the solution-finding business, even in surprising situations. It isn't unusual, for example, for someone to call because bees have moved into his garden. We can point the inquirer to a local keeper who will come and scoop the bees up without harming the hive and without using harmful pesticides. Another day it may be that someone is baffled as to how to make the best use of a relative's fur coat now bequeathed to her. We can offer to send the coat to a refugee in Afghanistan, to a poor person in Appalachia, to a homeless woman in a cold city in the winter; use it in a library display against trapping; or cut it up as bedding to keep orphaned wildlife warm in a sanctuary.

Throughout this book, I will share information and expertise from PETA and many other organizations and individuals as well. So, in addition to the information here at your fingertips, you'll learn about books, Web sites, and additional resources to explore.

What a total delight to share this information about the wealth of options; to encourage the kinds of changes that, when extended into our communities, one good deed at a time, multiply like bubbles in a pot put to simmer on the stove.

The goal of this book is to help people who, like me, want to make the most out of not only the special occasions but the everyday parts of their lives, even their chores. It is meant to provide positive change opportunities that will enhance our lives in ways generations before us were denied. It shows a way to live life to its fullest and most meaningful by becoming a more caring person in many ways, big and small. It is the only such handy reference book designed to assist busy adults, young people, families, and everyone else who wants to spread compassion and kindness.

So, time's a-wasting. Let's change the world!

PART ONE

Home and Garden

1.

Kindness by Design: Creating and Furnishing a Humane Home

May blessings be upon your house,
Your roof, your hearth and walls;
May there be lights to welcome you
When evening's shadow falls.

—MYRTLE REED,
A WINTER BLESSING

Yugoslavian-born interior designer Sasha (full name: Sasha Josipovicz) is a household name in Canada, making regular TV appearances and writing weekly columns in Canada's *National Post.* He has been lauded for creating exotic villas on Corfu in Greece, Harbor Island residences in the Bahamas, nightclubs, and even synagogues. He has also founded a company to save nineteenth-century brick buildings and is widely sought after by businesses and upscale home owners.

When Sasha walked into James Silver and Lisa Grill's home in Toronto, he was wearing white rabbit sandals.

"But they're Prada," said the star designer.

"I don't care what label they are—they're *rabbit,*" Lisa exclaimed.

Later, Sasha reflected on that moment. "They were a beautiful design," he said. "I never thought about it as a rabbit. But I never wore them again."

Lisa Grill and James Silver own a beautiful Victorian home in Toronto's trendy Little Italy district. Guests sipping fresh fruit cocktails on the upper patio can look out over the CN tower, the world's tallest structure, and onto downtown Toronto. The house has been made over to look fresh and contemporary, and is what Sasha calls "seductive and beautifully proportioned both inside and out." He should know because he redesigned it from below the floor to above the ceiling, and every part of it is cruelty free. Sasha admits that the experience of designing this special home opened his eyes to where fabrics and furnishings come from and the wide array of alternatives that exist: "In most of my homes I do lush curtains with silk or mohair. I do wool rugs. I find leather chairs. The way Lisa and James approached me, I didn't feel threatened; I didn't feel like I was on a guilt trip. These people were so passionate, they inspired me. I came up with a million different ideas."

For the curtains, Sasha and his clients chose linen, with nylon and bamboo window coverings. The bamboo is split and pressed, and the planks are sewn together to make horizontal blinds. The bamboo came from Sohji, a panda-safe bamboo company that uses a variety of bamboo that pandas don't eat.

Lisa and James wanted to avoid hard woods from the rain forest, so their stairs were done with natural sisal, which is not as slippery as wood and, as Lisa describes it, "has a tantalizing feel on your feet."

Although it would have been easy to get cotton or other fabric rugs, Lisa and James decided to leave most of the floors bare, with one exception: Sasha got a large leather manufacturer called Nienkamper to make a rug out of small slats of wood woven with rope. As Sasha says, "It is glorious and can replace any priceless wool Persian rug."

The couple found some chairs they liked in Thailand and bought some chair frames from Palazzetti, and Sasha chose the faux leather upholstery from Designer's Fabric Outlet in Toronto. The ultrasuede came from the Italian manufacturer Alacantara, considered leaders in ultrasuede. Sasha, who is now crazy about ultrasuede thanks to its superior feel and durability, has since done ultrasuede wallpaper for a client who wanted good acoustics in a room.

Some seasons ago, U.S.-based Pottery Barn, owned by Williams-Sonoma, retailer of goods for well-appointed kitchens, bedrooms, and baths, introduced a synthetic leather it calls Everydaysuede. Although Lisa and James did not use this one, it's worth knowing about: a microfiber that feels like suede but is entirely machine-washable. Its rugged durability and incredible softness combine to create casual, relaxed slipcovers that withstand the rigors of every-day living. It is strong and colorfast.

Ro-en Furniture made all the pillows for Lisa and James with foam, becoming so particular about the project and engrossed in it that they not only reduced the price (because the fabrics they used cost less than their usual leather) but decided not to use the same machine to stuff the pillows or the same scissors to cut the foam as were used to cut leather or work with feathers!

All the paints were latex rather than graphite, to keep the dogs and cats safe from toxicity, and all the dyes used were vegetable dyes. The bed linens are no-wrinkle, no-iron polyester from W Hotels.

Other design decisions included knocking down a lot of walls, which means, among other things, according to James, "lots of space for the dogs to run. It's all open. It's like being outdoors, and they love it!" Other "dog features" include vertical railings on the atrium level so that the dogs can't climb them and fall over the top, and freestanding lamps with very strong, sturdy bases to prevent the dogs from knocking them over.

Although most people haven't a clue that this impressive home is cruelty free, one conversation piece that's hard to miss is a most intriguing painting accompanied by a photograph of the artist who created it, a chimpanzee named Tom.

Lisa and James bought the painting at a fund-raiser for the charity Zoocheck and have since found out much more about Tom—that he was born in Africa but taken from his family by force and shipped to the U.S. when he was a child. He spent his first thirty years in the cold world of a laboratory, where records show he was "knocked down" (chemically restrained) 369 times. He suffered fifty-six punch liver biopsies, one open liver wedge biopsy, three lymph node biopsies, and three bone marrow biopsies. In 1984, he was injected with HIV.

According to his laboratory keeper, Tom gave up. He became ill and had no appetite. When he could summon his strength, he banged constantly on his cage walls. When he arrived at the Fauna Foundation, a wonderful refuge for primates in Canada, it was clear he lacked the social skills he would have learned from his mother and siblings in Africa. He wouldn't play or engage other animals or people.

Tom is very intelligent and understands most of what people say to him. These days, he loves to sit quietly and have a cup of tea and bask in loving words of encouragement. He has learned to laugh. When he came to the refuge, he had one toe that was white. After a year, given paints by the people who worked to rehabilitate him, he painted that toe black and started doing other artwork.

"It's a very angry painting," James says. "You can tell he was in a lot of pain, probably from all the testing that was done on him."

The living room opens up onto a patio with lots of stonework that is easy to maintain and also bamboo. Neighborhood cats come and hang out in the basement, and James gardens while the dogs, Madison, Bandit, and Lupe, try to make it difficult for him to concentrate. "I garden while the dogs play," says James. "Inside and out, we just love this home!"

The last thoughts should go to Sasha. He says, "Growing up in Eastern Europe, at the age of twelve you get your first fur coat. Now with all the faux, you can still achieve a perfect look without compromising animals' lives. Before knowing Lisa and James, I had a coat with a detachable fur collar. I took the collar off, and I'm not wearing it anymore. They are the people who taught me. Sometimes money goes where the conscience does not. I always tell people now, 'These alternatives are usually cheaper than the real thing.'

"It was an unusual experience for me, and a wonderful one. I'm going to show this house on TV and everyone will go mad!"

RESOURCES

Designer Extraordinaire

Sasha Josipovicz
The Element Group, Toronto
416-921-8899

Chimpanzee Rescue

The Fauna Foundation
PO Box 33
Chambly, Quebec
Canada J3L 4B1
450-658-1844
fauna.foundation@sympatico.ca
Donations gratefully received. Paintings by Tom and other artists available for sale.

Furniture, Furnishings, and Fabrics
Original Ultrasuede

Alcantara
Italy-based, with distributors throughout Europe.
www.alcantara.it

Faux Leather and Other Fabrics

Designer Fabrics
Toronto
416-531-2810
www.designerfabrics.ca

Bamboo Rug

Nienkamper
Go online and find the distributor in your area.
www.nienkamper.com

Furniture and Upholstery

Ro-en Furniture

Can be purchased by individuals through Roots, a Canada-based home and clothing store.

877-927-6687

www.roots.com

Panda-Safe Bamboo Window Coverings

Sohji

Montreal

514-528-4333

www.sohjico.com

Vinyl and Ultrasuede Wall Coverings

Versa

Kentucky-based

502-458-1502

www.lsiwc.com/index.htm

No-Iron Polyester Sheets

W Hotels

New York–based

800-453-6548

www.whotelsthestore.com

Everydaysuede

The Pottery Barn

www.potterybarn.com

Makers of Everydaysuede, a microfiber that feels like real suede but is an entirely machine washable, durable, colorfast slipcover material.

2.

Creating a Beautiful Garden to Attract Birds, Butterflies, and Other Natural Life

---

And other eyes than ours
Were made to look on flowers,
Eyes of small birds and insects small:
The deep sun-blushing rose
Round which the prickles close
Opens her bosom to them all.
The tiniest living thing
That soars on feathered wing,
Or crawls among the long grass
Out of sight
Has just as good a right
To its appointed portion of delight
As any king.

—CHRISTINA ROSSETTI,
"TO WHAT PURPOSE THIS WASTE?"

Those who contemplate the beauty of the earth find reserves of strength that will endure as long as life lasts.

—RACHEL CARSON

There are as many ways to create a garden as there are gardeners, but the ideas offered in this chapter are meant not only to encourage plantings that are beautiful to behold and relatively easy to maintain, but also to provide a haven for winged wildlife in an ever-more developed world

Creating a bird- and butterfly-friendly garden involves four key concepts:

1. keeping a part of the area natural;
2. using shrubs;
3. planting flowering food and adding minor attractions, like nesting boxes and seasonal feeders; and
4. if possible, adding a source of fresh water.

According to the Royal Society for the Protection of Birds (RSPB), one of the oldest organizations in the world of its kind, a bird-friendly garden does not have to be wild or overgrown. It can also look attractive all year round.

Birds these days have lost many of their natural sources of food and lodging, and so providing them with sustenance and opportunities to shelter and raise their young is a wonderful service. The RSPB recommends creating a natural habitat for birds that includes a feeding station. This can be as simple or elaborate as you like and as space allows. Ideally, the design would consist of:

- a couple of trees (it isn't hard to plant small trees like holly and ivy, which are important because they produce berries in winter and robins love to nest in them; rowan; fruit-bearing trees like pear, apple, cherry; or, if you have a large garden, a larch, willow, or ash);
- a thick yew, holly, or other hedge and a group of berry-bearing shrubs (perhaps an evergreen like a strawberry tree; a variegated holly such as "Silver Queen"; a deciduous bush or two like lilac, hawthorn, or blackberry; pyracantha or

cotoneaster, which provide a bird feast; and/or viburnum, snowberry, or elder); and
- some colorful cottage garden plants.

Any decent nursery will be able to guide you as to what will grow best in your soil and climate. When you plant your shrubs, scatter some bulbs about too. Thistle in a little wild area is a favorite food for some bird species, and teasels are popular among seed eaters.

Cover any bare walls, unsightly areas, and fences with climbing vines (they will need support at first) or plants like clematis, ivy—the perfect wildlife plant—and/or beautiful-smelling honeysuckle, all of which provide excellent nesting opportunities for many different species of birds, from robins to visiting finches. Leave a little pile of twigs, fallen leaves, and stones for the birds to use, pop in some bulbs and wildflowers, and then leave it all alone. You can watch from your window as your new visitors and permanent residents discover the place and settle in.

It is important to avoid chemical sprays, of course. Furthermore, consider not treating your garden as if it were in the Marine Corps by trimming any growth as soon as it sprouts. The key to creating a pretty haven is to let things grow a little wild and natural, a bit prairie or meadowlike, full of the surprises of nature. Birds will appreciate the opportunity to forage, eat the dropped seeds, and peck at fallen fruit if everything isn't tidied and swept up right away. If you are going to prune, avoid heavy pruning from about March to July, for this is when many species of birds (and little mammals who may find refuge among your leaves) are breeding and nesting.

Like all birds, hummingbirds benefit from plants that bloom at different times of the year, and they particularly seek out nectar-rich flowers. To attract them, plant some of their favorites, like cleome, trumpet vine, red petunia, impatiens, catmint, red ivy geranium, salvia, nasturtium, morning glory, fuchsia, and butterfly bush.

All birds love to bathe and splash about in clean water (though hummingbirds will not use a birdbath; they need a mister). If you can install a birdbath and keep it clean, not only will you provide yourself with ever varying programs of "bird TV," but you will provide all the winged residents with endless joy.

Butterflies are glad to have a refuge too, and their numbers are in decline. Like birds, all they need is a little food, shelter, and a place to lay their eggs.

According to butterfly gardener Krist Wetherbee, a safe and hospitable butterfly garden consists of flowers, of course, and also includes a sheltered area that provides protection from the wind and rain while allowing butterflies to absorb plenty of sunlight; provides a pesticide-free food source; and has some weeds and wildflowers in which butterflies can lay their eggs.

Here again, consultation will pay off, but butterflies certainly enjoy these easy-to-grow plants: butterfly bush, chrysanthemum, black-eyed susan, lantana, phlox, goldenrod, milkweed, marigold, purple coneflower, and lilacs and lavender, which smell divine. Butterflies will dip their tongues into all these flowers and nourish themselves on the nectar. It's also important to provide a food source for butterfly caterpillars, such as milkweed, fennel, parsley, violet, spirea, wisteria, and passionflower.

The little garden outside the window of my rented apartment in an old house in Takoma Park, Maryland, was so tiny you could set off to walk around it and be back at the door in twenty seconds flat, yet that garden provided the biggest distraction in the world whenever I sat down and tried to work at my desk. For all the activity at the birdbath, I could have been looking out at the skaters on the rink at Rockefeller Plaza! I came to know the regulars, discover the varying personalities, and learn each bird's routine and habits. My happiest moments were smiling at their antics, feeling the pleasure of recognizing someone who had been absent for a while, and watching a mother bird bring her baby for a refreshing drink for the very first time.

When I left that apartment, if I could have taken one thing, it would have been the garden.

RESOURCES

Royal Society for the Protection of Birds

UK Headquarters:
The Lodge
Sandy, Bedfordshire
SG19 2DL
United Kingdom
44 01767 680551
www.rspb.org.uk

The RSPB, Europe's largest wildlife conservation nonprofit, has been researching wildlife problems, promoting practical solutions, and working on behalf of birds and the environment since 1889.

Audubon Society

Main Office:
700 Broadway
New York, NY 10003
212-979-3000
www.audubon.org

The Audubon Society's national network of community-based nature centers and chapters works to conserve birds and other wildlife through scientific and educational programs, including "Audubon Adventures" for grade-school children and camps and workshops for families, adults, and children.

National Wildlife Federation

11100 Wildlife Center Dr.
Reston, VA 20190
800-822-9919
www.nwf.org

The NWF is not animal-friendly in all matters, but it does run the Backyard Wildlife Habitat Program, through which people can have their yards certified as "backyard habitats" if they provide certain things, such as water sources, nesting sites, etc. The NWF also puts out a handy little book called *Planting an Oasis for Wildlife.*

The Xerces Society

4828 SE Hawthorne Blvd.
Portland, OR 97215
503-232-6639
www.xerces.org
A nonprofit organization named after an extinct butterfly species and dedicated to conserving butterflies, bees, and other invertebrates.

Monarch Watch

University of Kansas Entomology Department
1200 Sunnyside Ave.
Lawrence, KS 66045-7534
888-TAGGING
www.MonarchWatch.org
Focuses on conserving monarch butterflies but has valuable information about other butterfly species as well. (Drawback: they have a "tagging" program in which they put stickers on butterflies' wings so they can track their migration.)

Stokes, Donald, Lillian Stokes, and Ernest Williams. *The Butterfly Book: An Easy Guide to Butterfly Gardening, Identification, and Behavior.* New York: Little, Brown, 1991.

3.

Creating an Eco- and Animal-Friendly Bathroom

This is oceans of fun!

—SPONGEBOB SQUAREPANTS

The "kese" (keh-sehzz) is a rough cloth mitt carried in a copper soap case, and is not only used to scour dirt from your pores, but it serves to deliver a bracing massage. The soaping web was specially woven out of hair or plant fibers.

—DESCRIPTION OF THE TURKISH BATH EXPERIENCE

Anyone who doesn't know what soap tastes like has never washed a dog.

—FRANKLIN P. JONES

Sea sponges are a vital part of ocean life. In fact, they are animals, made up of countless living cells—or rather, they are if they are left intact on the ocean floor. They are also nature's natural water filters, and today they are in grave danger of disappearing because of pollution and "harvesting" for bath shops. Those of us who try not to buy environmentally destructive products know to select faux sponges like those listed below, which are *not* collected from the seabed by being hooked and harpooned as real living sponges are.

But there is much more we can do to be kind to the earth and animals when we step into the shower or clean our teeth.

Let me introduce you to Leslie Fain. Back in the eighties, Leslie took a job at a Gillette laboratory in Rockville, Maryland. No one guessed that this rather glamorous young woman, with chic-cut short dark hair and a bell-like laugh, was a PETA undercover agent and that her shoulder bag contained a video recorder.

What Leslie captured on film was deeply upsetting to anyone who wishes to end needless suffering. Albino rabbits, as well as mice and rats—who certainly feel pain and suffering every bit as much as any animal, even though few people's sympathies go out to them—were used in what is known as the "basic four" tests. That is to say, they were restrained in stocks and heavy plastic collars, and then shaving foam and other products were sprayed into their eyes; dandruff shampoo was forced down their throats; suspected irritants were left on their shaved, scraped skin to burn through to their flesh; and the animals were placed in sealed chambers and forced to inhale gaseous forms of ingredients that made them go into convulsions and, in many cases, die.

When Leslie's footage and photographs were picked up by news stations, a storm of protest erupted and serious campaigning began to get Gillette to stop hurting animals in tests that no law required. PETA's consulting scientists pointed out that the tests could be replaced by modern alternatives, such as the use of human corneas from eye banks, human cell cultures, and the "Generally Recognized as Safe" list of ingredients and ingredient combinations compiled from human experience. Still, Gillette wouldn't budge.

PETA protested the company for ten long years, its members doing everything from climbing the flagpole outside Gillette's Boston headquarters office with a banner begging it to stop the tests to meeting with its top brass. In the end, Gillette did the right thing. It stopped all animal tests.

Today, if you ask Gillette about its decision, it will tell you that the challenge to use only nonanimal tests moved the company forward and pushed it to be more innovative and progressive in its science. PETA now holds Gillette up as a model company, a leader among the giants, and recommends its products as cruelty free.

While Avon and Revlon also stopped using animals in tests, and companies like the Body Shop and Paul Mitchell Systems have never used animals at all, there are, unfortunately, many other large companies that cling to old, cruel animal tests. Campaigns rage on against them (see www.peta.org for more information). Nonetheless, it is easy to wash your hair and groom yourself without hurting a single bunny or mouse. In fact, many hundreds of companies are listed in the "approved" section of PETA's free wallet guide to companies that do and don't use animals in this way.

One of the best mission statements I've ever read is that of the Body Shop. This business was one of the very first to be founded on the principles of human and animal rights and earth-consciousness, and its success is marvelous to note. The Body Shop supports native industries in local indigenous communities, like cooperatives run by Amazonian Indians who have lost their land. Its goals are to ensure that its business is ecologically sustainable; to contribute to communities in which it trades by adopting a code of conduct that ensures care, honesty, fairness, and respect; and to campaign for the protection of the environment and human and civil rights, and against animal testing within the cosmetics and toiletries industry. It gets my vote and my business!

RESOURCES

For an up-to-the-minute list of which companies conduct animal tests and which do not, always carry a copy of PETA's free, wallet-size cruelty-free shopping guide, available by writing PETA (501 Front Street, Norfolk, VA 23510, www.peta.org) or calling 757-622-7382. Companies listed as not testing have either signed a corporate Statement of Assurance or met the Corporate Standard of Compassion for Animals put out by the Coalition for Consumer Information on Cosmetics (CCIC), a group of seven animal-protection organizations, including PETA.

Organic Health and Beauty

www.organichealthandbeauty.com

New York's *Satya* magazine for the environmentally conscious consumer recommends this company this way: "Their name says it all—organic, wild-crafted products that are completely animal-free and don't use synthetic or petroleum ingredients."

Clear Conscience

(10 percent goes to PETA)

Cruelty-free contact lens solutions.

Tom's of Maine

PO Box 710

Kennebunk, ME 04043

800-367-8667

www.tomsofmaine.com

Toothpastes.

Gillette

www.gillette.com

Razors and shaving and oral care products, including Venus, Mach 3 Turbine, and Oral B.

The Body Shop

5036 One World Way

Wake Forest, NC 27587

919-554-4900

www.thebodyshop.com

The Drench Body Sponge is available from the Body Shop and is a thoughtful alternative to sponges removed from the sea. This one lathers very well and lasts longer than a real sea sponge.

Soap Dream

PO Box 6278

Albany, CA 94706

510-526-9668
www.soapdream.com
Natural and cruelty-free gift baskets of vegan soaps, body scrubs, body butter, lip balm, and much more. Ten percent goes to PETA.

LeapingBunny.org
www.LeapingBunny.org
To learn more about why cosmetics tests on animals do not protect the consumer, and to get the answers to other questions about animal tests and alternatives.

Vegan Essentials
www.veganessentials.com
HBG aftershave for men in bay rum, sandalwood, and other scents.

4.

Choosing Cleaning Products That Are Kind to More Than Your Floor

Where did the White Rabbit go?

—LEWIS CARROLL, *THROUGH THE LOOKING GLASS*

The comedian Phyllis Diller used to joke that the only thing domestic about her was that she was born in the United States. Phyllis said that she'd talk to anyone at all on the phone, even direct marketers or religious tract sellers, just to put off housework. Her beautiful tan, she said, came from the princess light on the handset.

Some people find cleaning therapeutic, and some find it just plain necessary. Whichever category you fall into, cleaning brings important choices.

Household, office, and institutional cleaning products, paper towels, and bathroom tissue can all be selected with a view to making life more pleasant not only in our own homes but also in the world outside them and in the laboratories where they are tested—often in incredibly cruel ways on albino rabbits, rats, and guinea pigs. Even the hardest cleaning jobs do not have to result in toxins entering our waterways via the drains or leaving chemical residues that last a decade. These days it isn't that hard to find products that are biodegradable, are non–animal tested, and do not contain ammonia, dyes, and chlorine.

Some commercial convenience products can be quite toxic without warning, so it is especially important to be wary of upholstery cleaners, odor maskers, oven cleaners, pesticides, and even air fresheners, if you have animals in the home. Certain chemicals in self-cleaning ovens will kill birds without warning, something no one will tell you at the appliance store. The fumes, however faint, from Teflon-coated pans, burner liners, drip pans, and other nonstick cookware have been shown to poison birds outright, so watch out. And reports from anguished guardians retell the stories of dogs who have gone into shock and been lost after sniffing a couch or chair sprayed with certain types of fabric deodorant.

"Earth Friendly Products" is not just a catchphrase. There is actually a company of the same name that creates products for home and personal use that are derived from environmentally responsible, replenishable resources. EFP does not test on animals or use animal ingredients.

Apart from such home products as dishwashing liquid and pellets, nonchlorine oxygen-based laundry bleach, and toilet bowl cleaner, retail-packaged Earth Friendly Products are available in refillable five-gallon bulk containers for major projects requiring industrial strength. There is zinc-free floor finish and floor stripper; Greasemate, a noncorrosive, nonacidic product that clears pipes and traps of grease, oil, and sludge; a noncombustible, nonflammable house and office cleaner called Uni-Dust; and even odor control Green Granules that absorb the kinds of messes no one wants to encounter but that hospitals and schools routinely have to deal with.

This company is by no means the only one, so below I have included a short list of other companies, distributors, and mail-order companies, together with an information source on bird deaths due to household chemicals.

How wonderful to have a clean conscience as well as a clean floor!

RESOURCES

Advanage Wonder Cleaner

800-323-6444

www.wondercleaner.com

All-purpose cleaner (vegan).

Allens Naturally

800-352-8971

www.allensnaturally.com

All-purpose cleaner, dish detergent, fabric softener, laundry detergent (vegan).

America's Finest Products Corporation

800-482-6555

All-purpose cleaner, fine-washables detergent, stain remover (vegan).

BI-O-KLEEN

800-477-0188

All-purpose cleaner, bleach, carpet cleaner, dish detergent, laundry detergent, stain remover (vegan).

Citra-Solv

800-343-6588

www.citrasolv.com

Air freshener, all-purpose cleaner, dishwashing detergent, car care, carpet cleaner, drain cleaner, furniture polish, glass cleaner, oven cleaner, stain remover (vegan).

Earth Friendly Products

800-335-3267

www.ecos.com

Air freshener, all-purpose cleaner, bathroom cleaner, bleach, cream cleanser, dish detergent, drain cleaner, furniture polish, glass cleaner, laundry detergent, stain and odor remover, toilet cleaner (vegan).

Ecover

800-449-4925

www.ecover.com

All-purpose cleaner, dish detergent, cream cleanser, laundry detergent, fabric softener, stain remover.

Environmental Working Group

www.ewg.org

Information on bird deaths from household chemicals.

Huish Detergents

800-776-6702

www.huish.com

Bathroom cleaner, bleach, dish detergent, fabric softener, floor cleaner, glass cleaner, laundry detergent, stain remover.

James Austin Company

800-245-1942

www.jamesaustin.com

All-purpose cleaner, bleach, carpet cleaner, dish detergent, drain cleaner, fabric softener, glass cleaner, laundry detergent, oven cleaner.

Method Products Inc.

866-9-METHOD

www.methodhome.com

All-purpose cleaner, bathroom cleaner, dish detergent, glass cleaner, shower cleaner (vegan).

Nature Clean (Frank T. Ross & Sons Ltd.)

416-282-1107

www.franktross.com

All-purpose cleaner, automatic dishwashing detergent, bathroom cleaner, bleach, carpet cleaner, fabric softener, fine-washables detergent, glass cleaner, laundry detergent, oven cleaner, stain remover, toilet cleaner (vegan).

Orange-Mate

800-626-8685

www.orangemate.com

Air freshener, all-purpose cleaner, glass cleaner (vegan).

Planet

800-858-8449

www.planetinc.com

All-purpose cleaner, dish detergent, fine-washables detergent, laundry detergent (vegan).

Seventh Generation

802-658-3773

www.seventhgeneration.com

All-purpose cleaner, carpet cleaner, cream cleansers, dish detergent, laundry detergent, bleach, glass cleaner, toilet cleaner (vegan).

Shaklee Corporation

800-SHAKLEE

www.shaklee.com

All-purpose cleaner, dish detergent, drain cleaner, laundry detergent.

Shop Natural

www.shopnatural.com

Natumate stain and odor removers, including skunk-odor remover.

Stanley Home Products

800-628-9032

www.stanleyhome.com

All-purpose cleaner, bathroom cleaner, brass/copper/silver/stainless-steel cleaner, carpet cleaner, furniture polish, glass cleaner, jewelry cleaner, laundry detergent, stain remover.

Whip-It Products

800-582-0398

All-purpose cleaner for home or industrial use, carpet cleaner, laundry detergent, oven cleaner.

5.

Choices in Car Interiors

The defendant is clearly one who insufficiently appreciates the value of the motor car to the human race. But we must not allow our natural detestation for such an individual to cloud our judgement.

—A. P. HERBERT, *MISLEADING CASES*

I have 117,000 miles on my Mercedes station wagon. It has carried me to all 88 counties in Ohio to gather signatures to prevent mourning doves from being shot and, when an egg farm's sheds collapsed on top of the birds during a hurricane, it carried dozens of chickens to their new animal-friendly "safe forever" homes.

—RITCHIE LAYMON, MERCEDES ENTHUSIAST

Not everyone's heart flutters to hear an engine start up, but if the car is sporty enough, my heart leaps like a gazelle in flight. That throaty hum from a well-built engine conjures up memories of days spent at automobile race tracks: I relive sitting in the viewing stands at the track in sunny Sebring, Florida, on a sizzling hot day; driving in an open convertible along the conifer-lined roads en route to the Watkins Glen Grand Prix in upstate New York; and my ears popping as the Formula One cars zoomed by the yachts moored alongside the winding street track in Monte Carlo, Monaco.

There is another aspect to cars that sparks the imagination, and that is what goes into creating the seats, the steering wheel, and the trim.

Sticking strictly to luxury cars for just a moment, did you know that manufacturing a Mercedes S-class car interior requires seven cows per car? That a Rolls-Royce takes fifteen? Or that Bader, a leather supplier that sells skins to DaimlerChrysler and other car companies, goes through nine thousand skins in a single day? In fact, according to the *New York Times* American tanneries serving the auto industry "buy 20 percent of the 36 million hides produced domestically. At about forty-five square feet per cow, that's fifty-eight square miles"—enough to cover the island of Manhattan two and a half times, with enough skin left over for headrests.

Car companies are using and promoting leather because leather is cheap these days, so the markup is high. The good news is that many car companies are switching over to synthetic leather that doesn't smell, "breathes" but doesn't "sweat," and now offers the feel and look of leather *if* that's what the customer desires. For sports-car fans, the imported Jaguar XKE comes with an additional kind alternative to leather, vinyl, and fabric, but Jaguars aren't alone in offering a choice. BMW and Audi were among the first to offer pleather instead of leather in their sporty models.

Although Jean Andrew has never given a hoot about cars, she never wanted one with a leather interior. She purposely chose a Mercedes SE model with the vinyl option. Her husband, Kenneth L. Andrew, lived and breathed cars, putting himself through school by selling miniature racing models. He passed his enthusiasm on to their daughter, Ritchie Laymon, as well as the family's interest in animals. Ritchie and her husband, Ron, once a professional auto racing photographer whose shots have appeared in *AutoWeek* and *Road and Track,* love cars and have eight dogs who think there's nothing better than to ride around all day with their folks. The dogs apparently consider the Mercedes SE the perfect "portable den."

Also in their garage, tucked away for special occasions, is a forty-year-old Jaguar XKE convertible restored to mint condition. The only thing that isn't original and in "authentic condition" is the Jaguar's interior. The leather was replaced with synthetic skin as soon as the Laymons got the car. The couple (and the dogs) love the durable, comfortable, easy-to-clean vinyl interior.

How did the Laymons decide to replace the leather? The Jag's bumper sticker reads, "NO FURS." One day, says Ritchie, someone left a note on the seat. It said, "NO FURS? But you have leather seats—hypocrite!"

The Laymons are also concerned about environmental and health issues connected with leather use. They learned that the mordants and other chemicals often used in leather preservation are linked to nervous disorders, asthma and other respiratory problems, and serious health concerns. According to an investigation by the New York State Department of Health, the National Institute for Occupational Safety and Health, and other agencies, those who work in tanneries may be greatly increasing their risk of testicular cancer, and the Highlander Research and Education Center determined that the incidence of leukemia among residents in an area near one Kentucky leather tannery was five times the national average, while birth defects and miscarriages were also very high.

Furthermore, animal skin used for leather is often kept from biodegrading by the use of a variety of dangerous substances, including mineral salts (chromium, aluminium, iron, and zirconium), formaldehyde, coal-tar derivatives, and various oils and dyes, some of which are cyanide based. All wastes containing chromium are considered hazardous by the U.S. Environmental Protection Agency (EPA) and other organizations.

A consumer revolution against leather car interiors has dawned only recently, in the United States and around the world. In 2002, Jeanne Daniels was so moved by the facts about leather's drawbacks and origin that she removed all the leather from her new Mercedes-Benz, replaced it with a luxurious synthetic material, and returned the skins to DaimlerChrysler's headquarters, with a letter that said she had concluded that "supporting cruelty to animals through the use of leather is no longer acceptable."

In late 2003, Indian member of Parliament Maneka Gandhi, the powerful daughter-in-law of the late Indian prime minister Indira Gandhi, sent the company a letter stating she was "contemplating a large campaign against DaimlerChrysler and its brands in India" that would involve "religious leaders and politicians as well as the heads of business associations and communities" if DaimlerChrysler did not at least start offering all models of its vehicles in nonleather there. The company promptly announced that it would start making its E-class available in nonleather in India and its S-class available in nonleather via import.

Poorva Joshipura, PETA's primary campaigns manager on this issue, who has spent time in slaughterhouses and cattle markets in Asia, thinks it inevitable that alternatives will be phased in as consumers demand them. In her dealings with car companies, she recommends Ultrafabrics' faux leather, letting them know that it is not only beautiful and soft but up to six times more durable than animal leather.

As they say at Le Mans, "Gentlemen and ladies, start your engines!"

RESOURCES

Ultrafabrics LLC (L)

400 Executive Blvd.
Elmsford, NY 10523
888-361-9216 (Sales and Marketing)
877-309-6648 (Customer Service)
Fax: 914-347-1591
email@ultrafabricsllc.com
www.ultrasuede.com
Motto is "So like leather, only better." Soft, supple, and sensuous to the touch, resistant to stains and discoloration, machine-washable and dry-cleanable.

6.

Selecting the Purest Candles: Those Without Tallow, Paraffin, or Beeswax

Romantic light of flickering flames

Fragrance doubly sweet

Evokes passion's memory

Wherein we often meet.

—DONA LOU PEARSON, "CANDLELIGHT"

Shopping for candles—whether to light the table for that special romantic evening, votive candles to float in the bath, or ones to pop in the kitchen drawer just in case the lights go out—means thinking about what goes into them.

The main ingredients to avoid are beeswax (which is taken [animal rights activists would say "stolen," and rightly so] from the industrious bees' hive), tallow (a slaughterhouse product), and paraffin wax (a petroleum product that is associated with health risks). Today there are wonderful decorative and practical household candles, all easily available, that are made from soy and other ingredients that are kind to the environment as well as to your health, and which do not depend on killing, harming, or exploiting animals.

According to environmental watchdogs, there are three main reasons to avoid buying petroleum (paraffin) products. These are:

- petroleum smoke/exhaust contains many carcinogenic toxins and produces ugly black soot;
- petroleum is not a renewable resource and it is of a limited supply; and
- burning petroleum products creates air pollution and contributes to global warming.

According to the state of California, paraffin candles can release seven toxins, including toluene and benzene, which are labeled probable carcinogens by the EPA. One air-quality researcher, David Krause, has documented evidence that candle soot particles contain many of the same compounds given off by burning diesel fuel.

No one knows for certain when candles were first invented, but in Roman times candles were made of the pith of certain rushes, peeled except on one side, and dipped in animal fat. Today, tallow candles are still made from "rendered" sheep or beef fat from around the animal's kidneys—so little wonder they can go rancid, can cause irritations in sensitive people, and smell distasteful once you know exactly what it is your nose is picking up.

A fine alternative to animal tallow is vegetable tallow, obtained from various plants. Chinese vegetable tallow is obtained from the seeds of the tallow tree, and Indian vegetable tallow is a name sometimes given to piney tallow.

Vegetable wax is also a safe ingredient. This is simply a waxy excretion on the leaves or fruits of certain plants, such as the bayberry.

By the Middle Ages candles were common. Tallow, beeswax, and vegetable wax (such as bayberry in North America, candleberry in the East, and waxberry in South America) were later supplemented by whale oil (spermaceti) and by stearin or stearic acid in the early 1800s (this is still obtained from factories that process the carcasses of dogs and cats killed in animal pounds and shelters), then by paraffin in the mid-1800s.

Somewhere along the way, people learned to pour beeswax over the wicks. Here's why we should all avoid it: Whether we are taking honey, royal jelly, pollen, propolis, or wax from bees, these incredible little insects—capable of complicated communication and a sophisticated social network—suffer and die needlessly.

First, most beekeepers blow smoke into the hives to slow the bees down and make them docile. Next, a "bee brush" is used—often crudely—to sweep away the bees who rush from the hive and who can easily succumb to the smoke and damage their legs and wings. Bee farmers then remove the honey and the honeycomb (which is, of course, the hive's main source of nourishment) and replace it with cheap white sugar. The honeycomb yields animal wax, which is then used in candles and in certain other products, including some polishes, crayons, and lip balms.

It's easy to pick out "clean candles," as candle ingredients are usually clearly marked, but sometimes you do have to poke about a bit or ask sales assistants to call the manufacturer for more details than those given on the labels. Instead of beeswax-coated wicks, you can also buy paper, hemp, and cotton wicks.

The next time you buy or light a candle, you can really shine!

RESOURCES

Vegesoy Candles from Jenni Originals

480-753-5194 or toll-free 877-95-JENNI; fax 480-753-5196

Favored by Alicia Silverstone and Brooke Shields, these candles are handmade with "specially formulated superior wax derived from soybeans and all natural vegetable ingredients." Environmentally safe and much cleaner burners than paraffin. One hundred percent biodegradable.

Royal Products Inc.

718-417-9696

Sabbath candles can be purchased by the case; also available in kosher markets.

Ethicalwares.com

www.ethicalwares.com

Vegan candles in the shapes of pyramids, cones, and rounds.

7.

Capping Your Chimney/ Sealing Your Attic

Surely, the squirrel, drawn
to the warmth of the chimney's mouth
on a winter night,
had no consequence in mind,
no more than the guests,
gathered round the hearth
deep in the house, mistook
laughter and conversation
for ecstasy.

—DANIEL LUSK, FROM "A SORT OF PROOF,"
A POEM AGAINST WAR

On the very first day Jean Goldenberg moved into her home in Chevy Chase, Maryland, she and her family woke up to bumps in the night. There was someone moving about in the attic.

Putting on her robe and taking her flashlight, Jean pulled down the attic steps and climbed up. Lifting the ceiling door carefully, she shone the light into the empty room and scared a family of raccoons half to death!

After the initial shock on both sides of the flashlight, all hell broke loose. The raccoons, five or six of them, flew about the room, colliding with each other as they tried to find their escape route to the outside world and away from this hideous demon with the single glow-in-the-dark eye.

The next morning Jean called around and was told that mothballs are a good raccoon deterrent. She filled a huge cardboard box with them and put it up in the attic.

That night Jean heard the raccoons moving about, then silence. After a while, she heard a new sound, like the mothballs being rolled around on the floor and then some bonks. After an hour or so, the raccoons' rough-and-tumble began again. Jean put in earplugs and figured she couldn't expect instant miracles.

The next morning Jean returned to the attic and looked in the cardboard box. It was empty. These raccoons, disliking the mothballs intensely, as advertised, and not realizing that they were delivered as a humane eviction novice of sorts, had rolled them one by one to a crack in the eaves—the one through which they came and went—and pitched them out. The ground below was littered with mothballs.

Because so many trees have been felled to make our houses where once deer roamed and raccoons and other wildlife flourished, animals move, out of sheer necessity, into whatever shelter they can find. If you can adopt a "live and let live" attitude and put up with some minor inconvenience, you will be doing a service to homeless wildlife. But if damage is severe and you feel you must act, there are a few things to know.

"Pest control" and "wildlife removal" services are often not what you might think. Their representatives may soothe customers by saying they "release trapped animals into the woods," but unfortunately there's a good chance they drown them in cold water, turn the raccoons over to a hunt club as practice bait for the hounds, or otherwise cruelly dispose of them. The fact is that animals don't do well released into what small patches of woods are left; they do not know the terrain, have no nest, den, food source, or family there, and may try desperately to find their way home to their infants who were left behind. In many areas, it is illegal to release animals.

The solution is relatively easy. Most animals who want to share the warmth and safety of your home go out during the day and get active at night. That means that while they are out and about, you can bring in a carpenter and seal up any cracks and crevices they are using to enter the house. When they come back, they will have to seek new shelter, but at least they'll know the neighborhood. Evictions should *not* take place in spring, especially in April and May, if you have reason to believe that a mother animal is raising infants. Wait until they are old enough to come and go with their mother before sealing off entryways.

Home repairs to deter raccoons and squirrels can include capping the chimney, fixing the roof, and putting latticework or quarter-inch mesh hardware cloth on all vents, crawl spaces, attic gables, and other exterior accesses to buildings. Capping your chimney is extremely important, as animals seeking safe places to hide or give birth may make their nests in it. Come winter, if you open the flue over burning logs, baby animals can drop into the fire and be burned.

If an animal, like a raccoon or squirrel, falls down your chimney and can't get out (so that's what that scratching noise is!), try dangling a very long thick rope with big knots in it down the chimney, tie it to the top, and leave it there in the hope that the trapped animal can use it to climb out. After a day or two, if that doesn't work, action must be taken or the little creature will die of dehydration. If you open the flue, cushion the landing and have a laundry basket handy to pop over whoever shows up at the bottom; then slide something firm under it and release your rescued one outside.

Local humane societies may be of help—but again, beware of wildlife control companies.

The Fund for Animals offers these tips on how to coexist with urban and suburban wildlife:

- Make trash cans unappealing. Cover them securely and keep them in the garage until trash day if possible, or pour ammonia or pepper in the trash can to discourage foraging.
- Do not keep food outdoors. Feed your dogs and cats indoors, or outdoors in the daytime, and remove the food

before evening, when raccoons are more likely to be scavenging.

- Trim tree limbs away from the roof and trim vegetation to prevent it from covering foundation walls, all of which make for easy climbing onto your roof and up to your attic.
- A portable radio in an attic or crawl space or other raccoon "den" for a couple of days will generally cause the raccoon to pack up and move to quieter surroundings.
- Protect fish ponds by covering them with nylon netting in the evenings when raccoons are most likely to develop an appetite for one of their favorite delicacies.

The Fund for Animals reminds us that in addition to being entertaining to watch from a distance, raccoons are great at helping control rodent and insect populations.

RESOURCES

The Fund for Animals
www.fundwildlife.org
Urban wildlife advice.

PETA
757-622-7382
Contact PETA for Wildlife Fact Sheet #7–"Living in Harmony."

www.helpingwildlife.com
A resource for anything and everything related to PETA's work to educate people about wildlife.

8.

Dealing Kindly with Mice and Other Uninviteds

I think mice are rather nice.
Their tails are long, their faces small.
They haven't any chins at all.
They nibble things they shouldn't touch.
And no one seems to like them much.
But I think mice are nice.

—ROSE FYLEMAN

One scorching hot day, D. O'Hara was looking out of her back window. She had put water out for a neighborhood cat, but as she watched, she saw another animal at the dish. It was a mother rat. The rat took a drink, then laid her head on the cool rim of the water bowl and fell fast asleep.

The mother rat had had her babies in a nest of eucalyptus leaves near the O'Haras' porch, and Ms. O'Hara could watch from her window as the mother groomed them and taught them to shell the unsalted peanuts put out for the birds.

The mother rat, like most mothers of any species, took impressive care of her brood: dipping their little paws in the cool water and smoothing the fur around their ears and faces. Each baby put his or her arms around the mother's neck and paid attention while being bathed. The mother also taught them to dart and run if danger approached.

Everyone told Ms. O'Hara that the rats would become a problem, so she swept out the nest, only to see the mother rat work tirelessly to build another and gather more food to store for her family. O'Hara felt like a heel.

Rodents who remain outside are one matter, and they have been there—elaborate efforts to kill them off with poisons notwithstanding—since the beginning of time, or at least since people first started storing grain. For the most part, they don't bother us, and vice versa. However, rodents who venture inside the house are a different story.

When rats or mice come indoors—which one must admit is a smart move in the heat of summer or when snow and ice descend—they can wreak a lot of havoc: They can chew holes in clothes and gnaw furniture legs, and they leave droppings wherever they go, kitchen or bedroom. There is no question that some action has to be taken, but what?

Those sticky glue traps sold in hardware stores are *not* the answer. Veterinarians in Maryland signed a petition to outlaw them on the grounds of their cruelty. Mice, even the occasional squirrel or bird, walk into them and get stuck. As they struggle to disengage themselves from the glue, the situation gets worse and they find their limbs and sometimes their faces stuck fast. In many cases, animals caught this way are left to die, panicked and exhausted from the struggle, of dehydration or starvation, or are cavalierly tossed into a Dumpster, trap and all, to boil in the sun, freeze, or eventually meet the trash truck. These traps should be illegal everywhere.

The most common trap is the spring trap, and that, too, while being unthinkable to employ on a larger mammal—say a dog or cat—is sold and set as a matter of routine. However, much like going to a bullfight because it sounded like fun and then realizing it is a horridly cruel spectacle, many people eventually regret doing something so gruesome to rodents. Those with a heart often find their hearts sinking when they remove the small body from that cheap device.

I'm sure I wasn't the only person moved by an essay, "A Better

Mousetrap," written in the *Washington Post* by the author Gregg Levoy some years back. Levoy was raised in a household "equipped with pest spray or rolled-up newspapers for every genus and species" where his father would "sometimes crouch in an upstairs window, Luger in hand, and try to pick off tomcats." In the essay, Levoy wrote that after experiencing pain firsthand, he decided to live his life without administering it.

He stopped stripping the leaves off twigs anymore as he walked along the sidewalk, and he worked around the ant colony when he cleared the backyard. He said he sometimes felt so isolated from the "proverbial web of things," living in the city, that a part of him was glad to have something resembling an ecosystem about him.

"Also," said Levoy, "I cannot shake the feeling that somewhere there is a tally being kept of these things—my cruelties, my compassions—and that it will make a difference somewhere down the line when I go to cash in my chips. Besides, there is a slight question, in my mind, of relativity. Who is the pest here, me or the mouse?"

One day he was standing at a checkout line in a hardware store when an elderly man tapped him on the shoulder. "Good for you," the man said, surveying Levoy's $17.50 Havahart box trap. "You'll probably come back as a mouse."

Well, whether or not we believe in reincarnation, we can all deal with rodent problems humanely. For most of us, the solution lies with kinder "box traps" that can be used to capture rodents without harming them and allow us to remove these uninvited guests from our homes. Being caught will frighten the animals, as will being separated from their families and loved ones, so it is imperative to check the traps often and to handle them as quietly and gently as possible once a mouse or rat has been caught. The trap can then be carried to a sheltered part of the outdoors (where there is shade and protection from aerial predators) or, better, to an interim terrarium set up with a little cardboard privacy box and food and water, until you can catch the whole clan. That way they can be released together.

Then, be sure to seal up any holes or cracks through which they may have entered your home, so you don't have to do the whole thing all over again!

RESOURCES

Ketch-All Company

www.ketch-all.com or www.realgoods.com/shop

Ketch All Mouse Trap ($20)

This trap uses no bait. Simply wind the knob to catch mice twenty-four hours a day and release. This is a heavy-duty galvanized steel trap, with a simple goofproof design. Each mouse should be removed immediately after being caught in order to prevent injury to another mouse that enters. Measures 5 ½" H x 9" L x 7 ¼" W.

Pro-Ketch Mouse Trap ($16)

Made from tough galvanized steel, this trap captures multiple mice without ever resetting. Placing bait inside entices mice to enter. As they walk in, the teeter-totter–style ramp lowers to allow mice in, but snaps back once they step off so they can't exit. Clear view lid allows easy monitoring.

Larger traps are available from this company.

H. B. Sherman

www.shermantraps.com

Folding and nonfolding traps (the folding one is very handy). Prices range from $11.99 to $35.00, depending on size and material of trap.

PETA

www.petacatalog.com

With the Humane "Smart" Mousetrap ($10) you can catch mice alive and unharmed. A little dab of peanut butter is our recommended lure, and we have lots of pinprick holes in the trap.

Tomahawk Live Trap

www.livetrap.com

The Tomahawk Humane Mouse Trap ($20) is constructed of 28-gauge galvanized sheet metal for maximum resistance to rust and corrosion. This trap can be used for mice, shrews, voles, small chipmunks, or any other small rodent.

An Ounce of Prevention

You can prevent mice from reentering the premises by patching all holes larger than a quarter inch in diameter, sealing cracks in the walls and floor, and closing gaps around plumbing, doors, and windows. This should help to prevent the need to deal with the problem of removing mice again.

9.

Dealing Kindly with Insects in the Home

"Day, kill that spider!"

"No," Day replied to his lawyer friend, "I don't know that I have a right. Suppose a superior being said to a companion, 'Kill that lawyer.' How should you like it? And a lawyer is more noxious to most people than a spider."

—THOMAS DAY, *THE HISTORY OF LITTLE JACK*

God in His wisdom made the fly
And then forgot to tell us why.

—OGDEN NASH, "THE FLY"

The comedian George Carlin says that animal rights activists are the sort of people who would invent a cockroach spray that doesn't kill cockroaches. It just fills them with self-doubt so that they have to go away and think about things.

Perhaps that's why I wish life were the way it is depicted in the Acts of John in the Apocryphal New Testament. In it, we learn that the apostle John, his party having stopped at an inn to rest for the night, found himself unable to sleep because of bedbugs. John, being a very kind man, pleaded with the bedbugs to leave him in peace. The next morning John's companions awoke and found a big cluster of insects waiting by the door, having spent the night on the floor. The men woke John, who thanked the tiny insects for allowing him to sleep in peace and bade them return, which they did, scurrying up the bed legs and disappearing into the joints!

I'm not enough of a believer to buy that, but I do like the Sufi story of Abu Yazid, who every so often used to walk several hundred miles to a bazaar in Hamadan. Once, when he returned home, he discovered a colony of ants in his bag of cardamom seeds. Abu Yazid carefully packed the seeds up again and walked back across the desert, not to return the seeds to the merchant but to return the ants to their home.

When we stop and think about and watch small life-forms, we cannot but be in awe, as beautifully and simply suggested by Ogden Nash or as Olive Schreiner was when she watched a little ant for more than half an hour. She said that the ant was "trundling along a dried ball as large as itself. I followed it for nearly 100 yards, being blown over and over by the wind, regaining its feet, never leaving hold of its ball, climbing over stones and sticks and through grasses till it got to the hole. I never knew one's heart could go out in such a curious way to such a small spec of matter."

Cockroaches can be a problem, even in the best of places. The ones in Florida are nearly the size of condors, but even they are rather intriguing if you can get over your prejudices and look at them without that theatrical shudder we think we are supposed to let loose. Their wings are quite delicate. Yes, the Florida ones can fly. But they are polite and shy and scuttle away into the drains, out of sight, if they can avoid you.

Of the more than four thousand species of cockroach in the world, only a handful are considered "pests." Among them are the European cockroaches and the German cockroaches who came to stay in my warehouse. I tried all sorts of "cures," including bay leaves and even talking to them (something my friend swore worked for her when she did social work in a tenement in Maryland), but they had decided to populate the planet with their offspring, starting at my place, and wouldn't listen.

I shall never forget the borax. That was a mistake. I hadn't wanted to use an insecticide, a poison, and had taken bad advice to buy this instead. The forty thousand nerve endings in their antennae, their keen sense of smell (so keen that they can identify different people by body odor alone!), and the little ears on their rears weren't enough to warn the cockroaches away from the borax. They ate it and disintegrated slowly in front of me, no doubt in great pain as their small bodies burst asunder from some mysterious internal reaction. I felt hideously guilty, removed the refrigerator, and forbade everyone from eating in the office (a cockroach can live for about a year on the carbs in a cracker crumb), and in time, those who survived the hideous borax moved on to greener pastures.

Stephanie Boyles is PETA's wildlife biologist and an expert on moving insects out of people's homes. A most reassuring soul, she advises that fortunately, it is possible to control most insects safely and naturally with products that many of us have in our kitchen cabinets right now.

Besides knowing how to deal with challenges as vexing as wasps building a nest on a porch, armies of invading ants, and the ubiquitous cockroach, there is something else Stephanie knows about: the satisfaction of compassionately solving these problems. "People feel incredibly excited not to kill," she says. "They are grateful to have made a call and found a humane solution to their problem." Finding out how easy it is to be kind is a wonderfully uplifting feeling.

Well, off we go then, determined to try our damnedest to live up to these immortal words from Albert Schweitzer: "Each of us must live daily from judgment to judgment, deciding each case as it arises as wisely and mercifully as we can."

Here's how to deal with:

Ants

Pour a line of cream tartar, red chili powder, paprika, or dried peppermint at the place where ants enter the house—they won't cross it. You can also try washing countertops, cabinets, and floors with equal parts of vinegar and water and putting a little paprika at the edges.

Some people swear by cinnamon oil, peppermint oil, mint oil, lavender oil, a mixture of olive oil and cayenne pepper, or catnip.

Moths

A humane and great-smelling alternative to mothballs is to place cedar chips around clothes or to store sachets made out of dried lavender or equal parts of dried rosemary and mint in drawers and closets.

Flies

To repel flies, hang clusters of cloves in a room, or leave an orange skin out. However, you may invite them back, as with ants, if you don't keep living areas clean, sweep up crumbs promptly, vacuum, wash dishes right away, empty garbage promptly, and store food in tightly sealed containers.

Spiders

If you must evict them, carefully trap them in an inverted jar and release them outside.

Cockroaches

Place whole bay leaves in several places around infested rooms, including inside kitchen cabinets. Apparently bay leaves smell like dirty socks to cockroaches and they would rather not be around them. For serious infestations, you may need to resort to an insect growth regulator, called Gentrol, which nips the cockroach reproductive cycle in the bud, leading them to produce sterile offspring. Given that one German cockroach mother and her offspring can add thirty-five thousand new lives to the world in a year, birth control is a must.

Mosquitoes

Taking B-complex vitamins or eating brewer's yeast daily (in tablets or powder) can keep you mosquito-bite free in the summer months. Oil of citronella and pennyroyal mint oil are both effective repellents when diluted with vodka or vegetable oil and dabbed onto the skin. Mosquitoes dislike fresh basil and pennyroyal, so these can be usefully applied on porches and around the home.

RESOURCES

Holidobler, Bert, and Edward Osborne Wilson. *The Ants.* Belknap Press, 1990.

The definitive scientific study of one of the most diverse animal groups on earth. Full of amazing facts about the social behavior of these fascinating beings.

10.

Saving Little Visitors Who Get Trapped in the Swimming Pool or Pond

---

The first thing ninety-four per cent of the population does on acquiring a country place is to build some sort of swimming pool. The other six per cent instantly welches on the deal and stops payment.

—S. J. PERELMAN

Dawn Shewchuk of Plymouth, Connecticut, went out to her pool and found . . . a frog, sitting on a lily pad. She doesn't have lilies growing in her swimming pool, but she had placed a pretty plastic lily pad floater, called a Frog Saver, in it after being saddened to see frogs and insects become trapped in the pool and die there, unable to crawl up the sheer and slippery sides.

Dawn took a picture before releasing him out of the pool and said he was, she hoped, "the first of many rescues."

Dawn's frog isn't the oddest find in a backyard pool. Cindy Riggs of Miami reports finding a bedraggled squirrel staring hopefully at her from her plastic lily pad, which had come loose from its anchor and floated into the center of her pool; and Art Binder of Maine found a small opossum sitting on his floating chaise longue one morning. Someone else wrote to the makers of the Frog Saver to say that one morning she had found lizards, who may have fallen from an overhanging branch while playing, sitting on the Frog Saver. All animals were successfully rescued and released, although none would stick around to be dried with a towel!

PETA advises anyone with a pond or pool to leave a little "stairway," a ramp, rock, or platform that can rest in the water to serve as an emergency escape route for trapped wildlife. In a bowl of water, the help line can be as small as a stick; in a birdbath it can be a large pebble; and in a pool, well, the lily pad is not only functional but pretty, although any pool furniture can serve the same purpose.

In winter, pools should be drained and covered to prevent accidents such as animals falling in.

RESOURCES

PETA

www.petamall.com
Frog Saver Lily Pad (about $15)
Frogs trapped in pools swim around the edge in search of escape. This "lily pad" gives them just the leg up they need and can be snapped onto the pool ladder or attached to the wall. Made of 100 percent recycled plastic.

11.

Being Kind to Your Lawns and the Life in and on Them

The wind cannot read.

—CHINESE SAYING

She goes but softly, but she goeth sure;
She stumbles not as stronger creatures do;
Her journey's shorter, so she may endure;
Better than they which do much further go.
She makes no noise but still seizeth on
The flower or herb appointed for her food,
The which she quietly doth feed upon,
While others range and gare, but find no good.
And though she doth but very softly go,
However 'tis not fast, nor slow, but sure;
And certainly they that do travel so,
The prize they do aim at, they do procure.

—JOHN BUNYAN, "UPON THE SNAIL"

Howard Lyman is a self-proclaimed "fourth-generation reformed farmer, stockman and feedlot operator" who emerged from University of Montana determined to use his agricultural degree to redo his family's organic farm as an "agribusiness," using all the new chemicals that were then coming onto the marketplace on his crops and his cattle. Some years later, he looked at the land under his feet and found it was "deader than a doornail. No worms, no insects, no life. I had killed the soil and all the animals who once made it churn and thrive. It was now sterile and chemically saturated. What had I done?"

Mr. Lyman, who went on to become president of EarthSave and wrote a moving book called *Mad Cowboy,* had many thousands of acres to ruin, but the lessons he learned may allow us to stop ourselves before we behave in the same way to the manicured lawn in front of our house or to the wonderful garden out back. For there are other, gentler ways to proceed. This is especially important because the insects, birds, even wandering dogs and cats, cannot read those signs that say "Chemically Treated," nor can the rains that carry those chemicals via the storm sewers into the rivers and streams to poison fish and frogs and water-dwelling mammals and birds.

Let me relate two absolutely chilling stories from the press. First, the *New York Times* in 1986 reported how a champion ice skater, Christina Locek, was sunning herself in her Illinois backyard when a lawn care company began spraying insecticides onto a neighbor's yard. The article described how the spray drifted into Ms. Locek's yard, across her and her cat and dog. The cat died within minutes. The dog died within a few hours. Ms. Locek collapsed and is now permanently disabled and no longer able to compete. An extreme example, but one that offers an idea of how toxic some of these chemicals are, even in small doses.

The second story is about fungicides. The *Washington Post* reported an incident that occurred when navy lieutenant George Prior was spending his vacation golfing. One evening he developed a headache and a rash, followed by a high fever and vomiting. He entered a hospital. His skin blistered and peeled away, his organs failed, and he died. The cause of death was toxic epidermal necrolysis, a skin reaction apparently caused by exposure to a fungicide that had been applied to the golf course.

One study showed that Kansas farmers who apply 2, 4-D, a weed killer, in 1,500 over-the-counter products, had a risk up to seven times higher than average of developing non-Hodgkin's lymphoma, a rare cancer. The Environmental Protection Agency (EPA) and clinical researchers continue to "review" the possible risks associated with 2, 4-D, which one agency does not currently classify as a human carcinogen.

Birds and wild animals suffer even more than humans do. Ward Stone, a New York State wildlife pathologist, says, "You can follow label directions to a T and still kill birds." Classic symptoms of pesticide poisoning in birds are shivering, gasping, excessive salivation, seizures, wild flapping, and sometimes screaming. Birds often have these reactions out in the open, while small mammals may crawl into their dens to suffer and die.

EPA officials caution that their agency's registration of a pesticide does not guarantee that the product does not carry health risks. In 1999 the Northwest Coalition for Alternatives to Pesticides surveyed nineteen then-recently registered pesticides. Their conclusion as reported in their *Journal of Pesticide Reform*? That seven cause cancer, six cause genetic damage, one causes miscarriages, one causes birth defects, one causes cataracts, one causes liver and kidney damage, with eight being toxic to fish, one to shrimp, and one to oysters, and five being potential groundwater contaminants.

Whenever we wish to find what I call a "non–Wyatt Earp" approach, there invariably is one.

A chemical-free lawn, like a tree, detoxifies the air of pollutants and brings better health to four- and two-legged property occupants. A lot of unseen underground activity by worms and microorganisms makes a lawn healthy. If you allow this biological activity to go on unharmed by pesticides, roots will be stronger and chemical fertilizers unnecessary.

The members of McHenry County Defenders, a recycling group of Woodstock, Illinois, advise: "Grass clippings, left to decompose on the lawn, can contribute about 1.8 pounds of nitrogen per 1,000 sq. feet—for free! These clippings will not cause thatch.

Grass clippings are 85% water and will begin to decompose in a week or less. Within two weeks, nitrogen from the clippings can be found in new grass. Grass clippings also reduce water evaporation from the lawn and keep the soil temperature cooler."

They urge us not to turn a lawn into a chemical "junkie" waiting for its next nitrogen fix and suggest fertilizing with organic fertilizers to maintain growth rather than concentrating on creating "an advertising agency's version of a perfect landscape!" Good soil, they point out, grows good grass. "Improve your soil, then add clover and other nitrogen-fixing plants to your lawn seed mix to make your lawn self-fertilizing" is their advice.

Sow grass in fall, when the weather is cooler and there is little competition from weeds. Keep the seeds moist. A mixture of grasses that do well in your particular area is recommended, rather than a single variety. Zoysia, a spreading perennial grass, grows in thick, chokes out weeds, and stays green without watering.

Carla Bennett, PETA's columnist of "Ask Carla" fame, says, "Never walk on wet or soft lawns. Where the soil is compacted, use an aerator, available at rental stores, to punch small holes in the ground, or walk over the soil in shoes with cleats. Raking removes thatch and other dead organic material that smothers grass. Using a sharp blade, mow high; a grass height of two inches will shade out crabgrass and many weeds."

It's best to leave grass clippings on the lawn after you mow. This natural, free fertilizer breaks down easily and provides up to one-half the nitrogen and potassium a lawn needs to green up and thrive. Earthworms and natural organisms eat the clippings to provide a natural cycle of fertilizing and aeration.

Even leaves can be left in place if they are ground up with a lawn mower. Leaves also provide winter protection for tree roots. If you water, replace sprinklers, which waste water, with soaker hoses or "impulse" sprayers, which shoot water out in an efficient jet as the head turns. Plant ground cover in difficult areas.

Mulch exposed ground with wood chips, hay, or pine needles to keep moisture around plants.

- Increase activity in spent soil areas by top dressing them once in spring and once in fall with organic matter such as compost, leaf mulch, or peat moss. This makes plants healthier and more resistant to insects, drought, fungi, and disease.

Carla Bennett is adamant that lawns can survive with little or no fertilizer. There are now excellent new organic fertilizers on the market, but beware of harmful petroleum-based products that are represented as "organic" because they contain a little manure. In a natural, healthy lawn, the grass will be slower-growing, stronger, and more drought-resistant. Clover is not a weed and should be left in peace to grow. Its root nodules contain bacteria beneficial to the lawn and plants. And don't worry about dandelions or other weeds, Carla advises. Weeds are judgment calls. Dig them out by hand if you don't like them.

The joys of a great yard are made even sweeter when it's a natural, healthy, and kind space.

RESOURCES

www.environmentalfactor.com
Chemical-free turf care

www.AskCarla.com

www.McHenryco.def

12.

Do It Yourself: How to Avoid Commercial Cleaners

Accuse not Nature, she hath done her part;
Do thou thine!

—JOHN MILTON, *PARADISE LOST*

These days, whether we're dealing with a spot on the rug or fumes in the oven, we tend to reach for a chemical solution (literally as well as figuratively). It doesn't have to be that way! This may surprise you, but vinegar is one of the most powerful cleaning agents there are, and not only for hardware and fabric. Vinegar may even help give the human body a little more sparkle.

I first heard of vinegar as a "folk remedy" from an old lady who lived next door to my grandmother in Kingston, England, who used to swear that swallowing a teaspoon of vinegar every day was, like an apple a day, the antidote to illness. She is not alone in singing vinegar's praises. There is a Web site (see below) that boasts "44 Things to Do with Vinegar," and some of them are quite surprising.

For example, you can remove skunk odor from a dog by rubbing full-strength vinegar into his coat; vinegar polishes car chrome, relieves symptoms of colds if poured into a vaporizer, unclogs a steam iron, and freshens cut flowers.

Once, on vacation in Cancún, I overdid my first day at the beach. By the time I got off the bus and tried to walk the block or so to my hotel room, people were staring at me. That's because I looked like hell, or at least as if I had spent my day roasting in hell's fires.

The housekeeper disappeared into the kitchen and returned with squashed tomatoes floating in vinegar. Using the universal language of two people who can't understand each other through words, she indicated that I should smear the stuff all over my sizzling skin. To this day, I think she threw in the tomatoes as a joke, but tomatoes or not, that concoction took the sting out and allowed me to touch my flesh without screaming! People still stared at me, but this time it was because I smelled like salad dressing.

There are many cheaper and more ecologically sound ways to clean things and take care of your person and possessions than to buy commercially produced products that contain harsh compounds and chemical toxins. If you are interested in a more natural approach to housekeeping, here are a few ideas:

All-Purpose Cleaner

- Mix vinegar and salt to make a good surface cleaner.
- Pour some baking soda and vinegar on a damp sponge. It will clean and deodorize all kitchen and bathroom surfaces.

Deodorizer

- Place partially filled saucers of vinegar around the room.
- Boil one tablespoon of vinegar in one cup of water to eliminate unpleasant cooking odors.
- Baking soda is excellent for absorbing odors.

Removing Grease Spots

- Immediately pour salt on grease spots to absorb and prevent staining.

Removing Scratches

- Mix equal parts of lemon juice and vegetable oil, and rub against scratches with a soft cloth until they disappear.

Oven Cleaner

- While the oven is still warm, pour some salt on grimy areas. If the areas are dry, dampen with water before applying the salt. When the oven cools down, scrape the grime off and wash clean.
- Spray grimy areas with water or vinegar-water and apply a layer of baking soda. Rub gently with fine steel wool and wipe off. Rinse with water and wipe dry.

Toilet Bowl Cleaner

- Sprinkle baking soda into the bowl, then drizzle with vinegar and scour with a toilet brush. This combination both cleans and deodorizes. NOTE: Do *not* mix this combination with store-bought toilet cleaners. The combination will create toxic fumes.

Glass Cleaner

- Mix equal amounts of water and vinegar in a spray bottle. Wipe the glass with newspaper for a streak-free shine.

Drain Cleaner

- For a clogged drain pour a handful of baking soda down the drain, add one-half cup of vinegar, and close with a plug for twenty seconds. Rinse with hot water.

RESOURCE

44 Things to Do with Vinegar
groups.msn.com/veggiechat/crueltyfreecleaners.msnw

PART TWO

Fashion and Beauty

13.

Choosing Cosmetics That Give Everyone Something to Smile About

There is a garden in her face
Where roses and white lilies blow;
A heavenly paradise is that place
Wherein all pleasant fruits do flow.
There cherries grow which none may buy,
Till "Cherry ripe" themselves do cry.

—THOMAS CAMPION, "CHERRY-RIPE"

Lips that seem so kissable
Unpermissible unzippable unzip!

—LYRICS TO "UNZIP" BY ABC, AUSTRALIAN ROCK GROUP

Once in a while my job requires that I fly off to England to visit two wonderful old friends: Anthony Lawrence and Hilly Beaven, designers who work in the Soho district of London. Our meetings are supposed to be all about putting together a magazine, but before we get down to brass tacks, we order up pints of bitter in a local pub, reminisce, and catch up. Hilly's stories often focus on her adventures flying a single-engine Beagle Pup, and Ant's stories are about his misadventures in the search for the world's most interesting woman. It is thoroughly enjoyable fun, but something else I enjoy as part of those visits is that when I get off the tube at Oxford Circus and head to Hilly and Ant's studio, the route takes me down Carnaby Street.

Every time I round the corner onto this most famous of London streets, I feel as if forty years have slipped away. My feet hit the cobblestones and I look up from the windows of the little shops to the colorful banners and flags hanging overhead and think of the Swinging Sixties. The Beatles and the Stones were battling to top the music charts, and it was on Carnaby Street that you shopped for clothes and makeup if you wanted to look anything like the world's very first "supermodels."

The first big catwalk star was Jean Shrimpton, "the Shrimp," and then came Twiggy. Both women were photographed on Carnaby Street, all eyes and lips. Their lips were painted stark white to match the geometric circles on their micromini dresses or their white PVC thigh boots, and they drew long fish-bone lines in blue pencil on the skin beneath their black, mile-long false eyelashes.

Lips and eyes will always rule, but there's one difference between then and now. We now know that there is a lot more to choosing cosmetics than simply picking out a color.

If you are opposed to animal tests, you will want to look for the Corporate Standard of Compassion (CSC) cruelty-free logo, a leaping bunny. This logo means that the product has passed the highest standard in that every single ingredient is guaranteed not to have been tested in animals' eyes or in other cruel ways. Look, too, to see if product companies have printed "Not tested on animals" and "No animal ingredients" in their promotional materials, and don't be afraid to ask at cosmetics counters. Clinique, for example, is cruelty free, and sales assistants are proud to show you written proof. In shopping for any brand, if assistants seem to waffle or are unsure, ask to see the pledge in writing. Although it is the twenty-first century, animal tests are still abominably cruel and carried out in much the same way as in the 1920s, when they were first devised as a crude way to test for toxicity. But the alternatives are there, lots of them, and so are those companies that choose to use them. Today we have human skin patch tests, computer analysis, human corneas, databases containing human experiences with chemicals, and sophisticated assays that can give us more accurate information faster; yet some companies, even some big ones, still haven't modernized their testing methods.

And there is more: If you are a vegetarian, a vegan, or someone who objects to overfishing, or if you do not wish to contribute even a few dollars to the destruction of ocean lives (including those of seals and turtles caught in giant fishing nets), you may wish to watch out for the source of the shimmer in lipstick and, for that matter, in nail polish. It can be from a harmless synthetic or it can be what is sometimes called "pearl essence." Pearl essence is the silvery stuff found in fish scales, mostly herring scales, and is a by-product of large-scale commercial fish processing. The herrings thrash about aboard ship, having been dragged in by net, and their scales are removed and shoved into bags on deck.

Another frightening ingredient, given the worries of mad cow disease being transmitted from the animals' brains and spinal tissue, is the "cerebroside" used to create "luminosity" in some brands of cosmetics. It comes from "cattle, oxen or swine brain cells or other nervous system tissue," according to the Food and Drug Administration. Luckily, there are many companies that wouldn't dream of putting anything derived from an animal into a cosmetic, and other companies that offer you a choice. Urban Decay, for example, a company with its finger on the pulse of edgy "alternative culture," creates nail polishes in "All-American urban landscape–inspired colors," like, believe it or not, Roach, Rust, Oil Slick, and Acid Rain. To them, the very idea of adding animal ingredients is out, out, out of the question.

Aveda is another animal ingredient–free company. It was founded by a once fast-living Austrian hairdresser named Horst Rechelbacher, who took his doctors' advice about his reckless lifestyle so seriously that he quit his first high-stress job and traveled to the snowcapped Himalayas. There he studied Ayurvedic medicine and learned about healing herbs, essential oils, and other ancient remedies of India.

Horst and his newfound Indian associate Shiv Nath set out to achieve environmental awareness and appreciation within the beauty industry. That is why Aveda relies solely on plant-based ingredients, and uses essential oils and pure flower and plant essences in its cosmetics for cleansing and healing. They even look out for the welfare of beetles at Aveda. In one brochure, you can read this: "Some colors, for example, are very difficult to create without using carmine, but the company decided that crushing insects to derive the ingredient is unethical."

The word *aveda* means "knowledge of nature" in Sanskrit and also means "health" in ancient Greek, but the company's products are ultramodern in color and style, allowing you to make strong statements with chocolate- or plum-colored lipstick or wow them subtly with the gentle shades of rose and oat. Best of all, perhaps, is that all Aveda lipsticks smell glorious because they contain breath-freshening essences of real peppermint, cinnamon, basil, and anise.

Speaking of ancient beauty knowledge, have you ever tried kohl? If you do, do *not* do what my friend Linda did, and put it on your lips! Kohl is used by Asian and Arab women, men, and even children to make the eyes sparkle and keep the eyes cool and free from irritation. In the past several years, kohl has also made an appearance in the American marketplace. When I was in India recently, I picked up a tube of surma, a black kohl cosmetic that looks like lipstick, and gave it to her. Mistaking it for lip moistener, Linda smeared it all over her lips. Only when she looked at herself in the mirror and saw that her lips were pitch black did she realize why people had been giving her some very odd looks.

M.A.C. cosmetics is one of the growing number of cosmetics companies that uses kohl in eyeliner, but you can find "pure" kohl in liquid or "lipstick tube" form in many Asian grocery stores or on the Web.

I mustn't forget to mention the makeup brush! Synthetic bristle brushes are easy to find, but beware of brushes made from real animal hair, including mink from dirty fur ranches and pig farms (usually fancily named "boar bristle"). Some sales assistants will tell you that most horsehair brushes are made from hair obtained by brushing horses' manes. The truth is that they come from horse slaughterhouses. Urban Decay is one of the companies that save the day, and the animals, by offering fabulous animal-free brushes.

Beautification, it is said, goes from your brows to your toes. And toes must never be forgotten, so let me end with the silly tale of Loring Harkness, a twenty-something college student.

When Loring was preparing to fly off to an important job interview, his two older sisters said, "You know, Loring, it brings good luck when boys paint their toenails." The sisters insisted that they were not teasing, so Loring, not normally prone to do silly things, decided that their advice was harmless and raced to his girlfriend's house to ask her to paint his toenails. This she did, using Miss Glitter nail polish in Sea Green and Petunia, and alternating the colors, toe by toe. Loring isn't sure if that's what did the trick, but he did get his dream job. He says he hasn't painted his toenails since, but he'd definitely consider it.

Whether or not you paint your toenails, the operative word in Loring's story is "harmless." Whenever we use cosmetics, whether to prepare for a job or because we are going out on the town, we can be safe in the knowledge that our choices have resulted in no harm to any living being.

RESOURCES

Urban Decay

www.urbandecay.com

Products such as innovative Face Case, XXX Shine Gloss, Urban Camouflage Concealer, Lip Gunk, and Eye Shadow are available in Sephora, Ultra, and select boutiques nationwide.

Aveda

www.aveda.com

Cosmetics, hair products, and spa treatments.

Avalon Organic Botanicals

www.avalonnaturalproducts.com

Facial cleanser.

M.A.C. Cosmetics

www.maccosmetics.com

Kohl eyeliner and eye shadows.

Coalition for Consumer Information on Cosmetics (CCIC)

www.leapingbunny.org

For information on the cruelty-free logo and the Corporate Standard of Compassion for animals.

14.
Some Thoughts About Wool

"What is it you want to buy?" the Sheep said at last,
looking up for a moment from her knitting.
"I don't quite know yet," Alice said, very gently.
"I should like to look all round me first, if I might."
"You may look in front of you, and on both sides, if you like,"
said the Sheep: "but you can't look all round you—unless
you've got eyes at the back of your head."

—LEWIS CARROLL, *ALICE IN WONDERLAND*

When I was only a little sprite of a girl, my father's occupation took us to some rather craggy outposts, such as the Orkney Islands and the Scottish Highlands, where flocks of sheep lived on the hillsides and drank from the ice-cold streams or "burns" that fed the lochs. The winter mornings were brisk, to say the least, and I remember waking up shivering, reluctant to put even one toe out of bed until the fires had been lit and the coal glowed with warmth, filling the rooms with a fine layer of dust!

Then, full of "a good hot breakfast," which always included Scotch porridge oats, I ventured outdoors. Like all the children, I must have looked like an advertisement for a wool company, bundled up in a braided Shetland "jumper" (that's a sweater to you!) and thick, hand-knitted Argyle knee socks. The outfit was invariably topped off with a woolen tam-o'-shanter pulled hard down over my ears and a knitted scarf to keep out the chill and wind.

My mother, like the Sheep in *Alice in Wonderland,* is a master knitter, and she was responsible for all my "woollies." She would sit down after dinner and knit away, oblivious of the fading light. There were pullovers and vests for my father, cardigans for her, and all my various bits and pieces. Her needles clicked together like the sound of a tiny metronome, and I can almost see her, talking to my father, the dog, and me, amazing two out of three of us by not even glancing down as the intricate patterns materialized beneath her fingers. Now and then, she might get up to measure a length of knitting against my arm or waist, or to ask if we approved of the mix of colors she had woven into flowers or stripes or who knew what intricacies.

My favorite homemade woollies were the little pink bed jackets I got to wear when I came down with a bad cold and so stayed at home, propped up on pillows, being fed hot drinks like Marmite tea. These delicate jackets made me feel like a fairy princess, with their lacelike designs and the pretty pink ribbons threaded down the front.

At the same time I was growing up, so was Patty Mark. Patty lives in Australia, halfway around the world from me, down through that bore hole we English children were always told to dig so that we could slide through it and out the other side to visit the kangaroos. Patty fell in love with sheep when she was a girl and has spent much of her life rescuing them and other "livestock" from various farming calamities.

It was Patty who taught me where wool really comes from and, in the process, gave me quite a lot to think about. Most wool sold in the world's shops, whether in balls or made up into garments, comes from Australia, although most of the sheep in Australia are the offspring of involuntary immigrants from Scotland. They are of a breed called merinos, who are suited for life in colder climes, and so don't do very well in the searing heat of summer in Australia. There, such thick-coated breeds are prone to "fly-strike"—maggot infestations caused when blowflies lay their eggs in the folds of the deep pile wool. But in 1923 Australian farmers, who nowadays keep a hundred thousand sheep or more to a "field," came up with an ingeniously simple but most painful way of dealing with the problem, a procedure called mulesing. This involves using a pair of shears to cut off a dinner plate–size patch of the lamb's rump, flesh and all, for that is the place where the blowflies lay most eggs.

No pain relief is given to the sheep used in these huge farming operations, where every procedure involves lots of manpower and lots of sheep. So tiny lambs who are mulesed, their backsides bleeding and raw, collapse to the ground for about three days, dealing with their pain as best they can. Then, when they are able to stand, you see them staggering about, crablike, until the wound heals. Sometimes the farmers slap creosote (tar) on the wounds to stop the bleeding, but that likely only hurts the lambs even more.

Patty loves sheep very much, which means that seeing them mulesed, having their tails cut off, losing a teat to the shearing blade, or left with a broken leg in the fields cuts *her* like a knife. She rescues as many as she can, driving them to the vet in her old jeep. I'll never forget Patty telling me how "politely" the sheep sit on the backseat. Then she nurses them back to health and lets them live out their days safely on her vegetarian farm.

The worst treatment "wool sheep" get is reserved for last. When their most productive wool years are over, thousands upon thousands of these old, and sometimes ailing, sheep head for the Middle East and North Africa. They are crammed tightly on board huge multitiered, open-deck ships. You can just imagine what they must feel during the voyage, seeing a vast ocean all around them. They are not tended, nor do they all drink for the weeks-long journey; and not only do many die en route, but sick animals are reportedly often tossed to the sharks while still living.

Upon arrival at the docks in Iran, the survivors are herded "on foot" into the marketplaces or shoved and thrown, if they cannot move, onto trucks bound for faraway live animal bazaars. All are killed in the Muslim halal manner, left to bleed to death, their throats slit with a knife.

In the U.S. and Europe, the end may not usually be as hideous, but the fact remains that sheep are a business. They are not kept as beloved "pets," and it is not economically viable to treat them carefully for their aches and pains. Moreover, they too are mutilated without painkillers when they are castrated and have their tails "docked" (cut off). My father was the first person to tell me about pneumonia in sheep—he had listened to the sheep hacking and coughing through the winter on the English farm next to his boyhood home. That pneumonia was the result of sheep being exposed to the damp and the cold because the farmer had decided to get one last shearing in so he could sell that wool before the worst of winter hit.

I also found a study of sheep by a researcher named Keith Kendrick, who concluded, "We may have underestimated the importance and complexity of a sheep's social environment and intelligence." He drew that understated conclusion after discovering that sheep recognize each other by facial features, as we recognize our fellows, and that they can remember at least fifty other sheep and ten human beings for more than two years! The research also showed that sheep are able to imagine the faces of absent friends, and that a picture of a friendly face (a picture!) reduces the stress of being alone.

Leafing through my news clippings files recently, I found a story about Jim Watts, a farmer in Wiltshire, England, who devised a plan to spare a flock of sheep from attacks by foxes. He got his hands on some old fur coats, spray painted them luminescent orange, and put them on the sheep. This apparently baffled the foxes. Unfortunately, as what you've just read above bears out, it's not the foxes who are the biggest threat to the millions of sheep used for wool; but what *we* wear can protect them from needless cruelty. And manufacturers are coming through with plenty of great choices. You can ditch the itch of wool, feel as if you're five pounds lighter, and look stunning, if you switch to a natural fiber.

There are all manner of synthetics, but take cotton: Cotton is nonirritating, never itchy or scratchy, and so a godsend to people allergic to wool. It absorbs body moisture and evaporates it to the surrounding air, allowing our bodies to breathe and keeping us cool in summer and dry and warm in winter.

Cotton is also strong and durable, an ideal fabric to launder, being 30 percent stronger when wet and able to withstand repeated washings in the hottest water. It is free of static electricity, which causes fabrics to cling and soil easily and your hair to stand on end when you pull a wool garment over your head. Cotton fibers also accept the fastest dyes, providing you with vibrant, colorfast yarns. And it's great for knitting.

Because cotton fiber is less elastic than other fibers, Cotton Clouds (cottonclouds.com) advises knitters to knit tightly to avoid stretching and to use a thin cotton or four needles to hold shape best. You can add body to cotton knitting by using either a garter, seed, or plaited stitch or knitting into the back of purl stitches on a simple stockinette stitch.

RESOURCES

The Plymouth Yarn Company

PO Box 28
500 Lafayette St.
Bristol, PA 19007
215-788-0459
www.plymouthyarn.com
This company distributes hand knitting yarns to shops across the USA. Its product is 100 percent acrylic.

Yesterknits

www.yesterknits.com
Supplier of vintage British crochet and knitting patterns. The company also gives advice on pattern conversion and will send anyone a free pattern.

15.

Avoiding Bits of Fur on Collars and Cuffs, and Sidestepping Shearling, the "Sheepy Fur"

Whenever there is a popular animal skin or hide, someone comes up with a faux version of it. And there are so many people with environmental or ecological concerns, people who don't want real shearling.

—JAQUI LIVIDINI, A SENIOR VICE PRESIDENT AT SAKS FIFTH AVENUE, *NEW YORK TIMES*, DECEMBER 24, 2002

The only foxes on the runway should be the models.

—BRAZILIAN SUPERMODEL FERNANDA TAVARES, TELLING REPORTERS DURING A NEWS CONFERENCE WHY SHE WON'T MODEL OR WEAR FUR

The ageless April tales
Of how, when sheep get old,
As their faith told,
They went without a pang
To far green fields, where fall
Perpetual streams that call
To deathless nightingales.

—WILLIAM KERR

Even in ages gone by, few people wished to be labeled "a wolf in sheep's clothing."

Today, no environmentally friendly or animal-conscious dresser wishes to be seen in sheep's *or* wolf's clothing, wanting not even a whiff of wolf or coyote on that ski parka collar, and certainly never a shearling coat. Disingenuously named to create the misimpression that it is simply shorn fleece, "shearling" is not that at all. It consists of the *skins* of several sheep, including their wool. (For what's wrong with wool alone, please see chapter 14: "Some Thoughts About Wool," page 67.)

Rather desperate to keep the fur trade going (its trade publications report enormous losses and the closure of fur "ranches"), the fur industry has taken to dying fur to mask it and to selling it as linings and as trim, as well as trying to expand its sales with shearling.

Shearling coats are made by killing sheep and then stitching their hides together, just as a mink coat is made by killing minks and stitching them together to form the whole. The hide has to be tanned using a virtual cauldron of mordants that pollute the water as effectively as they stop decomposition (see chapter 16: "Shoe Shopping," page 75.)

Because faux fur is so cleverly made nowadays, it can be hard to spot the fake from the real McCoy. If activists in Beverly Hills, California, had prevailed in their efforts, furriers would be required, at least in that city, to label even the smallest bit of fur so as to allow consumers to see where that fur came from. Consumers could then have made an informed choice as to whether to buy a coat with a collar "made from an anally electrocuted red fox," for example.

The truth apparently hurt more than the thought of the method used to dispatch the poor victims of fur, and the "truth in labeling" measure was defeated. So it is up to us as compassionate consumers to make sure no wisp of trapped coyote or glove lining of strangled rabbit (for that is, indeed, how the majority of rabbits are killed) ruins our outfit.

RESOURCES

Weatherproof Garment Co.

www. weatherproofgarment.com

Modern technology has made great strides in replacing animal products with humane synthetics. Weatherproof Garment Company has developed a faux shearling that it calls microshearling. Microshearling is a synthetic fabric that has the feel of sheep skin but is made of polyester microfiber. This new fabric consists of a layer of specially treated polyester that is bonded to a thick layer of a synthetic pile fabric. In look and feel, microshearling is practically indistinguishable from the "real thing." Its advantages over genuine shearling are many: It is resistant to rain, wind, and snow, and because it is completely synthetic, it is animal-friendly, too.

Fur Replicas

262-790-1895

www.furreplicas.com

An assortment of faux fur capes, wraps, jackets, and muffs for rent or sale. Prices range from $18 to $82 for a four-day rental period.

16.

Shoe Shopping

Throw out your old shoes and good luck walks in your door.

—GREEK PROVERB

Have you ever clung to a pair of shoes even though those shoes have seen far better days? One morning long ago, going out on a rainy, slushy fall day, I looked down at my beloved Bass Weejuns, scuffed and battered but still my favorites after years of hard outdoor life. There was no way around it. It was time for them to go. At this point, not even the Salvation Army would have said thank you if I put them in the giveaway box.

The problem was my Weejuns were the last bit of leather in my closet. I had decided some years before that if I wouldn't eat the flesh of cattle, then I shouldn't wear their skins either. Out went all the boots and pumps and strappy leather sandals. But I didn't miss them. It had been so easy really. I found a wonderful selection of velvet and satin heels for evening wear. When I went to France I stocked up on all the fabulous fabric shoes so easily found in small village shops and in shoe departments of Paris stores like Printemps. I have the most remarkable collection of funky beach shoes and trendy yet practical cotton office and travel shoes that come in all colors and are lightweight in my luggage (a few pairs can even get popped into the washing machine!). Closer to home, in fact about seven minutes away by car, I could pop into the mall to browse in a variety of stores that netted me faux leather boots, dress shoes with cork heels, and even comfy fabric flats.

My Weejuns were different. I'd told myself I needed them and hoped they would last forever because I wasn't sure I could find nonleather shoes hardy enough to take their place in the horse barn or climbing a hill. I found a dozen excuses to put off the shopping trip because I feared it would be fruitless. Could I find nonleather shoes that would mold to my foot, breathe, and stand up to the rigors of my work? Then, as so often happens when one is searching, a messenger appeared. While attending a luncheon one afternoon, I happened to meet a man who had the answers. He had been in the leather business for years, in fact his father had taught him his trade, but he'd made a switch and invested in what he was sure then was the wave of the future: man-made materials. He was convinced they would replace the hide. I had a million questions for him.

He listened patiently and then laid to rest all my concerns, one by one. Yes, I could find nonleather shoes that would rival my Weejuns for comfort and sturdiness. For that matter, he assured me, I could find shoes of man-made material for just about any occasion. Whether I was looking for a pair of what my mother used to call "court shoes" to wear to a fancy dinner or for kicking up my heels on the dance floor, for casual or comfy styles, for conservative office brogues, running shoes, cross-trainers, or even ultrahardy footwear for arduous trekking, there was a wealth of wonderful choices.

All the old arguments in favor of leather, like those in favor of fur, he told me, have evaporated as synthetic skins have been perfected for look, feel, and breathability. Products such as plastic leather (pleather) and faux suede are being used widely for garments and shoes, as well as for sports balls and luxury car seat covers. As an added bonus, most of the alternatives to leather are lighter, warmer, and cheaper than leather.

Like me, my messenger was deeply affected by the treatment of cattle, pigs, and other animals killed for their flesh and skin. But he also made me realize that my choice of footwear could save the environment and even improve the health of workers and their children in this country and in faraway lands. Leather is tanned with harsh chemicals that pollute waterways and are apparently linked to cancer for workers and those living downstream from such factories. Animal skin is turned into finished leather through the use of formaldehyde, coal tar derivatives, cyanide-based oils and dyes, chromium, and other toxins that poison water systems and the humans and wildlife exposed to them. A New York State Department of Health study found an apparent association between testicular cancer and employment in animal skin tanneries.

Finally, my "messenger" answered the question that had nagged at my conscience for some time. Are man-made materials, particularly petrochemicals, more environmentally destructive than "natural" leather? He laughed.

"Leather is certainly absolutely natural on the animal who was born in it," he said. "And when that animal dies, his hide certainly does dissolve back into the soil. But if you throw a pair of leather shoes into the woods, they don't biodegrade. They sit there for years, a decade or more."

I learned that this was because they've been treated with mordants, harsh chemicals that retard decomposition. As for synthetics, while they are not as pure as going barefoot, they are far less damaging to animals and the earth, not to mention to rivers and streams and those who depend on them.

Since then, I've found that I can also opt for the truly natural shoes of ultrachic recycled rubber or wonderful natural fibers and fabrics like cotton, cotton corduroy, satin, velvet, canvas, and even woven straw or jute. I've also visited the original home of Sir Paul McCartney's shoe provider, a funky store called Vegetarian Shoes, nestled in the trendy seaside town of Brighton in England. There, if you buy a pair of their purple and black vegan Dr. Martens, the shoes are popped into brown paper bags instead of shoe boxes. Like father like daughter. Stella McCartney's first line of vegan shoes so impressed a Manolo Blahnik representative who visited her Manhattan shop that he declared, "They must be of leather!" But they are not.

After this meeting, I didn't let even twenty-four hours pass before I tossed my Weejuns, grabbed my faux suede handbag, and headed out to the stores. As my messenger had predicted, I found several pairs of hardy work shoes to choose from, and not one of them had brought death to an animal or suffering to people.

RESOURCES

Moo Shoes

212-254-6512
www.mooshoes.com
Offers a wide variety of nonleather shoes, belts, and wallets.

Steve Madden

888-SMADDEN
www.stevemadden.com
Offers many nonleather women's shoes. Sells shoes in Steve Madden stores, in major department stores, and online.

Vegetarian Shoes

www.vegetarian-shoes.co.uk
This company, which Sir Paul McCartney patronizes, carries more than fifty styles of synthetic leather and synthetic suede shoes, including genuine nonleather Dr. Martens bad boy boots and shoes, nonleather Birkenstocks, dress shoes, hiking boots, work boots, pleather jackets, and belts.

Payless

877-474-6379
www.payless.com

Boasting possibly the world's lowest-priced selection, Payless carries a wide variety of trendy styles of shoes and boots. So cheap, you can buy three pairs for the price of one somewhere else! And they imitate many of the top designers' styles but use imitation leather, so you can get fashionable shoes at a fraction of the price.

For funky ultratrendy shoes, I recommend DragonFly Shoes (www.dragonflyshoes.com), and Funk e Feet (www.funkefeet.com), which, very endearingly, marks all vegan selections with a little cow symbol.

A Propos . . . Conversations (www.conversationshoes.com) offers pretty, feminine vegan fabric shoes for women.

For synthetic pumps there's Life Stride (www.browngroup. com/lifestride), which you can usually find at department stores such as Famous-Barr, Foley's, Hecht Co., Robinsons-May, Belk's, Boscov's, Rich's-Lazarus-Goldsmith's, Carson Pirie Scott, Proffitt's, and Younker's. You can call 1-800-766-6465 for a retailer near you. Delias (www.delias.com) has a wide selection of feminine faux leather and faux suede boots and shoes.

My top picks for athletic shoes are New Balance (www.newbalance.com) for comfortable synthetic running, tennis, and basketball shoes; for hiking boots, Garmont USA (www.garmontusa. com); Airwalk (www.airwalk.com) for synthetic snow boots and skateboarding shoes; and SiDi USA (www.sidiusa.com) for nonleather bicycling shoes. Road Runner Sports (www.roadrunnersports.com) sells nonleather running shoes including Brooks, Asics, New Balance, Saucony, Reebok, Mizuno, Adidas, and Etonic.

Spalding Sports (www.spalding.com) carries synthetic leather volleyballs, basketballs, softballs, soccer balls, and footballs. You can even get vegan ballet slippers from Capezio (www. capeziodance. com); the 626 Tapette and 625 Jr. Tyette for women are both synthetic.

17.

Finding the Perfect Soap

I used your soap two years ago; since then I have used no other.

—SOAP ENDORSEMENT IN *PUNCH* MAGAZINE

I test my bath before I sit,
And I'm always moved in wonderment
That what chills the finger not a bit
Is so frigid upon the fundament.

—OGDEN NASH

When the scents from the soap aisle rise up around you and caress your nostrils or when you turn on the tap after a hard day and look forward to sinking your aching limbs into a sudsy hot bath (not the chilly bath imagined by Ogden Nash), who would think that you can make a world of difference just by choosing your soap carefully?

There are at least three areas to consider in choosing a soap: What is in it, how was it tested, and does buying it help improve the world? Many companies offer soaps that satisfy all three.

First, what's in it? Well, I don't know about you, but I don't want pork fat, lard, and other tallow ingredients smeared on my face, yet most commercial soaps use tallow from animal carcasses boiled down, or "rendered," in giant vats. I'll take palm oil, coconut oil, or anything else from a tree in my soap, but not that. Cocoa butter soap, which comes from the seeds of the cacao tree, is smooth and soft and delightful, as is olive oil soap, reputedly Queen Cleopatra's favorite, along with pure African shea butter soap (shea butter is extracted from the shea tree)—perhaps brought back by Anthony from Syria. More on the healing properties of shea butter later. Queen Victoria, by the way, made the most of her imperial connections and is believed to have been quite taken by pink northern Indian soaps made from wildflowers and natural tree oils.

Second, the list of companies that do not test their soaps on animals, but use ingredients and ingredient combinations known to be safe, is now very long, and new soaps seem to come onto the market every day. Look for the "no animal testing" and "no animal ingredient" labels or check PETA's list of soap companies that do and don't test soaps cruelly.

Third, buying soaps from a cooperative helps your community, but some conscientious soap companies give back a portion of their proceeds to people in dire need. The best example is probably the Body Shop.

The Body Shop has its own foundation, supported by profits from soap sales. Among its charitable works is the development of income-generating activities to support the work of the Amazoncoop, a cooperative of Indian tribes. These activities include the Eco-Lodge at Tataquara, Brazil; the Cyber Café, which allows them to learn computer skills; and the development of the Green Pharmacy, replacing 60 percent of pharmaceuticals with traditional herbal remedies.

The Amazoncoop now gives employment to dozens of people, including Indians living in the town of Altamira, Brazil, who lost their land at the beginning of the last century and have few choices in their lives. Many of these people have never had the opportunity to have a steady job or be treated with respect. The Body Shop says that challenges are great and work is diverse, but the small team leading this project is completely dedicated and has great hopes for the future.

Now, back to shea butter for a moment. Despite its popularity today, traditional uses of shea butter are being preserved because a vast number of people in Africa and elsewhere around the world are using African shea butter for everything from traditional healing ceremonies to spiritual cleansing. In some households, shea butter is even used to prepare dishes. Many people from all walks of life have used unrefined African shea butter for their skin and hair. It also helps remove stretch marks, scars, burn marks, and dark patches.

Living in a part of the world where we have so much and so many options, it feels great to be able to help others just by taking a bath!

RESOURCES

The Body Shop

www.bodyshop.com

Cocoa butter soaps, translucent glycerin ones, and rich cleansing bars.

PETA

www.peta.org

For PETA's free list of companies that test on animals and those that don't.

18.

Bighearted Options to Exotic Skins

Mock crock and fake snake make the best
fashion statement, which is "Live and let live!"

—TWIGGY IN A LETTER TO THE
WORLD'S TOP COUTURIERS FOR PETA

I once kept a newspaper clipping in my desk about Pearl and Mel Pederson. This delightful couple from Illinois had an alligator named Alice who lived with them for forty-two years.

According to the clipping, Alice loved taking bubble baths and, according to the Pedersons, loved the couple dearly and played games with them.

Alice must have been six feet long from the tip of her tail to the end of her snout, but what I remember most is her silly smile. Perhaps, like dolphins, she wasn't really smiling at all and it was just that her mouth had natural crinkles in it, but it certainly looked as if this alligator, with her snaggly teeth sticking out at the sides, knew she was in clover and was very happy with her life.

I doubt anyone ever caught the Pedersons with an alligator bag or wearing alligator shoes!

Keeping alligators as pets does not usually work out well, for when the beasts grow up and start to bite, or won't fit into the aquarium or the bathtub any longer, they may find themselves flushed down the toilet or let loose in the neighborhood to look for small prey to eat.

When people decide to turn their hides into bags, belts, and footwear, that is even more perilous a proposition for the animals. Most alligators used in the fashion and trinket industries—and crocodiles raised commercially in Africa and elsewhere overseas for the same purpose—are farmed in highly unsanitary conditions. They are bred in cement pits and kept crammed almost on top of one another in their own waste.

In the wild, alligators are excellent mothers, guarding their eggs from all comers and, once the babies are hatched, carrying them, one by one, down to the water. Gator and croc moms also help struggling babies hatch by using their tremendously powerful jaws to crack the eggs, ever so gently.

When the end comes, the wild ones are hooked on enormous steel gaffs, have their mouths taped shut, and are dragged on board hunting boats, strung up, and skinned. In captivity, they are usually hit repeatedly on the head, sometimes with a sledgehammer and sometimes with a baseball bat by youngsters employed on the cheap to do the business's dirty work. Because few people care about what alligators or crocodiles go through, many are skinned alive.

When Britain's Princess Anne was asked about her role as patron of the Royal Society for the Prevention of Cruelty to Children, she said, "You don't have to like children to know they should not be mistreated." I feel the same way about reptiles.

Growing up in India, my family and I met quite a few snakes, and not always under the most polite circumstances. For example, a cobra made her nest in an outdoor lavatory and gave my mother quite a turn. On another occasion, when I was out walking near an enormous termite mound, a big snake poked his head out for a look around, inches from my own head. Both of us had a nasty shock, and then he popped his head back inside, no doubt to continue his supper.

A favorite tourist scam involving snakes, or perhaps not involving snakes, was run by a sightseeing guide who charged people a fee to take them into the forest to look for python tracks. I went on one of those outings once, and in a surprisingly short time, we spotted some marks in the sandy soil. When the guide had moved out of earshot, my friend, a cyclist, pointed out that that those "python tracks" looked remarkably like the tracks that would be made if you rolled a bicycle tire carefully along the ground.

Like snakes or not, the animal protection group Beauty Without Cruelty has made a deeply disturbing video of pythons, cobras, and other snakes being nailed to trees and skinned alive. Some of the skinned snakes are still alive two or even three days later. The skin is made into belts and purses, sometimes even pants, and sold for high prices in the West.

In India, Sri Lanka, China, and other Asian countries, capturing snakes and removing them from their natural environment—which is very tempting to do when a middleman is offering money and you are poor—has caused an imbalance that has resulted in a rise in the rat and insect populations.

The look is one thing, the reality another. If filmmakers can switch to fake gators and crocs, as indeed most of them have, so can fashion. Luckily, it is always possible to wear a patterned fake skin that looks like the real thing, although I'm not sure why anyone would wish to look as if he or she didn't care.

Life is all about options, and kindness is certainly the best option of all.

RESOURCE

For designer faux, check out Moschino, Todd Oldham, and many of the top names in bags, wallets, and accessories.

19.

Recognizing Animal Ingredients and Alternatives to Them

I spit it out!

—SOPHIE LOVIT, AGED SEVEN, UPON HEARING THAT HER JELL-O WAS MADE FROM BOILED HOOVES.

It might be useful to take a quick look down the list that follows and see if there are any surprises, as the oddest ingredients are finding their way into foods and cosmetics these days. Not all of them are readily recognizable, either. Who would know that "natural flavoring" can mean blood? Only Dracula might wish for that in a packet of potato chips or a cookie.

I guarantee that the origins of many commonly used ingredients found on this list would stump Uncle Ned in a family parlor game. Who would ever dream that some colorings are made from ground-up beetles, or that a makeup brush could come from the hair inside a cow's ear?

Where applicable, kinder alternatives to objectionable ingredients are listed with the definition. Manufacturers are turning to these alternatives more and more. If an ingredient can come from *both* an animal and a plant source and the label fails to identify which source the company has used, I recommend erring on the side of caution. Also keep in mind that the information here (and throughout this book) is not intended to diagnose or serve as a prescription for any illness or disease. If you suffer from any medical conditions, you should see your physician before adopting any of my suggestions. Drop a line to the manufacturer, asking for clarification. The more queries the company gets, the more likely it is that, if the company is using a less "savory" ingredient, it'll make the switch.

Happy label reading!

Adrenaline. Hormone from adrenal glands of hogs, cattle, and sheep. In medicine. Alternatives: synthetics.

Alanine. See **Amino Acids.**

Albumen/Albumin. In eggs, milk, muscles, blood, and many vegetable tissues and fluids. In cosmetics, albumen is usually derived from egg whites and used as a coagulating agent. May cause allergic reaction. In cakes, cookies, candies, and the like. Egg whites sometimes used in "clearing" wines. Derivative: albumin.

Aliphatic Alcohol. See **Lanolin** and **Vitamin A.**

Allantoin. Uric acid from cows, most other mammals. Also in many plants (especially comfrey). In cosmetics (especially creams and lotions) and used in treatment of wounds and ulcers. Derivatives: alcloxa, aldioxa. Alternatives: extract of comfrey root, synthetics.

Alpha-Hydroxy Acids. Any one of several acids used as an exfoliant and in antiwrinkle products. Lactic acid may be animal-derived (see **Lactic Acid**). Alternatives: glycolic acid, citric acid, and salicylic acid are plant- or fruit-derived.

Ambergris. From whale intestines. Used as a fixative in making perfumes and as a flavoring in foods and beverages. Alternatives: synthetic or vegetable fixatives.

Angora. Hair from the Angora rabbit or goat. Used in clothing. Alternatives: synthetic fibers.

Animal Fats and Oils. In foods and cosmetics. Alternatives: olive oil, wheat germ oil, coconut oil, flaxseed oil, almond oil, and safflower oil.

Arachidonic Acid. A liquid unsaturated fatty acid that is found in liver, brain, glands, and fat of animals and humans. Generally isolated from animal liver. Used in companion animal food for nutrition and in skin creams and lotions to soothe eczema and rashes. Alternatives: synthetics, aloe vera, tea tree oil, calendula ointment.

Arachidyl Proprionate. A wax that can be made from animal fat. Alternatives: peanut or vegetable oil.

Bee Pollen. Microsporic grains in seed plants gathered by bees, then collected from the legs of bees. Causes allergic reactions in some people. In nutritional supplements, shampoos, toothpastes, deodorants. Alternatives: synthetics, plant amino acids, pollen collected from plants.

Bee Products. Produced by bees for their own use. Bees are selectively bred. Culled bees are killed. A cheap sugar is substituted for their stolen honey. Their legs are often torn off by pollen-collection trapdoors. Millions die as a result of all these practices.

Beeswax. Honeycomb. Wax obtained from melting honeycomb with boiling water, straining it, and cooling it. From virgin bees. Very cheap and widely used. In lipsticks and many other cosmetics (especially face creams, lotions, mascara, eye creams and shadows, face makeups, nail whiteners, lip balms). Derivatives: cera flava. Alternatives: paraffin, vegetable oils, and fats. Ceresin, aka ceresine, aka earth wax. (Made from the mineral ozokerite. Replaces beeswax in cosmetics. Also used to wax paper, to make polishing cloths, in dentistry for taking wax impressions, and in candle making.) Also, carnauba wax (from the Brazilian palm tree; used in many cosmetics, including lipstick; rarely causes allergic reactions). Candelilla wax (from candelilla plants; used in many cosmetics, including lipstick; also in the manufacture of rubber and phonograph records, in waterproofing and writing inks; no known toxicity). Japan wax (vegetable wax; Japan tallow; fat from the fruit of a tree grown in Japan and China).

Benzoic Acid. In almost all vertebrates and in berries. Used as a preservative in mouthwashes, deodorants, creams, aftershave lotions. Alternatives: cranberries, gum benzoin (tincture) from the aromatic balsamic resin from trees grown in China, Sumatra, Thailand, and Cambodia.

Beta-carotene. See **Carotene.**

Biotin. Vitamin H. Vitamin B Factor. In every living cell and in larger amounts in milk and yeast. Used as a texturizer in cosmetics, shampoos, and creams. Alternatives: plant sources.

Boar Bristles. Hair from wild or captive hogs. In "natural" toothbrushes and bath and shaving brushes. Alternatives: vegetable fibers, nylon, the peelu branch or peelu gum (Asian, available in the U.S.; its juice replaces toothpaste).

Bone Char. Animal bone ash. Used in bone china and often to make sugar white. Serves as the charcoal used in aquarium filters. Alternatives: synthetic tribasic calcium phosphate.

Bone Meal. Crushed or ground animal bones. In some fertilizers. In some vitamins and supplements as a source of calcium. In toothpastes. Alternatives: plant mulch, vegetable compost, dolomite, clay, vegetarian vitamins.

Calfskin. See **Leather.**

Caprylic Acid. A liquid fatty acid from cow's or goat's milk. Also from palm and coconut oil, other plant oils. In perfumes, soaps. Derivatives: caprylic triglyceride, caprylamine oxide, capryl betaine. Alternatives: plant sources.

Carmine. Cochineal. Carminic Acid. Red pigment from the crushed female cochineal insect. Reportedly, seventy thousand beetles must be killed to produce one pound of this red dye. Used in cosmetics, shampoos, red apple sauce, and other foods (including red lollipops and food coloring). May cause allergic reaction. Alternatives: beet juice (used in powders, rouges, shampoos; no known toxicity); alkanet root (from the root of this herblike tree; used as a red dye for inks, wines, lip balms; no known toxicity). Can also be combined to make a copper or blue coloring.

Carotene. Provitamin A. Beta-carotene. A pigment found in many animal tissues and in all plants. Used as a coloring in cosmetics and in the manufacture of vitamin A.

Casein. Caseinate. Sodium Caseinate. Milk protein. In "nondairy" creamers, soy cheese, many cosmetics, hair preparations, beauty masks. Alternatives: soy protein, soy milk, and other vegetable milks.

Cashmere. Wool from the Kashmir goat. Used in clothing. Alternatives: synthetic fibers.

Castor. Castoreum. Creamy substance with strong odor from muskrat and beaver genitals. Used as a fixative in perfume and incense. Alternatives: synthetics, plant castor oil.

Catgut. Tough string from the intestines of sheep, horses, and other animals. Used for surgical sutures. Also for stringing tennis rackets and musical instruments. Alternatives: nylon and other synthetic fibers.

Cera Flava. See **Beeswax.**

Cerebrosides. Fatty acids and sugars found in the covering of nerves. May include tissue from brain.

Cetyl Alcohol. Wax found in spermaceti from sperm whales or dolphins. Alternatives: vegetable cetyl alcohol (e.g., coconut), synthetic spermaceti.

Cetyl Palmitate. See **Spermaceti.**

Chitosan. A fiber derived from crustacean shells. Used as a lipid binder in diet products, in hair, oral, and skin care products, and in antiperspirants and deodorants. Alternatives: raspberries, yams, legumes, dried apricots, and many other fruits and vegetables.

Cholesterin. See **Lanolin.**

Cholesterol. A steroid alcohol in all animal fats and oils, nervous tissue, egg yolk, and blood. Can be derived from lanolin. In cosmetics, eye creams, and shampoos. Alternatives: solid complex alcohols (sterols) from plant sources.

Civet. Unctuous secretion painfully scraped from a gland very near the genital organs of civets. Used as a fixative in perfumes. Alternatives: see alternatives to **Musk.**

Cochineal. See **Carmine.**

Cod Liver Oil. See **Marine Oil.**

Collagen. Fibrous protein in vertebrates. Usually derived from animal tissue. Applied topically, can't affect the skin's own collagen. Alternatives: soy protein, almond oil, and amla oil (see alternative to **Keratin**).

Cortisone. Corticosteroid. Hormone from adrenal glands. Widely used in medicine. Alternatives: synthetics.

Cysteine, L-Form. An amino acid from hair that can come from animals. Used in hair-care products and creams, in some bakery products, and in wound-healing formulations. Alternatives: plant sources.

Cystine. An amino acid found in urine and horsehair. Used as a nutritional supplement and in emollients. Alternatives: plant sources.

Dimethyl Stearamine. See **Stearic Acid.**

Down. Goose or duck insulating feathers. From slaughtered or cruelly exploited geese. Used as an insulator in quilts, parkas, sleeping bags, and pillows. Alternatives: polyester and synthetic substitutes, kapok (silky fibers from the seeds of some tropical trees), and milkweed seed pod fibers.

Duodenum Substances. From the digestive tracts of cows and pigs. Added to some vitamin tablets. In some medicines. Alternatives: vegetarian vitamins, synthetics.

Egg Protein. In shampoos, skin preparations, and the like. Alternatives: plant proteins.

Elastin. Protein found in the neck ligaments and aortas of cows. Similar to collagen. Can't affect the skin's own elasticity other than by helping to keep in moisture. Alternatives: synthetics, protein from plant tissues.

Emu Oil. From flightless ratite birds native to Australia and now factory farmed. Used in cosmetics and creams. Alternatives: vegetable and plant oils.

Estrogen. Estradiol. Female hormones extracted from pregnant mares' urine. Used for reproductive problems and in birth control pills and Premarin, a menopausal drug. In creams, perfumes, and lotions. Has a negligible effect in the creams as a skin restorative; simple vegetable-source emollients are considered better. Alternatives: oral contraceptives and menopausal drugs based on synthetic steroids or phytoestrogens (from plants, especially palm-kernel oil). Menopausal symptoms can also be treated with diet and herbs.

Fatty Acids. Can be one or any mixture of liquid and solid acids such as caprylic, lauric, myristic, oleic, palmitic, and stearic. Used in bubble baths, lipsticks, soap, detergents, cosmetics, and all sorts of foods. Alternatives: vegetable-derived acids, soy lecithin, safflower oil, bitter almond oil, and sunflower oil.

Feathers. From exploited and slaughtered birds. Used whole as ornaments or ground up in shampoos. See also **Down** and **Keratin.**

Fish Oil. Used in vitamins and supplements. In milk fortified with vitamin D. Alternatives: yeast extract ergosterol and exposure of skin to sunshine. Fish oil can also be from marine mammals. Used in soap making. See also **Marine Oil.**

Fish Scales. Used in shimmery makeups. Alternatives: mica, rayon, synthetic pearl.

Fur. Obtained from animals (usually mink, foxes, or rabbits) cruelly trapped most commonly in steel-jaw leghold traps or raised in intensive confinement on fur "farms." Alternatives: synthetics. See also **Sable Brushes**.

Gelatin. Gel. Protein obtained by boiling skin, tendons, ligaments, and/or bones with water. From cows and pigs. Used in shampoos, face masks, and other cosmetics. Used as a thickener for fruit gelatins and puddings (e.g., Jell-O). In candies, marshmallows, cakes, ice cream, yogurts. On photographic film and in vitamins as a coating and as capsules. Sometimes used to assist in "clearing" wines. Alternatives: carrageen (carrageenan, Irish moss), seaweeds (algin, agar-agar, kelp—used in jellies, plastics, medicine), pectin from fruits, dextrins, locust bean gum, cotton gum, silica gel. Marshmallows were originally made from the root of the marsh mallow plant. Vegetarian capsules are now available from several companies. Digital cameras don't use film.

Glycerin. Glycerol. A by-product of soap manufacture (normally uses animal fat). In cosmetics, foods, mouthwashes, chewing gum, toothpastes, soaps, ointments, medicines, lubricants, transmission and brake fluid, and plastics. Derivatives: glycerides, glyceryls, glycreth-26, polyglycerol. Alternatives: vegetable glycerin—a by-product of vegetable oil soap; derivatives of seaweed, petroleum.

Guanine. Pearl Essence. Obtained from scales of fish. Constituent of ribonucleic acid and deoxyribonucleic acid and found in all animal and plant tissues. In shampoo, nail polish, other cosmetics. Alternatives: leguminous plants, synthetic pearl, and aluminum and bronze particles.

Hide Glue. Same as gelatin but of a cruder, impure form. Alternatives: dextrins and synthetic petrochemical-based adhesives. See also **Gelatin.**

Honey. Food for bees, made by bees. Can cause allergic reactions. Used as a coloring and an emollient in cosmetics and as a flavoring in foods. Should never be fed to infants.

Alternatives: in foods—maple syrup, date sugar, syrups made from grains such as barley malt, turbinado sugar, molasses; in cosmetics—vegetable colors and oils.

Honeycomb. See **Beeswax.**

Hyaluronic Acid. A protein found in umbilical cords and the fluids around the joints. Hyaluronic acid from animal sources is used in cosmetics. Alternatives: synthetic hyaluronic acid, plant oils.

Hydrolyzed Animal Protein. In cosmetics, especially shampoo and hair treatments. Alternatives: soy protein and other plant proteins.

Insulin. From hog pancreas. Used by millions of diabetics daily. Alternatives: synthetics, vegetarian diet and nutritional supplements, human insulin grown in a lab.

Isinglass. A form of gelatin prepared from the internal membranes of fish bladders. Sometimes used in "clearing" wines and in foods. Alternatives: bentonite clay, "Japanese isinglass," agar-agar (see alternatives to **Gelatin**), mica (a mineral used in cosmetics).

Isopropyl Palmitate. Complex mixtures of isomers of stearic acid and palmitic acid. See also **Stearic Acid.**

Keratin. Protein from the ground-up horns, hooves, feathers, quills, and hair of various animals. In hair rinses, shampoos, permanent wave solutions. Alternatives: almond oil, soy protein, amla oil (from the fruit of an Indian tree), human hair from salons. Rosemary and nettle give body and strand strength to hair.

Lactic Acid. Found in blood and muscle tissue. Also in sour milk, beer, sauerkraut, pickles, and other food products made by bacterial fermentation. Used in skin fresheners, as a preservative, and in the formation of plasticizers. Alternative: plant milk sugars, synthetics.

Lactose. Milk sugar from milk of mammals. In eye lotions, foods, medicine tablets, cosmetics, baked goods, medicines. Alternatives: plant milk sugars.

Lanolin. Lanolin Acids. Wool Fat. Wool Wax. A product of the oil glands of sheep, extracted from their wool. Used as an emollient in many skin care products and cosmetics and in medicines. (See **Wool** for cruelty to sheep.) Derivatives: aliphatic alcohols, cholesterin, isopropyl lanolate, laneth, lanogene, lanolin alcohols, lanosterols, sterols, triterpene alcohols. Alternatives: plant and vegetable oils.

Lard. Fat from hog abdomens. In shaving creams, soaps, cosmetics. In baked goods, French fries, refried beans, and many other foods. Alternatives: pure vegetable fats or oils.

Leather. Suede. Calfskin. Sheepskin. Alligator Skin. Other Types of Skin. Subsidizes the meat industry. Used to make wallets, handbags, furniture and car upholstery, shoes, and so on. Alternatives: cotton, canvas, nylon, vinyl, ultrasuede, pleather, other synthetics.

Lecithin, Choline Bitartrate. Waxy substance in nervous tissue of all living organisms, but frequently obtained for commercial purposes from eggs and soybeans. Also from nerve tissue, blood, milk, corn. Choline bitartrate, the basic constituent of lecithin, is in many animal and plant tissues and prepared synthetically. Lecithin can be in eye creams, lipsticks, liquid powders, hand creams, lotions, soaps, shampoos, other cosmetics, and some medicines. Alternatives: soybean lecithin, synthetics.

Linoleic Acid. An essential fatty acid. Used in cosmetics, vitamins. Alternatives: see alternatives to **Fatty Acids.**

Lipase. Enzyme from the stomachs and tongue glands of calves, kids, and lambs. Used in cheese making and in digestive aids. Alternatives: vegetable enzymes, castor beans.

Lipoids. Lipids. Fat and fatlike substances that are found in animals and plants. Alternatives: vegetable oils.

Marine Oil. From fish or marine mammals (including porpoises). Used in soap making. Used as a shortening (especially in some margarines), as a lubricant, and in paint. Alternatives: vegetable oils.

Methionine. Essential amino acid found in various proteins (usually from egg albumen and casein). Used as a texturizer and for freshness in potato chips. Alternatives: synthetics.

Milk Protein. Hydrolyzed milk protein. From the milk of cows. In cosmetics, shampoos, moisturizers, and conditioners. Alternatives: soy protein, other plant proteins.

Mink Oil. From minks. In cosmetics and creams. Alternatives: vegetable oils and emollients such as avocado oil, almond oil, and jojoba oil.

Monoglycerides. Glycerides. From animal fat. In margarines, cake mixes, candies, and many processed foods. In cosmetics. Alternative: vegetable glycerides. See also **Glycerin.**

Musk (Oil). Dried secretion painfully obtained from the genitals of musk deer, beaver, muskrat, civet, and otter. Wild cats are kept captive in cages in horrible conditions and are whipped to produce the scent; beavers are trapped; deer are shot. In perfumes and in food flavorings. Alternatives: labdanum oil (which comes from various rockrose shrubs) and other plants with a musky scent.

Myristic Acid. Organic acid in most animal and vegetable fats. In butter acids. Used in shampoos, creams, cosmetics, and food flavorings. Derivatives: isopropyl myristate, myristal ether sulfate, myristyls, oleyl myristate. Alternatives: nut butters, oil of lovage, coconut oil, and extract from seed kernels of nutmeg.

"Natural Sources." Can mean animal or vegetable sources. Often in the health food industry, especially in the cosmetics area, it means animal sources, such as animal elastin, glands, fat, protein, and oil. Alternatives: plant sources.

Nucleic Acids. In the nucleus of all living cells. Used in cosmetics, shampoos, and conditioners. Also in vitamins, supplements. Alternatives: plant sources.

Oleic Acid. Obtained from various animal and vegetable fats and oils. Usually obtained commercially from inedible tallow. (See **Tallow.**) In foods, soft soap, bar soap, permanent-wave solutions, creams, nail polish, lipsticks, many other skin preparations. Derivatives: oleyl oleate, oleyl stearate. Alternatives: coconut oil. (See also alternatives to **Animal Fats and Oils.**)

Oleyl Alcohol. Ocenol. Found in fish oils. Used in the manufacture of detergents, as a plasticizer for softening fabrics, and as a carrier for medications. Derivatives: oleths, oleyl arachidate, oleyl imidazoline.

Palmitic Acid. From fats, oils (see **Fatty Acids**). Mixed with stearic acid. Found in many animal fats and plant oils. In shampoos, shaving soaps, creams. Derivatives: palmitate, palmitamine, palmitamide. Alternatives: palm oil, vegetable sources.

Panthenol. Dexpanthenol. Vitamin B Complex Factor. Provitamin B_5. Can come from animal or plant sources or synthetics. In shampoos, supplements, and emollients. In foods. Derivative: panthenyl. Alternatives: synthetics, plants.

Pepsin. In hogs' stomachs. A clotting agent. In some cheeses and vitamins. Same uses and alternatives as **Rennet.**

Placenta. Placenta Polypeptides Protein. Afterbirth. Contains waste matter eliminated by the fetus. Derived from the uterus of slaughtered animals. Animal placenta is widely used in skin creams, shampoos, masks, etc. Alternatives: kelp. See also alternatives to **Animal Fats and Oils.**

Polypeptides. From animal protein. Used in cosmetics. Alternatives: plant proteins and enzymes.

Polysorbates. Derivatives of fatty acids. In cosmetics, foods.

Pristane. Obtained from the liver oil of sharks and from whale ambergris. (See **Squalene, Ambergris.**) Used as a lubricant and anticorrosive agent. In cosmetics. Alternatives: plant oils, synthetics.

Progesterone. A steroid hormone used in antiwrinkle face creams. Can have adverse systemic effects. Alternatives: synthetics.

Propolis. Tree sap gathered by bees and used as a sealant in beehives. In toothpaste, shampoo, and deodorant. Alternatives: tree sap, synthetics.

Provitamin A. See **Carotene.**

Provitamin B_5. See **Panthenol.**

Provitamin D_2. See **Vitamin D.**

Rennet. Rennin. Enzyme from calves' stomachs. Used in cheese making, in rennet custard (junket), and in many coagulated dairy products. Alternatives: microbial coagulating agents, bacteria culture, lemon juice, or vegetable rennet.

Resinous Glaze. See **Shellac.**

RNA. Ribonucleic Acid. RNA is in all living cells. Used in many protein shampoos and cosmetics. Alternatives: plant cells.

Royal Jelly. Secretion from the throat glands of the honeybee workers that is fed to the larvae in a colony and to all queen larvae. No proven value in cosmetics preparations. Alternatives: aloe vera, comfrey, other plant derivatives.

Sable Brushes. From the fur of sables (weasel-like mammals). Used to make eye makeup, lipstick, and artists' brushes. Alternatives: synthetic fibers.

Sea Turtle Oil. See **Turtle Oil.**

Shark Liver Oil. Used in lubricating creams and lotions. Derivative: squalane. Alternatives: vegetable oils.

Sheepskin. See **Leather.**

Shellac. Resinous Glaze. Resinous excretion of certain insects. Used as a candy glaze, in hair lacquer, and on jewelry. Alternatives: plant waxes.

Silk. Silk Powder. Silk is the shiny fiber made by silkworms to form their cocoons. With the exception of one innovative company called Ahimsa, worms are boiled in their cocoons to get the silk. Used in cloth. Also used in silk-screening (other fine cloth can be and is used instead). Taffeta can be made from silk or nylon. Silk powder is obtained from the secretion of the silkworm. It is used as a coloring agent in face powders and soaps. Alternatives: milkweed seed-pod fibers, nylon, silk-cotton tree and ceiba tree filaments (kapok), rayon, and synthetic silks.

Snails. In some cosmetics (crushed).

Sodium Caseinate. See **Casein.**

Sodium Steroyl Lactylate. See **Lactic Acid.**

Sodium Tallowate. See **Tallow.**

Spermaceti. Cetyl Palmitate. Sperm Oil. Waxy oil derived from the sperm whale's head or from dolphins. In many margarines. In skin creams, ointments, shampoos, and candles. Used in the leather industry. May become rancid and cause irritations. Alternatives: synthetic spermaceti, jojoba oil, and other vegetable emollients.

Sponge (Luna and Sea). A plantlike animal. Lives in the sea. Becoming scarce. Alternatives: synthetic sponges, loofahs (plants used as sponges).

Squalane. See **Shark Liver Oil.**

Squalene. Oil from shark livers. In cosmetics, moisturizers, hair dyes, surface-active agents. Alternatives: vegetable emollients such as olive oil, wheat germ oil, or rice bran oil.

Stearic Acid. Stearates. From cows and sheep and from dogs and cats destroyed in animal shelters and elsewhere. Most often refers to a fatty substance taken from the stomachs of pigs. Can be harsh, irritating. Used in cosmetics, soaps, lubricants, candles, hair spray, conditioners, deodorants, creams, chewing gum, food flavoring. Derivatives: stearamide, stearamine, stearates, stearic hydrazide, stearone, stearoxytrimethylsilane, stearoyl lactylic acid, stearyl betaine, stearyl imidazoline. Alternatives: Stearic acid can be found in many vegetable fats, coconut.

Stearyl Alcohol. Sterols. A mixture of solid alcohols. Can be prepared from sperm whale oil. In medicines, creams, rinses, and shampoos. Derivatives: stearamine oxide, stearyl acetate, stearyl caprylate, stearyl citrate, stearyldimethyl amine, stearyl glycyrrhetinate, stearyl heptanoate, stearyl octanoate, stearyl stearate. Alternatives: plant sources, vegetable stearic acid.

Steroids. Sterols. From various animal glands or from plant tissues. Steriods include sterols. Sterols are alcohol from animals or plants (e.g., cholesterol). Used in hormone preparation. In creams, lotions, hair conditioners, and fragrances. Alternatives: plant tissues, synthetics.

Suede. See **Leather.**

Tallow. Tallow Fatty Alcohol. Stearic Acid. Rendered beef fat. May cause eczema and blackheads. In wax paper, crayons, margarines, paints, rubber, and lubricants. In candles, soaps, lipsticks, shaving creams, other cosmetics. Chemicals (e.g., PCB) can be in animal tallow. Derivatives: sodium tallowate, tallow acid, tallow amide, tallow amine, talloweth-6, tallow glycerides, tallow imidazoline. Alternatives: vegetable tallow, Japan tallow, paraffin and/or ceresin (see alternatives to **Beeswax** for all three). Paraffin is usually from petroleum, wood, coal, or shale oil.

Turtle Oil. Sea Turtle Oil. From the muscles and genitals of giant sea turtles. In soap, skin creams, nail creams, other cosmetics. Alternatives: vegetable emollients (see alternatives to **Animal Fats and Oils**).

Tyrosine. Amino acid hydrolyzed from casein. Used in cosmetics and creams. Derivative: glucose tyrosinase.

Urea. Carbamide. Uric Acid. Excreted from urine and other bodily fluids. In deodorants, ammoniated dentifrices, mouthwashes, hair colorings, hand creams, lotions, and shampoos. Used to "brown" baked goods, such as pretzels. Derivatives: imidazolidinyl urea, uric acid. Alternatives: synthetics.

Vitamin A. Can come from fish liver oil (e.g., shark liver oil), egg yolk, butter, lemongrass, wheat germ oil, carotene in carrots, and synthetics. In cosmetics, creams, perfumes, and hair dyes. In vitamins, supplements. Alternatives: carrots, other vegetables, synthetics.

Vitamin B Complex Factor. See **Panthenol.**

Vitamin B_{12}. Can come from animal products or bacteria cultures. If buying Twinlab B_{12} vitamins, look for nongelatin dots. Alternatives: vegetarian vitamins, fortified soy milk, nutritional yeast, fortified meat substitutes. Vitamin B_{12} is often listed as "cyanocobalamin" on food labels. Vegan health professionals caution that vegans get five to ten micrograms per day of vitamin B_{12} from fortified foods or supplements.

Vitamin D. Ergocalciferol. Vitamin D_2. Ergosterol. Provitamin D_2. Calciferol. Vitamin D_3. Vitamin D can come from fish liver oil, milk, or egg yolk. Vitamin D_2 can come from animal fats or plant sterols. Vitamin D_3 is always from an animal source. All the D vitamins can be found in creams, lotions, other cosmetics, and vitamin tablets. Alternatives: plant and mineral sources, synthetics, completely vegetarian vitamins, exposure of skin to sunshine. Many other vitamins can come from animal sources. Examples: choline, biotin, inositol, and riboflavin.

Vitamin H. See **Biotin.**

Wax. Glossy, hard substance that is soft when hot. From animals and plants. In lipsticks, depilatories, hair straighteners. Alternatives: vegetable waxes.

Whey. A serum from milk. Usually in cakes, cookies, candies, and breads. In cheese making. Alternatives: soybean whey.

Wool. From sheep. Used in clothing. Ram lambs and old "wool sheep" are slaughtered for their meat. Sheep are transported without food or water, in extreme heat and cold. Legs are broken and eyes injured. Sheep are bred to be unnaturally woolly, also unnaturally wrinkly, which causes them to get insect infestations around the tail areas. The farmer's solution to this is the painful cutting away of the flesh around the tail (called mulesing). "Inferior" sheep are killed. When shearing the sheep, they are pinned down violently and sheared roughly. Their skin is cut up. Every year hundreds of thousands of shorn sheep die from exposure to cold. Natural predators of sheep (wolves, coyotes, and eagles) are poisoned, trapped, and shot. In the U.S., overgrazing of cattle and sheep is turning more than 150 million acres of land to desert. "Natural" wool production uses enormous amounts of resources and energy (to breed, raise, feed, shear, transport, and slaughter the sheep). Derivatives: lanolin, wool wax, wool fat. Alternatives: cotton, cotton flannel, synthetic fibers, and ramie.

RESOURCES

Buyukmihci, Nermin. *"John Cardillo's List of Animal Products and Their Alternatives." Cosmetic Ingredients Glossary: A Basic Guide to Natural Body Care Products.* Petaluma, Calif.: Feather River, 1988.

Mason, Jim, and Peter Singer. *Animal Factories.* New York: Crown Publishers, 1980.

Ruesch, Hans. *Slaughter of the Innocent.* New York: Civitas, 1983.

Singer, Peter. *Animal Liberation.* New York: Random House, 1990.

Winter, Ruth. *A Consumer's Dictionary of Cosmetic Ingredients.* New York: Crown Publishing Group, 1994.

———. *A Consumer's Dictionary of Food Additives.* New York: Crown Publishing Group, 1994.

PART THREE

Food and Entertaining

20.

Going Organic: Supporting Home Growers

Earth is here so kind, that just tickle her with a hoe, and she laughs with a harvest.

—DOUGLAS WILLIAM JERROLD, *A LAND OF PLENTY*

By eating foods with more life force—fresh picked, organic, and vegan—we will powerfully change ourselves, physically, mentally, and spiritually, positively influence those around us, and, most probably, transform the world we live in—one bite at a time.

—NANCY SORENSEN, DEVOTED GARDEN VOLUNTEER FOR THE LAST ORGANIC OUTPOST

Did you know that the average bite of food eaten in the United States has traveled 1,300 miles before it goes into your mouth? That provocative bit of information was offered on Pacifica Radio in a show hosted by Janice Blue out of Texas. That much travel uses up an awful lot of gasoline, puts wear and tear on the roads, and adds to that big hole in the sky that has replaced our protective ozone layer! The closer to home we can get our food, the less destructive our eating habits.

Texas! The state where cattle ranches stretch as far as the eye can see. The state where I got up one morning and stepped onto a foot warmer made from an elk's hide and looked up into the eyes of a gigantic bull whose head was mounted on the wall before me. Texas, where even the green beans come with pork in them and you still see the bodies of coyotes hanging on fence posts. Texas . . . well, you get the picture. Suffice it to say that if the organic movement is big in Texas, it has grown indeed, and what a glorious matter to celebrate!

In Houston, growers of fresh, organic fruits and vegetables, all grown from seed, come together to sell as well as to exchange information on wellness, horticulture, successful composting, and environmental preservation through marketplace choices. In fact, weekly farmer's markets are now thriving all over the country. Most are easy to find if you speak to any food co-op manager, check out community newspapers, or read the bulletin boards at health food stores.

Of course, if you are adventurous and have a green thumb, you can grow a garden of fresh, organic veggies and fruits or just plant a few tomato plants or other veggies in a window box. You can even build your own boxes for under $30 (see below) and buy organic seeds for everything from gourmet greens to fruit trees and garlic.

During the food shortages of World War II, Britons and Scandinavians feeling the pinch of food rationing planted "victory gardens" of veggies at home and in little borrowed or rented patches of soil called allotments or community patches, something that is becoming popular again now for different, happier reasons. That way you can become your own local, organic vegetable producer, cutting down the travel distance traveled by the produce you eat to just a few yards!

If you'd like to join consumer groups fighting government pesticide programs and such hot button issues as genetically modified foods, there are ones like the Organic Consumers Association, which can keep you abreast of developments (and efforts to curb developments that are unhealthy for the planet, animals, and human beings).

RESOURCES

Last Organic Outpost

www.lastorganicoutpost.com

Organic Consumers Association

www.organicconsumers.org

The Vegetable Patch

www.thevegetablepatch.com

Looking for the Web site full of organic vegetable gardening information? The Vegetable Patch offers practical information for online gardeners.

Seeds of Change

www.seedsofchange.com

Sells everything from fruit trees and flowers to herbs, and from compost starter to organic seeds for "ordinary" greens like kale and lettuce, and gourmet greens like Persian garden cress and mesclun.

Do-It-Yourself Network

www.diynetwork.com

Great source for window boxes.

Organic Bouquet

www.organicbouquet.com

Organic flowers and fruits by mail.

Books

Colement, Eliot. *Four-Season Harvest: Organic Vegetables from Your Home Garden All Year Long.* White River Junction, Vt.: Chelsea Green Publishing Company, 1992.

21.

Putting Organic-, Worker-, and Bird-Friendly Coffee in Your Pot

. . . wouldst give me water with berries in 't.

—WILLIAM SHAKESPEARE, *THE TEMPEST* (PERHAPS THE VERY FIRST REFERENCE TO COFFEE IN THE OLD WORLD)

Men trifle away their time, scald their chops, and spend their money, all for a little base, black, thick, nasty, bitter, stinking, nauseous puddle water.

—THE WOMEN'S PETITION AGAINST COFFEE, 1674

I have measured out my life with coffee spoons," wrote T. S. Eliot in "The Love Song of J. Alfred Prufrock." Lots of people could say the same, needing their morning cup of coffee to start their engines and sealing their day with a last drink of coffee after dinner. Coffee drinking is an international pastime. The Duchesse of Orléans in France was an outspoken fan who advocated coffee drinking because she believed it helped men, Catholic priests particularly, to remain chaste! In Germany, people took to coffee with such gusto that Johann Sebastian Bach felt moved to compose a sonata ribbing the coffee-mad ladies of Leipzig. In England, in its heyday, coffee drinking reached such proportions, with coffeehouses springing up so quickly, that letters to the editor of the *London Times* began appearing, lamenting the decline not only of the empire, but of the British national brew, tea. So, what should one look for in a coffee besides flavor?

One answer is a "Fair Trade" certificate on the bag. Another is the magic words "shade grown."

According to the community-minded people who started Fair Trade, "More and more people choose organically grown coffee not only because it helps to better sustain our environment, but also because they usually sustain better economic conditions for the growers. With coffee being the second most traded commodity in the world economy (after oil), a choice in what coffee to buy is not just a matter of taste and health, but a choice of considerable economic influence."

Hunger has become commonplace in coffee-producing communities like Chiapas, Mexico, with more than 75 percent of indigenous children suffering from malnutrition. In 349 of the 411 municipalities in Mexico where coffee is currently being grown, the farmers live in a state of poverty. Because the coffee processing and exporting infrastructure in Mexico is dominated by the government and large foreign companies, farmers are at the mercy of "coyotes" (middlemen) who purchase their coffee. Fair Trade works with farmers who have organized into cooperatives and, together, are building systems for processing and exporting. That's why the Fair Trade label is important.

As for shade-grown coffee, there is a double advantage: Its growers achieve a similar positive economic effect while not contributing to the destruction of tropical forests in Mexico, Central America, Colombia, and the Caribbean, often the last safe haven for songbirds, hummingbirds, and other native and migratory birds.

Growers of shade-grown coffee pay attention to the ecological sustainability of growing and harvesting methods. With shade-grown coffee, the growers have done their best to avoid depleting natural resources: They plant their fields and harvest the beans carefully so as to disturb only minimally natural flora and fauna. Whereas many big coffee companies cut down all the bushes and trees that are homes to birds and other animals, growers of shade-grown coffee allow that foliage to remain and also allow migratory birds to continue to rest along their traditional flight paths. And whereas some companies might cover the coffee plants with nets and put out poison for "bothersome" native wildlife, growers of shade-grown coffee either leave the birds in peace or use natural herbicides and pest-control methods.

Some say that a side benefit of shade-grown coffee is that shade slows the maturation of the bean, allowing a higher sugar content (and therefore a more flavorful bean) to develop.

RESOURCES

PETA's Free Bird Coffee and Coffee Club

www.petamall.com

PETA offers three varieties of coffee grown without pesticides, herbicides, or chemical fertilizers: Flying Free French Roast, Morning Birdsong Breakfast Blend, and No Ruffled Feathers Decaf coffee. A percentage of the proceeds from sales go to support PETA's Free Bird Campaign. PETA will send your choice of shade-grown arabica coffee bean coffees to your home or as gifts for others. Shipping is free.

Fair Trade

For a list of traders local to you who use Fair Trade coffee retailers:

1611 Telegraph Ave., Suite 900
Oakland, CA 94612
510-663-5260
Fax: 510-663-5264

Transfair USA

www.transfair@transfairusa.org

This is the only organization providing independent certification for fair trade products in the U.S. Look for the Fair Trade

Certified label—proof that the farmers who grew your coffee or tea received a fair price.

The Roasted Bean

888-294-8886

www.theroastedbean.com

This company allows you to select coffee by "taste profile" and provides free shipping from southern Florida.

JavaSoy

www.javasoy.com

Comes in French vanilla, Swiss chocolate almond, and other flavors, and became the first soy-based Colombia arabica coffee when it debuted at the Indiana State Fair in 2003. An eight-ounce cup of JavaSoy has half the caffeine of regular coffee, five grams of soy protein, and 2.2 milligrams of isoflavones, cancer-fighting plant chemicals.

White Wave Silk Soylattes

www.silkissoy.com

These are geared to consumers who want organic soy as part of their diet to reduce the risk of heart disease as well as customers who simply prefer the flavor. Available in most supermarkets.

Most coffee chains, even those that do not serve environmentally, animal-, and ecologically friendly coffees, now serve soy milk even if they do not list it on their boards, so don't forget to ask.

22.

Breakfast of Eco- and Animal Champions

In England oats are generally given to horses,
but in Scotland they support the people.

—SAMUEL JOHNSON, *DICTIONARY OF THE ENGLISH LANGUAGE* (ON PORRIDGE OATS)

If a man be sensible and one fine morning, while he is lying in bed, count at the tips of his fingers how many things in this life will give him enjoyment, invariably he will find breakfast is his first one.

—WITH APOLOGIES TO LIN YUTANG

One of the best breakfasts I ever found was a Scottish Sunday breakfast at the Metropole Hotel in Brighton, a little holiday town on the coast of southern England. The buffet was piled almost as high as the frightful waves that bashed against the rocky shore some five hundred yards outside the hotel's fortified storm windows.

It was January and we had bravely been out for our morning constitutional, walking against the wind, virtually alone on the promenade, the gusts blowing so hard that we had to walk with our heads down, unable to look up enough to know if the moisture hitting our faces was ocean spume or sleet.

Spotting the huge, elegant glass doors of the grand hotel and seeing the sign that read "Hot Breakfast Served Here," we ducked inside, price be damned. Shaking the water from our coats, we came face-to-face with a breakfast banquet that would have impressed Bonnie Prince Charlie and all the royals at Balmoral Castle.

But the best part was this: Even the "meatiest" traditional dishes, like haggis, black sausage, and the scramble, were vegan!

Even since I rescued a little pig on a farm in Maryland many years ago, the smell of bacon cooking in a pan has made me shudder. Pig flesh gives off a strong smell that I used to find inviting, but now I associate it with that little fellow and all those other little piglets who have to endure having their tails and part of their ears cut off on factory farms. It no longer calls to me; it repulses me.

James Cromwell, star of *Babe,* feels the same way, and since meeting his costar on the set of that movie, he won't put a piece of pig—or, for that matter, any animal—in his mouth anymore. He says that what the pig taught him was that all life is precious and that pigs are more intelligent than most dogs or even young children.

"Later, I drove through the stockyards of Texas on a motorcycle," says Cromwell. "It doesn't let you escape what surrounds you and what it smells and feels like—and what hit me was the realization that something that was alive and had feelings will suffer before a piece of it is placed on the plate."

Cromwell is upset not only about the stench but about the pollution from hog farms, depletion of earth resources, and other important issues.

"It goes further," he says. "The health of the planet is at stake, because the cruelty and waste that accompany the slaughter of billions of animals each year infect us all. We could produce consumer-healthy plant-based food at almost infinitely less cost. What does that say, really, about us and what we are doing to animals and ourselves?"

So much for bacon. What about eggs?

I don't know what the people who made the movie *Chicken Run* found out about real-life egg farms, but it was probably an eye-opening experience. Carla Bennett, author of *Living in Harmony with Animals,* calls the plight of the hens who grow up crowded together in sheds "like going from shell to hell." From personal experience I know how you have to cover your nose and try not to breathe in the laying sheds as the ammonia fumes from the accumulated waste of thousands of hens, all kept in constant light to produce an egg every twenty-two hours, assault your senses. I think of that now any time I smell an egg cooking.

But in Brighton, in the cozy hotel breakfast room, the smells were of hot buns, toast, Scotch porridge oats, syrups, fresh fruits, and other welcoming food. The breakfast should have come as no surprise, for Brighton is "vegan heaven," part old hippie commune and part ultra-progressive hideaway. It is so special that both the Tories and the Labour Party choose it as *the* place to hold their annual conventions, and it is where King George III went in the 1700s to "take the waters" for his health. In Brighton, he also built an enormous folly, the Royal Palace Pavilion in the style of the Taj Mahal. Within ten years its roof was leaking and its drains were clogged, but thanks to massive repairs, you can still walk through it and see the old four-poster beds in which a probably hungover King George took his own breakfast.

Brighton is also a haven where vegans want for nothing: Even the seaside fish and chip shops serve veggie pies and veggie burgers! As it turned out, even our own hotel had vegan "bangers"—sausages—on its breakfast menu.

Starting your morning with protein gives a body and your mood a good boost, but protein does not have to come from meat. Beans, for example, are packed with the stuff. And in England, as in much of South America, beans are a breakfast staple. Both come with tomato sauce, either as the "gravy" of the English baked beans, served on toast, or as salsa with the frijoles on a tortilla. In the U.S., the old bacon and egg breakfast, which would once have been worked off in the fields and ditches by laborers and, to some extent, by walking briskly to and from the office, now haunts the thighs, clogs the arteries, and contributes to the paunch of today's population. However, soy sausage, tofu scramble, and all manner of healthier, less fatty, yet protein-rich substitutes, many made from soybeans, are taking their place in humane and health-conscious households.

Here are some easy, superhealthy, cholesterol-free, and totally humane favorite breakfast dishes to try:

TAL'S TOFU SCRAMBLE

Tal Ronnen, vegan chef, says he often wraps the scramble in a tortilla shell and adds hot sauce as well.

1 lb. firm tofu, patted dry and mashed
1 cup of your favorite vegetables such as broccoli, fresh mushrooms, onions, or tomatoes; also great with vegetarian soy sausage, crumbled
⅛ teaspoon turmeric
1 teaspoon onion powder
½ teaspoon salt
black pepper to taste
2 cloves of garlic, minced
2 tablespoons nutritional yeast

Place the tofu and soy sausage (if using) in a lightly oiled sauté pan and cook over medium heat for 5 minutes. Add the remaining ingredients, stir well, and cook for 5 to 8 minutes, until the vegetables are cooked and the tofu is heated through.

Serves 4.

MEXICAN-STYLE BEANS ON TOAST (OR TORTILLA)

You can simply open a can of El Paso or Goya refried beans, warm them up in the microwave, spread them on toasted bread or a warm tortilla, and top with Herdez or another good salsa to taste, or you can do it the old-fashioned way:

2 cups dried pinto, black, or red kidney beans
2 onions, finely chopped

3 cloves garlic, finely chopped
1 bay leaf
1 teaspoon chili pepper
2 tablespoons vegetable oil
Salt and freshly ground pepper to taste

Place the beans in a saucepan with enough water to cover. And half the chopped onion, half the chopped garlic, the bay leaf, and the chili pepper and bring to a boil over moderate heat. Reduce the heat, cover, and simmer, adding more water as necessary. Cook until the beans are soft (could take as long as 2 hours). The beans should be fairly dry when done. Heat the oil in a skillet and sauté the remaining onion and garlic until tender but not brown. Add the onion mixture to the beans and mash the beans until they are creamy and have formed a thick, dry paste. Add salt and pepper to taste.

Serves 4 to 6.

"BLISSED" FRENCH TOAST

Tanya Petrovna of Native Foods (www.nativefoods.com).

1 ½ cups water
3 tablespoons soy flour or unbleached pastry flour
1 tablespoon corn starch
1 tablespoon organic sugar
¼ teaspoon almond extract
Pinch of sea salt
Pinch of cinnamon
2 tablespoons organic coconut shortening (Spectrum), melted (or you can substitute vegan margarine)
¼ teaspoon turmeric
French bread
Pure maple syrup

Puree all ingredients except bread in a blender. Put on stovetop and heat while whisking until thickened. Remove from heat; let cool slightly. Slice the French bread and soak slices in batter. Heat a skillet and add a touch more coconut shortening or margarine, then brown the soaked bread on each side. Serve with pure maple syrup.

Serves 3 to 4.

RESOURCES

Fabulous soy "bacon" and "sausages" are in most supermarket freezer cases. Here are some favorites:

Gardenburger Meatless Breakfast Sausage
www.gardenburger.com
This has a satisfying meaty homemade sausage taste and is made with all-natural soy and seasoned with herbs and spices.

GimmeLean! Sausage Style
Lightlife Foods
153 Industrial Blvd.
Turners Falls, MA 01376
1-900-SOY-EASY
www.lightlife.com
A fat-free and very tasty soy replacement for breakfast or anytime sausages, this crumbles well for casseroles and lasagna too.

Yves Canadian Veggie Bacon
1638 Derwent Way
Delta (Vancouver), BC
V3M 6R9

Canada
1-800-667-9837
www.yvesveggie.com
Delicious preservative-free "bacon" made from wheat gluten and other wholesome foods, perfect with frozen waffles (vegan varieties are available in most major grocery chains).

Books

The recipe for "Blissed" French Toast was adapted from Abbot George Burke's *Simply Heavenly*, a Saint George Press cookbook. (New York: Hungry Minds, Inc., 1997)

23.

Harmless Hors d'Oeuvres and Other Delights

Food is an important part of a balanced diet.

—FRAN LEBOWITZ, *METROPOLITAN LIFE*

Hors d'oeuvres, canapés, morsels, tapas, antipasti, kickshaw—the food equivalent of aperitifs, small morsels, elegant but not nourishing. (The word *kickshaw* is believed to be a corruption of the French *quelque chose,* literally "something.") How could there be any issue with these savory delights? Well, trust an animal-rights person to know there is, but also to know that there are as many wonderful replacements for the problem ones as there are different varieties of crackers to serve up pâtés! Let me touch upon a few of the worst offenders and then offer a few easy-to-make delights.

First, pâté. Sir John Gielgud loved dogs and birds, and it pained him greatly to go to society and theater events and see foie gras on the canapé tray. Foie gras is the fattened liver of geese and ducks, the lively birds Sir John enjoyed watching on the village pond near his country home in Wooten-Underwood, an hour's train journey from London's theater district. Sir John's unmistakable voice—the voice that carried Shakespeare's words in the characters of Hamlet and King Lear, out into the audience from the stage of the Old Vic Theatre—was put to use on many an occasion to convey his disgust over how foie gras is made.

The practice dates back hundreds of years to when the first French housewife decided to nail a goose's webbed feet to the kitchen floor and force-feed the bird corn mash until his liver become grossly distended, soft, and a "delicacy." Today, factory-farmed geese and ducks are hooked up to a hydraulic pump to receive their dosages, a procedure that leaves them frightened, upset, and often injured and unable to move. Not so "civilized" after all.

"Finger food" trends are often problematic. The sight of little pieces of cuttlefish (squid) on the salad bar, bits of octopus tentacles in batter or cut into slices with lemon dressing, or that caviar sparkling in a dish can spoil the appetite of a conscientious consumer. For cephalopods like squid and octopuses are magnificent, intelligent, truly magical animals who communicate with each other in ways we will probably never understand, using rapidly changing and incredibly intricate patterns of light and color, including dots, solids, stripes, and blotches. One squid, the Caribbean reef squid, can flash a different display on each side of its body when, for example, positioned between a potential mate on the one side (she sees soothing uniform gray) and a rival on the other (he gets a tiger-striped warning).

Young cuttlefish can even purposely blend into the background on the bottom of the sea, changing to a swirling pattern to match debris moving in a breaking wave! And the "octopus's garden" from that old Lennon-McCartney classic is not a made-up invention. Not only are octopuses good-natured and intelligent, but they are avid decorators, carefully collecting objects from the seafloor to stick up on the walls of their dens. These intriguing creatures can learn how to unscrew a jelly jar just by watching someone do it, and they have been known to gently kiss familiar divers on the lips with their tentacles when they have determined the divers are not harmful.

As for caviar, it is cut from the belly of a live mother sturgeon. No, thank you! But, if only to prove that there are kind alternatives to *everything,* along comes faux "caviar." Made of seaweed, this product actually looks and tastes like real lumpfish roe but is economical as well as ethical. It comes in red, black, and natural, and doesn't leak into other foods when used as a "garnish," as fish caviar does. (And needless to say, no one's belly is harmed to create it.)

Here are some suggestions for harmless tidbits that will disappear from cocktail trays in a flash:

CAPONATA CROSTINI

2 tablespoons olive oil
1 medium yellow onion, chopped
1 large eggplant, peeled and diced
1 red bell pepper, chopped
2 garlic cloves, minced
1 14-ounce can tomatoes, drained and chopped
Salt and freshly ground black pepper
2 tablespoons capers
1 tablespoon red wine vinegar
2 teaspoons sugar
1 tablespoon minced fresh parsley
8 pieces French bread, sliced ½-inch thick
¼ cup olive oil

Heat 1 tablespoon of the oil in a large skillet over medium heat. Add the onion, cover, and cook until soft, about 5 minutes. Remove the lid. Add 1 more tablespoon of the oil and stir in the eggplant. Cook, stirring occasionally until the eggplant begins to soften. Add the bell pepper, garlic, tomatoes, and salt and pepper to taste. Cook until the vegetables soften but still hold some shape, about 15 minutes. Stir in the capers, vinegar, sugar, and parsley. Taste to adjust seasoning.

Transfer to a bowl and cool to room temperature (if not serving right away, refrigerate, but bring back to room temperature before serving.)

Preheat oven to 400°F. Lightly brush one side of the bread slices with olive oil and place on a baking sheet. Bake until lightly browned, about 3 minutes. Remove from oven, spread the caponata onto bread slices and serve at once.

Serves 4.

HOT AND SPICY STUFFED MUSHROOMS

8 ounces white mushrooms
2 tablespoons olive oil
1 garlic clove, minced
4 hot cherry peppers, seeded and minced
2 cups fresh bread crumbs
1 teaspoon sugar
½ cup raisins
1 tablespoon minced parsley
Salt and freshly ground black pepper

Remove the stems from the mushroom caps and set the caps aside. Chop the mushroom stems and set aside. Preheat oven to 400°F. Heat 1 tablespoon of the oil in a large skillet over medium heat. Add the mushroom caps and cook for 2 minutes to soften slightly. Remove from the pan with a slotted spoon and set aside.

Return the pan to the heat. Add the garlic and cook until fragrant, about 1 minute. Add the reserved mushroom stems, cherry peppers, bread crumbs, sugar, raisins, parsley, and salt and pepper to taste. Cook for 2 minutes, mixing well. Add more oil if necessary for the stuffing to hold together.

Fill the mushrooms with the stuffing mixture and arrange on a lightly oiled baking sheet. Drizzle with any remaining oil, and bake until the mushrooms are soft and the tops are lightly browned, about 10 minutes. Serve hot.

Serves 6 to 8.

BASMATI-STUFFED GRAPE LEAVES WITH PINE NUTS AND DILL (DOLMAS)

1 8-ounce jar grape leaves
3 tablespoons olive oil
1 medium yellow onion, minced
¾ cup basmati rice
¼ cup toasted pine nuts
3 tablespoons minced dill weed
½ teaspoon ground cinnamon
Salt and freshly ground black pepper
1¼ cup vegetable stock
1 tablespoon fresh lemon juice

Remove the grape leaves from the jar and rinse under running water to remove the brine. Pat the leaves dry and trim off the stems. Set leaves aside. Heat 1 tablespoon of oil in a large skillet over medium heat. Add the onion, cover, and cook until soft, about 5 minutes. Stir in the rice, pine nuts, dill, cinnamon, salt and pepper to taste, and 1 cup of the stock. Cover and simmer, stirring occasionally, until the liquid is evaporated. Transfer the filling to a bowl and cool completely.

Place a grape leaf on a work surface shiny side down, with the stem end toward you. Place a tablespoon of the cooled filling near the stem end and fold in the sides of the leaf over the filling. Roll up the leaf away from you, firmly but not too tightly. Repeat the process using the remaining leaves and filling. Transfer the dolmas to a large skillet.

Pour the remaining stock, oil, and lemon juice over the dolmas, adding additional water to just barely cover them with liquid. Bring to a simmer and cook, covered, until tender, about 30 minutes. Remove from the heat, uncover, and let cool. Drain any remaining liquid and transfer to a serving plate. Serve at room temperature.

Makes 20 to 24.

CRUELTY-FREE PÂTÉ

1 tablespoon margarine or water
1 medium onion, chopped
2 pounds fresh mushrooms, finely chopped
4 cloves garlic, minced
2 tablespoons chopped fresh parsley, or 2 teaspoons dried
2 tablespoons chopped fresh rosemary, or 2 teaspoons dried
1⅓ cups bread crumbs
2 tablespoons lemon juice
Salt and pepper

In a large saucepan, heat the margarine or water and cook the onion for 10 minutes.

Add the mushrooms and cook for another 20 to 30 minutes, or until all the liquid has evaporated. Remove the mixture from the heat and add the remaining ingredients. Spoon into a serving dish and serve immediately.

Serves 6.

RESOURCES

Cavi★Art Faux Caviar
www.happycookers.com/wc.dll/products/divulge/3-4364.html

Pangea

www.veganstore.com

Organic Gourmet Pâtés, Nacho ChReese Dips, and Meditalia Roasted Eggplant Spread.

The PETA Celebrity Cookbook

www.petamall.org

Try artichoke dip, red-hot risotto, and other treats from the kitchens of Alicia Silverstone, Russell Simmons, Moby, and more.

24.

The King of Barbecue

"No, I don't have any spare ribs!"

—LITTLE PIGGY SAYING ON CHILD'S T-SHIRT

This is an account of how a woman who says she is so hopeless in the kitchen that she "burns water" wowed all comers at the American Royal Barbecue cook-off.

It was a bizarre turn of events. Paige Glidden is "twenty-something." She works at the national headquarters of Camp Fire USA, which certainly sounds as if it has something to do with cooking, but Paige is no cook. In fact, she says she has trouble preparing cereal and toast.

And, until an unlikely happenstance in 2002, she had never "done barbecue in real life."

Paige's coworker at Camp Fire USA and his team of cooks had plunked down the money to enter the most prestigious, and talked about, competitive cooking event in Kansas City—the biggest barbecue contest in the world, known as the World Series of Barbecue. At the last minute, however, they had to back out, and Paige found herself called upon to grab a cooking apron and look sharp about it.

As if this weren't difficult enough, Paige is a vegan, and no one had ever entered a *vegan* dish into the competition.

Luckily, Paige went "temporarily insane," as she puts it. "I just had the idea that all you have to do is buy some stuff. It didn't seem like a big deal!"

The event took place in the American Royal Arena, a famous arena in Missouri in the stockyard district that hosts rodeos, horse shows, and contests for shoeing horses. All contestants had to produce a certain number of categories of food to qualify, which meant that Paige and her crew, coworkers Alison, Carol, and Greg—none of them cooks—had to prepare a . . . brisket.

When they heard the news, they looked at each other and said, "Brisket. Okay. What *is* that?"

They learned that a brisket is a cut of beef taken from the breast section under the first five ribs of a cow. If you looked back to the 1913 edition of *Webster's Dictionary,* you would find this unappetizing description of a brisket: "Brisk'ket—a noun of Celtic origin, the breast of a slain animal, the front of the chest, the cartilaginous part of a bone extending from the fore legs back beneath the ribs."

A brief digression about brisket: I once introduced a *New Yorker* photographer to a brisket on the hoof one day, as we stood in a freezing cold field in New Jersey, sizing up cattle of various breeds, shapes, and sizes for their modeling potential. There were the "doughnut boys," who had been rescued after a plea from a bankrupt farmer's wife who had been keeping them alive on day-old doughnuts. And there was Beatrice, a redheaded Scottish Highlander with shaggy hair that covered her eyes and enormous horns. She had been saved from the butcher's grinder by a child at a fair who had grabbed her harness and run off with her, hiding out until PETA came up with the money to buy her and keep her safe forever.

We were having a hard time staying upright as curious cows jostled us for a closer look at the photographer's fragile equipment ("Oh, no, there goes the light screen again!") and cows who wanted the apples they knew full well we had buried in our jacket pockets.

Front and center was an enormous, friendly black bull named Willis, the "alpha bull."

To keep warm, we were shuffling our feet and I was rubbing my fingers—frozen even through my thick gloves—over Willis's warm brisket, that thick, tufty bit of cow that juts out of their chests way under their chins. Suddenly, Willis rolled out his pink tongue, over a foot of it, to grab an apple. The photographer, Jill, said, "Oh, good grief! Is that the tongue you get in a sandwich?" I told her it was indeed. She grimaced. Then I pointed out Willis's brisket and told her that corned beef was sliced right off that part of the animal's body.

"*That's* a brisket?" she said, "*That's* what you see in the deli case!" I had a feeling things would never be the same again for her at lunchtime in Manhattan.

But back to Kansas. On the day of the competition, a cool fall day, Paige and the gang found themselves surrounded by chickens in cages, pigs in stalls, and hundreds of booths, all cooking animals. She and her crew set up on a little sidewalk, grabbed a couple of grills, and started cooking.

"We were really into it," says Paige, who wore a "Love Animals, Don't Eat Them" T-shirt for the occasion. "It was an adrenaline rush because we had had zero time to get ready. Only afterward, when we looked back, did we realize how cool the whole thing was."

Their vegan brisket, which appeared beneath a big banner, proclaiming, "American Royal Barbecue Competition: First Vegan Entry" was a huge success (see recipe below). "We made it with tempeh and vegetables so that it was like a loaf, and then we slathered it in locally made barbecue sauce and grilled it really well," says Paige. "We did all the classic stuff."

The tasters' comments ranged from "What do you mean there's no cholesterol and no fat?" to "What do you mean there's no meat in this?" with lots of tasters saying in wonder, "Well now, if I didn't know this wasn't meat . . ." People took the "No, I don't have any spare ribs" buttons with the endearing piglet on them and went away, drinking their Boulevard Brewery beer and marveling to themselves.

Paige and her helpers did not win (no big surprise there), but they opened a lot of eyes. More than two hundred people tasted the vegan brisket, and the *Kansas City Star* and other newspapers covered their entry as a first in the history of the ARBC.

I don't know if it is true that the very first barbecue took place during the Depression, when a man named Henry Perry put ketchup on some cow ribs, dug an outdoor pit, and cooked them over it. What I do know is that times have certainly changed. So if you would like to put something on the barbecue that, as Paige puts it, "you never have to worry about being pink on the inside," here are a few great recipes for happier—and kinder—times at the grill.

LUCKY LUAU KEBABS

Pineapple and pork are commonly paired in Hawaiian fare, but you can enjoy the taste of the islands with these pig-friendly kebabs. Aloha!

Tempeh
Teriyaki sauce
Button mushrooms
Sweet potatoes
Walla Walla onions (or other sweet onions)
Fresh pineapple, cut into 1-inch chunks
Red and green bell peppers, cut into 1-inch squares
Cooked brown rice

Steam the tempeh over a pot of boiling water on the stove for 15 minutes, then let it cool. Cut the tempeh in half lengthwise, then cut it into 1½-inch pieces. Pour teriyaki sauce into a shallow container and add the tempeh slices. Marinate in the refrigerator, stirring occasionally, for at least 1 hour.

Meanwhile, trim any rough ends from the stems of the mushrooms. Steam the sweet potatoes until just done, let cool, then cut into 1-inch chunks. Parboil the onions, then cut into quarters.

Alternately thread the tempeh, mushrooms, sweet potatoes, onions, pineapple, and peppers on skewers. Brush with teriyaki sauce and grill for about 10 minutes, turning several times to cook evenly. Serve over brown rice.

Tip: Colorful kebabs served over pasta or rice make any get-together more festive. Grill at least four or five different vegetables, along with tempeh, tofu, or another "mock meat," and allow two full skewers per guest.

PAIGE'S "THROWN TOGETHER" FAUX BRISKET

Start with a nice big glob of wheat gluten.

Puree peas, carrots, a little cauliflower, and whatever other veggies you may have in your fridge. Add some potato flakes to help thicken it up if necessary.

Grab whatever veggie meats you have in the freezer: sausage, hamburger, buffalo wings, whatever. Give them a quick zap in the microwave to get the chill off of them and break them up into tiny pieces. When you get it down to what you think are small enough pieces, take them down to about half size again.

Zap some brown rice, lentils, black beans, and other starches from your pantry in the microwave just to get them blending together.

And the most important part: Find a good vegan BBQ dry rub. This is actually a lot easier than you might imagine. Just make sure it has plenty of garlic, onions, spices, salt, and sugar. At this point you can add a little (or a lot of) extra garlic, cayenne, liquid smoke, and hot sauce.

Grab your blob of wheat gluten, which should be close to formed, and massage in all of the other ingredients and seasoning. It will look weird and take some time, but patience pays off in the end.

Once everything is fully incorporated, take your ball of amalgamated ingredients, form it into whatever shape you like, and let it soak in a nice bath of BBQ sauce until you're ready to cook.

Before it goes on the grill, give it a few minutes under the broiler to sear it a bit; there's nothing like having to clean veggiecue out of the grill. If it still seems a bit too soft to go right over the coals, throw a layer of aluminum foil over the grate and give a splash of olive oil. That way the brisket won't stick or run between the grates. Keep it on the fire until it looks, smells, and feels done, douse it in sauce; and serve.

It's not a science, but it's a pretty good dinner.

RESOURCES

Atlas, Nava. *Vegetarian Celebrations.* New York: Little, Brown, 1996.

Chelf, Vicki Rae. *The Sensuous Vegetarian Barbecue.* New York: Avery Penguin Putnam, 1994.

Chesman, Andrea. *The Vegetarian Grill.* Boston: Harvard Common Press, 1998.

Gwynn, Mary. *Vegetarian Barbecue.* Markham, Ontario: Whitecap Books, 2001.

People for the Ethical Treatment of Animals. *Cooking with PETA.* Nashville, Tenn.: Book Publishing Company, 1997.

25.

A Lesson About Lobsters and Crabs

I am part of all that I have met.

—ALFRED LORD TENNYSON, "ULYSSES"

I learned something on my birthday. It was about lobsters, in a way, but it was also about human nature and feelings.

When I was newly married, my husband had taken me to a famous lobster restaurant in Philadelphia for the occasion and I remember feeling very romantic and happy that evening, the two of us in our lobster bibs, drinking white wine in this gorgeously appointed room.

The waiter brought a silver tray to the table and on it were some fine-looking lobsters. He invited me to select one. The lobsters waved their antennae at me, probably looking me over as I tried to assess them. I picked one.

"Broiled or boiled?" asked the waiter.

"Broiled," I said, without hesitation.

Back then I had no idea that it is standard to take the live lobster and to slit open his back; to pour salt, butter, and seasoning into the wound; and then to place him on the burning grill and slide him, alive, under the hot broiler.

The lobster returned to the table, accompanied by heaping side orders of scalloped potatoes and vegetables. Our wineglasses were refilled. I cracked open a big red leg and pulled out a long mound of buttery flesh, squeezed lemon onto it, and popped it into my mouth.

Suddenly, I burst into tears. To this day, I am astonished that it happened. My husband put his arm around me. What was the matter?

For some reason, it had suddenly struck me that I was no different from the people in China who point to the puppy or monkey in the hanging cages and pick out the one they wish to have killed, the one they want to eat. I had paid no more attention to these animals' waving antennae, the only sign they could make to be "heard," than those diners paid to the cries and frightened looks of the animals before them. I had selected my victim and had him killed, and I felt very small.

Apparently I am not alone in my experience. Years later, I read an account in the *New York Times* of a chef who set about cooking a large batch of lobsters for a holiday. He was unsettled to see that when he placed the first one in the boiling pot, the others waved their antennae at him and tried to escape, backing up and falling over each other. They didn't want to die.

My friend Cam McQueen told me of her epiphany. She had wandered into the kitchen in a commercial restaurant where live crabs, covered in batter, were lying beside a frying pan.

"One crab," she said, "had somehow separated himself from the group and was crawling away as fast as he could, although he couldn't see where he was going because his eyes were covered in batter. I realized then that every creature, no matter how small, values his or her little life."

Over time I came to learn a lot about lobsters and other sea animals. I learned that lobsters can live to be over a hundred years old, that they have a long courtship, that they help guide young lobsters across the ocean floor by holding claws in a line that can stretch for many yards, and that they have ganglia (nerves) throughout their bodies that certainly register pain; and I have found that, although theories abound, no one has ever come up with a satisfactory way to give a lobster a humane death.

That lobster in Philadelphia was the last one I ever attempted to eat, although I had been very partial to those I now call "sea animals" rather than "seafood." Having never lost interest in delighting in that particular taste but not being willing to kill for it, I jumped for joy when I found Harmony, a restaurant only a few blocks, as it turned out, from the restaurant where we sat on that fateful birthday evening. There, on the menu were "mock lobster," "mock crab," "sharks' fin" soup, and even "sea slug," those beautiful ladies of the rock pools with the ugly name. Everything was made of wheat gluten or soy.

My "shellfish" and "crustacean" dreams are now also easily realized via mail order, courtesy of May Wah, a retail supplier of fabulous Chinese mock meats that allow even an amateur cook to create "shrimp" cocktail, "jumbo shrimp" jambalaya, "lobster Thermidor," and more. And recently, in Norfolk, Virginia, where I live, Cora's—a modern yet truly southern restaurant—has put faux tuna cakes, which taste very similar to crab cakes, on its menu. They have shared their recipe with us and you'll find it below.

Whenever I hear news of a seventy-year-old "Albert" or even a one-hundred-year-old "Jimmy," one of the lucky few lobsters rescued from a tank and sent back to Maine to be released—where he is too big to legally be removed from the ocean—I celebrate with a glass of white wine and a faux lobster dish!

Now "all the fishes in the deep blue sea," and all the crustaceans, too, can rejoice in the opportunities there are to give them a break and leave them out there, in the rocks and waters, to live to a venerable old age.

FAUX TUNA CAKES

Recipe courtesy of Cora's Restaurant.

1 15½-ounce can chickpeas
1 12-ounce box tofu
1 tablespoon lemon juice
1 teaspoon granulated garlic (or 1–2 cloves fresh garlic)
1 tablespoon old bay
Salt and pepper to taste
1 12-ounce tube of Tuno (mock tuna made of soy, available in most health food stores and through www.healthy-eating.com)
2 pieces white bread, crusts removed, cubed
Flour
Bread crumbs, cornmeal, or ground-up fritters

Blend chickpeas in a food processor. Add remaining ingredients except Tuno, bread, and flour.

Strain the Tuno in a fine colander and get rid of excess water.

Combine the strained Tuno with the chickpea and tofu mixture, using a slotted spoon or your clean hand. Then fold in the cubed bread and small amounts of flour until the mixture is just sticky to the touch.

Dredge in bread crumbs or cornmeal, or ground-up fritters—anything you like. Form into patty cakes.

Pan fry or deep fry.

Serves 3 to 4 (makes about 6 or 7 8-ounce cakes).

FAUX FISH CAKES

Recipe courtesy of Chef Randy Holman.

1 pound extra-firm tofu
2 cups cooked brown rice
1 small onion, minced
6 tablespoons nutritional yeast flakes
2 tablespoons minced celery
2½ tablespoons soy sauce
1 tablespoon lemon juice
1 tablespoon sea salt
½ teaspoon dry mustard
½ teaspoon dill weed
¼ teaspoon white pepper
Pinch celery seed
¼ cup unbleached all-purpose flour

Mix the tofu, rice, onion, yeast, and celery in a large bowl. In a food processor, mix the remaining ingredients, except for the flour. Add to the tofu mixture, along with the flour. Mix well. Form into patties and broil or fry for about 4 minutes on each side.

Serves 8.

RESOURCES

May Wah Healthy Vegetarian Food
877-668-2668
www.vegieworld.com

The PETA Mall
www.petamall.com

26.

Substituting Mock Meats: Transition Foods for Macho Meat Eaters

We lost our corkscrew and were compelled to live on food and water for several days.

—W. C. FIELDS

Alcohol may have taken the place of food for W. C. Fields, but when it comes to finding something to take the place of a die-hard meat, dairy, and egg eater's high-cholesterol fare, do not despair! There are fabulous fakes that will go down the hatch without that stubborn carnivore even noticing that he or she has made the switch. I promise.

Linda McCartney used to say, "I cheated on my husband and you can too!" She was referring to how Paul hadn't a clue that she had switched from hamburger meat (called "mince" in Britain) to textured vegetable protein (TVP) in his spaghetti sauce and favorite mashed potato–topped shepherd's pie.

"When you go veggie," Linda told the *Animal Times* magazine, "there doesn't have to be a hole in the center of your plate where the meat used to be. I instantly filled that hole with 'fooled you' foods, the most exciting development in food in fifty years."

Today, Paul looks out of his window and sees the lambs on his farm gamboling about and can't understand how he ever ate meat. But of those first days, he says, "None of our family, none of the kids, ever noticed not having the meat." In fact, when actor Steve Martin visited the McCartneys' home, he refused the barbecue, saying, "I'm a vegetarian." Linda had to confess to him that the hotdogs and burgers on the grill were all made of soy.

Mock meats are the perfect transition foods. You can slather grilled onions, relish, mustard, and chili (made with soy crumbles) on that "not" dog and the most macho meat eater will wolf it down if you don't mention it is healthy and vegan! And if your resistant eater doesn't wish to be classified as a "health nut," at least *you* can know that one-quarter pound of TVP contains only 59 calories (as opposed to 250 calories in just three ounces of ground beef) and 0.2 grams of fat (there are 20 grams of fat in three ounces of ground beef).

For additional handy facts when the time comes, there is this: The Centers for Disease Control estimate that there are about 76 million cases of food poisoning in the U.S. every year—and most of them can be traced to fecal contamination of meat and products grown in soil treated with animal waste.

These days, all you have to do is look and you will find Fakin' Bacon (no difference in a BLT with *Nay*onnaise—yes, that's soy "mayonnaise"—pickles, lettuce, and tomatoes); soy sausage "crumbles" that can easily take the place of ground beef or pork in casseroles, tacos, or spaghetti sauce, or on top of pizza; even soy cheeses in flavors ranging from jalapeño to mock cheddar. What's more, faux meats do not have to be cooked thoroughly to kill bacteria like E.coli, salmonella, and trichinosis, as meat does, because they aren't there in the first place!

So if you want to fill your kids' lunch boxes with "fit in" food; entertain those poker night players with juicy "steak" sandwiches, or fix that working stiff a heaping plate of sloppy Joes and mash, take a tip from Linda McCartney: Smile knowingly and say nothing. When they find their belts need tightening a notch or two or their cholesterol has gone down, you might mention the changeover then, with a big smile!

"SAVE THE CHICKENS" SALAD

1 pound Chic-Ketts mock chicken
½ cup diced green and red pepper, celery, and/or red onion
pinch of parsley
pinch of chives
¾ cup vegan mayonnaise

Dice or tear the Chic-Ketts mock chicken (or use a food processor). Mix in the diced vegetables, herbs, and vegan mayonnaise. Chill. Serve as a sandwich filling or with crackers.

"BETTER THAN BEEF" STROGANOFF

½ cup chopped onion
1 tablespoon olive oil
12-ounce package Burger Style Recipe Crumbles
1 10¼-ounce can mushroom gravy
2 4½-ounce cans sliced mushrooms, drained
⅛ teaspoon garlic powder
¼ teaspoon pepper
⅛ teaspoon salt
½ carton Tofutti "Better Than Sour Cream"
¾ cup white cooking wine
1-pound bag egg-free pasta

In a large skillet, brown the onion in the oil. Add the remaining ingredients, stir, and cook over medium heat for 15 minutes. Boil the pasta. Drain. Serve the sauce over the noodles.

Serves 4.

TOFU SOUR CREAM

1 10-ounce package silken tofu, drained
3 tablespoons vegetable oil
1 teaspoon brown rice syrup
Juice of 1 lemon
1/2 teaspoon salt or to taste

Blend all ingredients together until very smooth in a blender.

RESOURCES

Books

Robertson, Robin. *The Vegetarian Meat and Potatoes Cookbook.* Boston: Harvard Common Press, 2002.

Mock Meat Ideas

Chic-Ketts
www.worthingtonfoods.com
Chic-Ketts is a completely meatless, precooked, vegetable protein product, free of animal fat and preservatives. It is ideal in casseroles, soups, stir fry, and more.

Morningstar Farms Burger Crumbles

www.morningstarfarms.com
Burger Style Recipe Crumbles are a blend of vegetable and grain proteins that provide a tasty, low-fat alternative to cooked ground beef. Fully cooked and recipe ready, they can be added to your favorite recipe.

Nayonnaise

Available in most health food stores.

27.

The Fun of Ethnic Eating

Variety is the spice of life,

That gives it all its flavour.

—WILLIAM COWPER,
"THE TASK"

A Washington paper once asked me some quickly shot questions. I remember two of them: "What color is your car?" Answer: "Rust. Real rust. I need a new one." "What's your favorite Washington restaurant?" Answer: "The Meskerem, where they serve mouth-watering Ethiopian food."

Let's face it, to most of us, travel is interesting and exciting, and food is too, but if you need only step outside your door to savor the taste of different cuisines from different lands, who's complaining?

I've eaten a lot of different foods in my time and travels, always anxious to discover native foods that bring fond memories, like the traditional peasant's soup of fresh vegetables in Portugal or the *horta* (dandelion) salad in Greece (see below). At other times, exotic foods have been brought almost to my own door, courtesy of whichever refugees were fleeing whatever hideous civil war.

Chinese refugees brought steamed dumplings into my life; Kashmiris brought deliciously flavored sweet rice with almonds and currants; from Lebanon, which was once a paradise of palm trees and hills for walking, came hummus, that irresistible chickpea appetizer, drizzled with olive oil and tasting of garlic and lemon. It is now sold in cans at specialty stores and even in many big supermarkets.

Ethiopians introduced me to their unique cuisine: sumptuous dishes of delicately spiced lentils, potatoes, tomatoes, and greens that you snatch up from a huge, round plate with *injera*—soft, thick, flat pancakes that look like thick napkins. Washington's Meskerem is special, perhaps, but the city has more Ethiopian restaurants per capita than any other city in the country. Restaurant critic Phyllis Richman summed it up best when she recommended Ethiopian food by writing, "Cheap, easy, tasty, and you can eat it with your hands."

When I was a child, long before I became a vegan, my father and I seemed to be using a knife and fork to work our way through the animal kingdom. We lived mainly in England, and were big on steamed Cornish mussels plucked from the rocks, calf's brains on toast, kippered herring, and lambs' kidneys. In Scandinavia, he introduced me to cheeses so ripe he used to like to say that "they will walk away without you."

Perhaps my somewhat nomadic upbringing accounts for the joy I get from trying new foods from other countries. For vegans, "eating ethnic" is a fabulous choice, because Ethiopians, for example, are expected to forswear all meat during Lent and so have mastered countless vegan dishes. Among Italy's finest sauces are the marinara, puttanesca (you can usually request it to be made without the anchovies), Arrabiata, and aglio olio (garlic and oil). In Asia, you can pop spice- and herb-infused pan leaves into your mouth from roadside stands and eat big slices of *darian,* the notorious Malaysian "stinky" but delicious fruit. India is the land of a million veggie dishes, and China is where the secrets of cooking with tofu originated. I could go on until the dinner bell sounds, but suffice it to say that you can find a wealth of healthy (and compassionate) fare when you explore ethnic eating. Here are a few ideas for recipes and cookbooks:

SIMPLE LEBANESE HUMMUS

To accompany this dish, you can drizzle a little good-quality olive oil over it, sprinkle it with a bit of chili powder, and/or garnish it with a few black olives, or three or four whole chickpeas.

1 14-ounce can chickpeas (garbanzo beans), rinsed and drained
2 tablespoons tahini
1 teaspoon pressed garlic
3 tablespoons fresh lemon juice

Be sure to skin the chickpeas before you start. If you do this then your hummus will be wonderfully creamy and tasty. If you don't, then it won't be half as good.

To skin the chickpeas: Put chickpeas in the bottom of a large bowl, and cover with water. Press down and rub fairly hard with the flat of your hand in a circular movement, massaging the skins off the chickpeas. The skins should come off and float to the top of the water, and pouring off the water will then remove the skins. Repeat until you've got rid of most of the skins. Drain the skinned chickpeas well.

Put chickpeas in a blender or food processor with the tahini, garlic, and lemon juice, and blend until smooth. Add salt to taste.

Makes 1 cup.

TASTY SPINACH AND POTATO CURRY

1½ pounds potatoes
1 pound fresh spinach or kale (10 ounces weighed without stalks) or frozen but thawed
1 medium onion
2 garlic cloves

2 medium tomatoes

½ teaspoon turmeric powder

2 teaspoons cumin seeds

1 teaspoon red chili powder (or to taste, and depending on its heat!)

Vegetable stock or water

1 teaspoon grated fresh ginger root

Scrub potatoes and boil them in their skins until almost but not quite fully cooked. Leave to cool, then cut into small cubes.

Meanwhile, if using fresh spinach or kale, remove the coarse stalks, then rinse and cook gently for 10 minutes, in just the water clinging to the leaves in a covered pan. Cool and chop (reserve any remaining liquid). For frozen spinach, just defrost and chop.

Chop the onion finely, crush or finely chop the garlic, and finely chop the tomatoes (keep them all separate). Measure the spices out into a small bowl. Brown the onion in a little vegetable stock or water until golden brown—about 10 minutes—topping up with hot water as necessary. Let it stick slightly from time to time to get that fried smell. Add the ginger and garlic to the pan and stir for a minute. Add the spices, and a little more water if necessary. Cook for a few minutes, then add the tomato. Cook gently 3 to 5 minutes.

Add the potatoes and spinach or kale, mixing well. Cover and simmer gently, stirring occasionally to prevent sticking, until the potatoes are cooked to your liking and the spices have permeated the vegetables.

Serves 3 to 4.

GREEK DANDELION SALAD

15 young dandelion leaves

1 small onion

8 black olives

2 tablespoons olive oil

1 tablespoon apple cider vinegar or lemon juice
Salt to taste

Steam the dandelion leaves and onion until soft. Add olives and top with the oil and vinegar or juice. Season with salt.

Serves 1 to 2.

RESOURCES

Holmin, Dalal A., and Maher A. Abbas. *From the Tables of Lebanon: Traditional Vegetarian Cuisine.* Nashville, Tenn.: Book Publishing Company, 1997.

Le, Kim. *Asian Vegan Cooking: A High-Energy Approach to Healthy Living.* Woodbury, N.Y.: Barron's Educational Series, 1997.

Morse, Kitty, and Deborah Jones. *Vegetarian Table: North Africa.* San Francisco, Calif.: Chronicle Books, 2002.

Polemis, Aphrodite. *From a Traditional Greek Kitchen: Vegetarian Cuisine.* Nashville, Tenn.: Book Publishing Company, 1992.

28.

Bees, Honey, and Some Thoughts About Sweeteners

A week must elapse from the day of her birth before she will quit the hive; she will then perform her first "cleansing flight," and absorb the air into her tracheae, which, filling, expand her body, and proclaim her the bride of space.

—AMY TOTH, *THE HONEY BEE DANCE LANGUAGE*

Cruising along the supermarket shelves, looking for that kind of old-fashioned jam that is bursting with pips, the kind my grandmother used to boil up from the raspberries my grandfather grew in his allotment in Surrey, I come to the jars of honey. I think immediately of two women, one I know and one I've never met.

Nermin Buyukmihci is a friend's sister. I met her one summer in upstate New York under a huge spreading tree nicknamed the Tree of Wisdom. Nermin had set up a card table and was giving a talk about bees. It was hard to stay awake that afternoon, but as soothing as her words were, what I learned was such an eye-opener that it stopped me from dozing off in the warmth of the sun.

Nermin spoke gently of her observations of, and respect for, bees: for their organization, their industry, and their complex ways of communicating via the bizarre-looking "waggle dance," and for their role in pollinating plants that people and other animals depend on for food. To bees, Nermin is the sort of champion Jane Goodall is to chimpanzees. With her flowing golden hair backlit by the sun, I wouldn't have been surprised to see bees come swarming about her.

She asked the listeners to consider that what goes into honey is the bee version of blood, sweat, and tears; for honey, to the bees, is precious life itself. She spoke with such sincerity, gentleness, and feeling that at one point, when she talked about the "bee brush"—a wire-tined brush used by beekeepers to brush away fallen bees who are smoked from the hive when their honey is to be stolen—I thought she would cry as she described how the bees' legs and wings are torn off as they are swept out of the "honeystealers'" way. "Stolen"—that was the word she used. I couldn't smile, because she was right. The bees make it, it belongs to them, and we take it. And we take more than just honey, Nermin reminded us; we also take beeswax, propolis, royal bee jelly, and honeycomb. We clean them out of house and home, food, and medicine. I left the talk a former honey-eater!

The other woman who springs to mind is Amy Toth. From what I've read, she's the sort of teacher children go mad for. Not the ones I had in elementary school, who would rap your knuckles for giggling but the kind who like to *make* you giggle.

She teaches her young students through a terrific role-playing exercise about the dance performed by bees who must communicate to the rest of the hive where to find the best flowers. (I can see this rather fun game being adapted for stiff executives at a corporate retreat!)

Amy can't very well explain to her young class that symbolic communication is one of the most sophisticated forms of communication, that it involves not only signaling and receiving but coding environmental information in a way that is understood by the receiver. But she does tell the kids the meaning of each bee dance move, a simplified version of which goes like this:

When they return to the hive with pollen and nectar, worker bees perform an elaborate dance. If the source is a fairly long way away from the hive, the bees dance in a figure eight, waggling their bodies about to carve out the shape that tells a tale to the viewing audience. If the source is oriented to the right of the sun, the dance will be oriented forty-five degrees to right of vertical; if to the left of the sun . . . well, you get the picture. The distance of the straight waggle run is apparently in direct proportion to the distance from the hive to the source.

Amy helps her students build a "hive" by positioning desks or chairs in a circle with a break in the circle for the entrance. A queen bee is designated (usually a teacher), and students adopt the various roles of real bees: workers, including cleaners, guards, and foragers. Other students are "flowers," being positioned somewhere outside the hive and given yellow balloons to represent pollen grains. Amy acts as a foraging scout, leaving the "hive" first and locating the "flowers." When she's found the "flowers," she returns to the "hive" and performs a "horizontal abstraction" of the bees' actual waggle dance. The rest of the "foragers" then pour out of the "hive" armed with the knowledge gleaned from Amy's dance of where to find the flowers with their valuable nectar and pollen.

Amy points out that bees are, these days, factory-farmed animals who, despite having the ability to fly relatively freely, are nevertheless subjected to many of the cruelties of the farming industry. Queen bees are artificially inseminated with sperm obtained from decapitated male bees, have their wings clipped to prevent escape, and are routinely slaughtered every one to two years as their egg-producing ability declines. Add to that the fact that hives, which northern farmers used to ship to Florida and other warm places to "winter over," are now often cast into the fire, with new stock brought in when warm weather comes again.

Bees owe a debt of gratitude to Nermin and Amy. Thanks to them, many people, myself included, have learned respect for bees, to the extent that we are glad to leave honey in the beehive, where it truly belongs.

GOLDEN SYRUP BEE BUNS

¼ cup chopped walnuts
¼ cup Golden Syrup
½ cup melted margarine
1 10-ounce can frozen biscuits
¾ teaspoon cinnamon

Heat oven to 350° F. Combine nuts, syrup, and ½ cup of melted margarine in a bowl. Pour mix into an ungreased casserole dish or pan.

Separate this biscuits, sprinkle with cinnamon. Bake for 30 minutes or until golden brown. Serve warm.

Serves 4.

RESOURCES

Sweet is as sweet does: If your taste buds are used to honey, they will need to adjust, and adjust they will, in a very short time, to another sweet flavoring. Try maple syrup or molasses, or one of the "natural sweeteners" like SugarNot, available in almost every health food store.

Rapadura
800-207-2814
www.rapunzel.com
Quality organic cane sugar.

The Ultimate Sweetener

800-THEMEAL

www.ultimatelife.com

No trees are cut down for this 100 percent birch sugar, which contains no honey, corn syrup, fructose, animal products, or artificial ingredients.

Amy Toth

amytoth@life.uiuc.edu

29.

Baking Kind Cakes: Replacing Ingredients That Hurt Animals

What am I missing? Cake! I need cake!

—GRACE ADLER, *WILL AND GRACE*

Ooh, Black Forest cake: It brings me memories of the once unspoiled little Swiss town of Interlaken, nestled between the Thunersee and the Brienzersee. I stayed in a magnificent chalet-style hotel whose restaurant balcony overlooked lush green Alpine pastures, waking up in the morning mists to the gentle tinkling of brass sheep bells. Later that day, I sat as if in the treetops, dipping my fork into luscious kirsch-laced dark chocolate cake topped with Black Forest cherries.

That cake came a few days after a relaxing car journey through Holland and Denmark, where huge creamy concoctions beckoned from every bakery. After I arrived in Switzerland, the temptation continued, with playful chocolate bears, marzipan roses, and marshmallow mice calling from village confectionery windows as I walked to feed the swans on the water, inhaling the scent of warm sweets.

In stark contrast to my Alpine journey was another visit I made to an entirely different sort of world, one of the giant factory farm sheds, this one in California, where hundreds of thousands of birds are confined to produce eggs. It was a terrible shock to me to see with my own eyes the hens who supply eggs to kitchens the world over. At the time I still had a childlike vision of the chicken-farm hens pecking at wholesome grain, free to dust-bathe in the farmyard, preen their feathers in the sunshine, and when the time was right rest in the deep straw of a nesting box to lay their eggs.

All of that went out the window when I stepped into that vast shed. I gazed in horror at row upon row of cages, stacked atop each other like packing crates. In each one were seven hens. It sounds impossible, I know, for so many animals to fit inside a space the size of a file drawer, but there they were, so crowded they couldn't even stretch their wings. Their food, laced with antibiotics to prevent the infections that thrive in such conditions, was in a long trough, and the hens had to poke their heads through the wire bars to eat. I stared in horror at the beaks of the hens as they tried to peck at the grain. Every one was cut off. The university agriculture professor showing me around explained that it was a universal practice in the egg industry to cut off much of the beaks of the chickens because otherwise the chickens would injure each other in fights.

"Why do they fight?" I asked. His explanation was that when a farmer puts birds in a single cage the birds can't do what they'd do in nature: establish a pecking order. There isn't enough room. Fights ensue.

I thought about the hens I had once known on an old-fashioned farm that belonged to friends of mine. Those hens were curious animals who peered intently at me when I visited, coming right up to inspect me as if to say, "Who are you and what brings you here today?" With my friends they were affectionate, and they loved to perch in an open window and listen to classical music from the stereo. And they were all very clear about their own space. The term pecking order comes from chickens, who among themselves decide which part of the farmyard belongs to whom, and woe to any hen who trespasses!

One thing I knew for sure on the day I saw that egg-laying "factory": These hens were miserable shadows of the animals they should have been. They couldn't even stand comfortably on the wires at the bottom of the cages, whose floors were slanted so that the eggs would roll out to a conveyor belt that rumbled past. They were a pathetic and disturbing sight as they scrambled over each other as best they could, treading on each other's backs, squawking, stressed, their bodies scrunched against the wire. In some cages, I saw that a head or foot had been thrust through the wire, no doubt in a fight, and the bird was stuck, unable to free herself. I knew then that I couldn't ever buy another egg from a grocery store.

When these two worlds—the idyllic holiday with its delectable sweets and the hen "farm"—collided, the first casualties were my favorite recipes. I remember sitting in my kitchen one Saturday afternoon, realizing that I had just two hours before a houseful of guests would arrive and wondering what on earth I could serve for dessert. I searched madly through my cookbooks, longing for the taste of a melt-in-your-mouth cake just cooled from the oven but fearing that whatever I concocted would taste like sawdust. It would have been easy to dash out to the store for a dozen eggs . . . except that I couldn't bring myself to give one penny to the misery I'd witnessed.

That evening I made do with fresh fruit for dessert and resigned myself to a future without the wonderful baked goods that I loved. But of course I am only an amateur cook. It took a professional—one who prepares lavish meals for some of the most prominent men and women in our government—to show me just how wrong I was. Chef Dennis Jaricot at the Willard Intercontinental Hotel, the "Hotel of Presidents," makes the most scrumptious blueberry cake and other mouth-watering desserts without so much as an egg white or any animal ingredients. His secret has become my ally in the kitchen: silken tofu. Whipped up in a blender and added to a recipe with the proper flavorings, it is the perfect "egg" or "cream" in the best cake recipes.

Discovering that eating eggs was a choice and not a necessity made me wonder about the other "necessities" I took for granted. Was

I supporting cruelty to animals in ways I had never considered? And if I was, couldn't I find better alternatives? The rich pastries and chocolate delights of the Alps started me on a journey that brought heartbreak, frustration, and, ultimately, an awareness of new possibilities.

I know now that there is always a better way, and that if we search, we can always find or create a kind alternative to the cruel act.

BLACK FOREST CAKE

Adapted from *Vegetarian Times*, December 1993.

Cake Ingredients

1 cup water

1 cup light maple syrup

½ cup applesauce

1 teaspoon vanilla

1 teaspoon vinegar

2 cups whole-wheat pastry flour or unbleached white flour

¾ cup cocoa powder

1 tablespoon baking powder

1 teaspoon baking soda

Syrup

½ cup water

¼ cup light maple syrup

2 thin lemon or orange slices

⅓ cup liquid from jar of cherries

Icing

¾ cup raw cashews

¾ cup water

2 teaspoons vanilla

½ cup light maple syrup
10 ounces firm tofu
3 ounces semi-sweet chocolate, melted
16-ounce jar pitted cherries, drained

CAKE: Preheat oven to 350°. Combine liquid ingredients in a large bowl and whisk well. Sift dry ingredients together and whisk into liquid mixture. Pour into greased and floured 9" cake tin and bake for 35 minutes or until springy. Cool cake completely and remove from pan. With a serrated knife, cut cake horizontally to make 3 thin layers.

SYRUP: Combine first 3 ingredients in a small pot and boil for 3 minutes. Let cool and then add cherry juice.

ICING: In a blender, combine cashews, water, and vanilla. Blend till smooth and creamy. Add light maple syrup and tofu and blend again. Set aside 2 cups for the vanilla icing to go on top and sides of cake. To the rest of the mixture, add melted chocolate and 3 tablespoons of the prepared syrup. Blend till smooth. Chill both icings before using.

TO ASSEMBLE: Carefully remove the top 2 layers of cake. Brush some prepared syrup onto bottom layer and spread half of chocolate icing over it. Place the middle cake layer on top and brush with syrup and icing. Put down a layer of cherries and dot with a little vanilla icing to help the top layer stick. Place the top layer on the cherries and brush again with syrup. Frost top and sides with vanilla icing. Decorate with cherries and pipe rosettes if desired. Chill several hours before serving. The cake can be kept covered if not being served till the following day. However, the frosting may discolor after about 3 days.

Serves 12.

RESOURCES

Egg Replacer

Tofu is wonderful for egg substitutions that call for a lot of eggs (like quiches). For each egg called for in a recipe, substitute ¼ cup whipped silken tofu to your cooking. You can buy commercial egg-replacer powders, such as Ener-G Egg Replacer. This can be used often in baking, but is usually best in recipes that call for only 1 or 2 eggs. For use in sweet baking, try substituting ½ of a ripe banana, mashed, or ¼ cup applesauce to replace each egg in a baked recipe. These will flavor the recipe, so make sure the fruit will taste good in whatever you are making.

To use things you have in your kitchen: For 1 whole egg, beat together 2 tablespoons water, 1 tablespoon oil, and 2 teaspoons baking powder. You may also try 1 tablespoon arrowroot and 1 tablespoon soy flour mixed with 2 tablespoons water, or 2 tablespoons flour, ½ tablespoon shortening, and ½ teaspoon baking powder mixed with 2 teaspoons water. For 1 egg white, dissolve 1 tablespoon plain agar powder in 1 tablespoon water. Whip, chill, and whip again.

Vegan Margarines

Some brands of margarine that are easy to find may not be vegan. However, many store-brand or generic spreads and shortenings do not contain animal products. Avoid ingredients such as whey, lactose, and vitamin D_3, which may be animal-derived. For your baking needs, try using Fleishmann's unsalted margarine (stick), Spectrum Naturals (tub), Willow Run soy margarine (stick), or pure vegetable shortening grocery brand tubs.

Milk and Cream Substitutes

Like egg substitutes, the best milk and cream substitutes to use when baking will vary for different recipes. For most recipes (for example, cream sauces), soy milk will do just fine.

For buttermilk, simply mix 1 teaspoon white vinegar into 1 cup soy milk. For a rich, creamy taste in sweet cooking, try using vanilla- or chocolate-flavored soy milk in place of dairy milk. These also work very well as a coffee creamer. Depending on the desired flavor of your dessert, rice, oat, almond, and even coconut milk can also work well in recipes that don't need to be boiled intensely.

Ready-Made Baked Goods

If you don't feel like cooking, nip around to your local supermarket and you can find vegan baked goods galore. If you have a Dollar Store near you, you will find apple and cinnamon cookies and twists and all manner of vegan baked goods on the shelves. Here are a few other suggestions (check labels, though, as ingredients can change from time to time):

- Barry's Bakery makes six varieties of French Twists as well as other cookies. French Twist flavors include Original (cinnamon), Maple French Toast, Chocolate Chip, Mocha, Wild Raspberry, and California Almond.
- Uncle Eddie's rich cookies come in chocolate chip, oatmeal, and peanut butter flavors.
- Keebler Vienna Crème-Filled Fingers go beautifully with a hot cup of tea or coffee.
- Krispy Kreme Pies: cherry, apple, and, best of all, coconut cream—available in grocery stores and gas stations.

- Little Debbie makes a "cake doughnut" that's vegan, and available in convenience and grocery stores and gas stations.
- Newmans-O cookies are organic and made without trans fats.
- Rich Foods: Chocolate fudge stripe cookies.
- Sara Lee has several varieties of vegan pastries.

Two cakes are definitely better than one! While you are buying the ingredients, what about thinking twice? That is, think about doing twice as much good by baking two cakes and giving the second one to a shut-in, a serviceperson living on a fixed income, or the volunteers or other hard workers at a local charity. This will multiply your kindness and share it with others.

30.

Preparing a Romantic Candlelight Dinner

Those who wish to lead virtuous lives should abstain from truffles.

—ANCIENT FRENCH PROVERB

They emerged depleted from a Turkish Bath of emotions.

—ANONYMOUS DESCRIPTION OF A LOVERS' FEAST

I love cooking with wine. Sometimes I even put it in the food.

—ANONYMOUS

Whether you want to melt the ice, or passions are too hot to keep the champagne cold in that bucket, a romantic dinner must include foods that you hope have aphrodisiac properties because, whether those properties are real or not, that hope alone can be suggestive enough to excite more than your appetite.

In Chapter 6, "Selecting the Purest Candles" (page 30), you can find the perfect candles to light the room and your table, so let's get to the menu and the reasoning behind it: I'm going to take a (fig) leaf out of Millennium's book. Millennium is a fine San Francisco restaurant that offers a monthly dinner consisting of five courses of "aphrodisiac" foods served up in a romantic setting. This restaurant uses foods the Greeks originally identified as having magic powers to ignite the loins, and includes oyster mushrooms, avocado, and, of course, chocolate, which many women find holds an allure that, like falling head over heels in love, cannot be fully explained.

Because Millennium is a vegan restaurant, what diners eat there leaves the lovers (or lovers-to-be) full of energy and vitality, rather than snoring on the couch afterward. And avoiding a meaty, creamy meal is important for more than ethical reasons: As the Physicians Committee for Responsible Medicine reminds us, meat and dairy products do not just clog the arteries to a man's heart but to *all* of his vital organs!

Researchers have established that though erections can be inspired by just about anything under the sun, ultimately they depend on blood flow. And just as blockages in the arteries to the heart can cause a heart attack and choked-off blood to the brain can lead to a stroke, when the arteries to the genitals are clogged, that part of the body will not work so well either. When the arteries are impeded only slightly, it takes longer to get an erection. As the obstruction worsens, complete impotence occurs. By age sixty, erectile dysfunction affects one in four American men. Artery blockages, a major cause of erectile dysfunction, are linked to one of America's most popular food categories—meat. The good news is that such blockages can be prevented, and even reversed, by changes in diet and lifestyle.

Breakthrough research by Dean Ornish, M.D., has shown that a combination of a low-fat vegan diet, moderate exercise, stress management, and no smoking lets the arteries begin to clean themselves out in 82 percent of patients. Many of the other factors contributing to impotence, including diabetes, obesity, and hypertension, can also be influenced by a menu change. Side effects from various medications are another root cause of impotence. In fact, two of the worst culprits are blood pressure pills and cholesterol-lowering drugs, both prescribed for conditions that could be dramatically improved by a vegetarian diet. With the right food and exercise, many men can cut back on, and even discontinue, drug therapy.

In other words, vegan diets are *natural* Viagra!

Quite cleverly, the cost of the Millennium meal can include a night's stay in the adjoining Savoy Hotel for just about $180 all-inclusive except for the tip and taxes, but you will already be at home, so even your bill will be easy on the heart.

A sample meal at Millennium, in which each course carries a lovers' theme title, might consist of smoked baba ghanoush antipasto, followed by an avocado, jicama, and sesame salad with kumquat dressing. For appetizers you could have oyster mushroom calamari and hot and sour "shark fin" (faux, of course) soup with ginger, lily buds, and banana blossoms.

Add a wild-mushroom-and-hazelnut-stuffed artichoke and chipotle grilled seitan roulade for the entrée, and for dessert, chocolate molten soufflé with raspberry crème anglais, rose petal "ice cream," or coconut tapioca pudding.

Millennium's favorite romantic nightcap: a Chinese herbal "love potion" made with lemonade, cranberry, pomegranate juice, ginseng, cornus, moutan, and light spices.

That meal is enough to make the most resistant love interest melt. And, speaking of melting, if you are at home, after enjoying the recipes listed below, you might liquefy some dark chocolate in the microwave; mix it with a little vegan cream and a dash of Cointreau. That will result in a delicious chocolate dip for strawberries, figs, apricots, cherries, dates, brazil nuts, and almonds, and one quite suitable for licking off each other's fingers.

Finally, if anyone is still feeling tense, I suggest having a book on massage and some massage oil handy (see Resources).

Now to Fabio, the modern Casanova whose shirtless body of bodies, chiseled chin, and flowing mane have graced more romance novel jacket covers than any other man in history. Lucky for us, Fabio created a Valentine's Day meal for PETA that can easily be cooked in an apartment kitchen and used for any night of the year. Beneath the recipes, you will find other bits and pieces that may be useful in conjuring up a magical evening.

Here are Fabio's romantic recipes:

ASPARAGUS AMORE WITH WALNUTS

½ lb. fresh asparagus
2 teaspoons red wine vinegar
3–4 tablespoons walnut oil
Salt and black pepper to taste
Chopped, lightly toasted walnuts

Cook the asparagus, covered, in a small amount of boiling water for 2–3 minutes, until crisp but tender. Drain and rinse with cold water.

Meanwhile, whisk together the vinegar, oil, salt and pepper. To serve, drizzle this vinaigrette over the asparagus and garnish with the chopped walnuts.

Serves 2.

TANTALIZING TOMATO AND WHITE BEAN CROSTINI

7 sun-dried tomato halves
1 clove garlic, coarsely chopped
1 15-oz. can white beans
1 tablespoon paprika
1 tablespoon minced fresh sage leaves
1 tablespoon olive oil
Salt and cayenne pepper to taste
Thick toasted slices of Italian bread
Fresh sage leaves

Place the tomato halves in a bowl, cover with boiling water, and let stand for 15 minutes.

Drain the tomatoes and coarsely chop.

In a food processor, combine the tomatoes, garlic, beans, paprika, sage, oil, salt, and cayenne pepper. Process until smooth.

Spread the bean mixture over the bread slices. Garnish with sage leaves.

Make 1¾ cups spread.

RIPE-FOR-ROMANCE RASPBERRY "CHEESE" CAKE

2 8-oz. containers plain nondairy cream cheese
1 cup sugar
Juice of 1 lemon
Dash of vanilla
Graham cracker (digestive biscuit) crust
Fresh raspberries or canned cherry pie filling

Preheat the oven to 350° F.

Blend together the nondairy cream cheese, sugar, lemon juice, and vanilla and pour into the graham cracker crust. Bake for 60 minutes. Allow to cool.

Cover the top of the cake with the fresh raspberries or cherry pie filling and chill several hours.

Serves 8.

RED-HOT RISOTTO

1 large onion, thinly sliced
2 green onions, finely chopped
½ red pepper, diced
2 cloves garlic, minced
1⅓ cups Arborio rice
2½ cups vegetable broth
⅔ cup (¼ pint) dry white wine

Salt and white pepper to taste
Soy Parmesan cheese (optional)

In a lightly oiled, heavy pot, fry the onion, green onions, and red pepper until soft and nicely browned. Add the garlic toward the end of the cooking time.

Add the rice. Then add the broth and wine a little at a time while stirring, and bring to a boil. Reduce the heat to low and simmer, uncovered, stirring occasionally until thick and creamy, about 30 minutes. If needed, add a tiny bit of water at a time until the rice reaches the desired consistency. Add salt and white pepper to taste and soy Parmesan cheese, if desired.

Serves 4.

FABIO'S PORTOBELLO PASSION

8 tablespoons (1 stick) margarine
2 large Portobello mushrooms
2 tablespoons vegetarian Worcestershire sauce
4 cloves garlic, finely chopped
¼ cup (4 tablespoons) pine nuts
2 small red or yellow bell peppers, chopped
1 small zucchini (courgette), chopped
½ cup fresh peas
1 cup sprouts
1 tablespoon finely chopped basil or 1 teaspoon dried basil leaves, crushed
¼ teaspoon salt and white pepper to taste
Pinch cayenne pepper

For the Sauce

⅓ cup chopped shallots or onions
1 cup soy milk
½ cup dry white wine or vegetable broth

¼ cup orange juice
1 teaspoon grated orange peel

Preheat the oven to 375° F.

In a large skillet, melt 2 tablespoons of the margarine over medium heat and cook the mushrooms with the Worcestershire sauce for 4 minutes, turning once. Remove the mushrooms and arrange them on a baking sheet. In the same skillet, melt 2 more tablespoons margarine over medium-high heat and brown the garlic and pine nuts. Add the bell peppers and cook 4 minutes, stirring occasionally, until almost tender. Stir in the remaining vegetables, sprouts, basil, salt, white pepper, and cayenne pepper. Evenly spoon the vegetable mixture onto the mushrooms. Bake for 10 minutes.

For the sauce, melt the remaining margarine over medium heat and cook the shallots for 4 minutes, stirring occasionally, until just golden. Sir in the soy milk, wine, orange juice, and orange peel. Bring to a boil over high heat. Reduce heat to medium and continue boiling, stirring occasionally, until the mixture thickens, about 3 minutes. Strain.

To serve, spoon the sauce over the mushrooms.

Serves 2.

RESOURCES

The Lovers' Dinner

Millennium Restaurant
580 Geary St.
San Francisco, CA
415-345-3900

The Body Shop

www.thebodyshop.com
usa.info@the-body-shop.com

Hundreds of retail locations around the world.

The Body Shop offers massage oils and a series of books on body care. Their practical and easy-to-use format provides simple solutions for everyday stresses.

Vegan Erotica

801-560-8238

www.veganerotica.com

Vegan erotica offers everything from cruelty-free lubricants to bondage gear custom-made from animal-friendly pleather. Their Web site also features CONDOMI condoms, which are manufactured with cocoa powder instead of casein (a milk protein), making them the only condom to be given the seal of approval by the Vegan Society. Available in a wide range of flavors, textures, and sizes and in packs of six ($3), twelve ($5.75), and twenty-four ($10).

Secret Garden Publishing

www.secretgardenpublishing.com

Erotic Massage: The Touch of Love by Kenneth Ray Stubbs. With more than a hundred illustrations, *Erotic Massage* presents detailed, long, flowing strokes for lovers. With almost half a million copies sold, this book appears in many languages and many countries around the world.

Secret Gardens Unscented Massage Oil/Secret Garden Scent Oil: a high-quality blend of apricot, sunflower, macadamia nut, safflower, grapeseed, jojoba oils, and vitamin E. Blend with your favorite Secret Gardens Scent Oil for a custom-scented massage aid that will relax tired muscles and delight the senses. Eight-ounce bottle.

Yo-Organic Plus

604-990-9700

Flavored lubricants with hemp oil and no animal products.

PART FOUR

Recreation and Vacations

31.

Traveling Safely with Animals or Leaving Them Safely Behind

Now, that's ironic!

—ONE CAGED PARROT TO ANOTHER AS THEIR PEOPLE HEAD OUT THE DOOR, AIRLINE TICKETS IN HAND

Look excited, look excited! Oh never mind!

—DOG TO GOLDFISH AS HE HEARS THEIR PEOPLE RETURNING HOME

Travelers who want to treat their animal companions with kindness should consider several issues, which I'll cover here: boarding, pet-sitting, flying and driving, and finding "animal-friendly" lodging.

First, if you absolutely must leave an animal behind when you go away, the very best thing is to leave him at home, where he feels comfortable. Boarding is a traumatic experience for most animals: Not only do they lose you, but they lose the safety and comfort of their home at the same time. Although you may like and trust the person who runs a certain kennel or cattery, imagine for a moment (all other aspects aside, like overcrowding, impatient staff, the risk of fire) being the cat or dog who must live on concrete or in a cage while you are off on holiday. A vet's office is also a bad place to leave an animal who is not ill: The sounds of pain and fear and the smells of illness can be disturbing to your pal. And who knows what he or she may pick up while "hospitalized."

No, home is where the heart is, where security lies, and where comfort can be found, so that is where a dog or cat should stay if at all possible.

This means finding a dog or cat or hamster "sitter." Pick this person as carefully as you would choose someone to look after your baby, or as a French chef chooses vegetables. You cannot be too careful. Being listed in the Yellow Pages doesn't mean anything more than being able to find the money to buy an ad, but if you do choose a "professional" sitter, check references very, very carefully and check in with the Better Business Bureau and chamber of commerce to make sure there are no complaints against the outfit you have in mind. A sitter should not be too young, remote, or unknown. The best chance of pinpointing a good one is to turn to a reliable relative or someone who has animals and whom you have known for aeons.

It is not neurotic but prudent to check up on your sitter, no matter if you are in Timbuktu (there are phones there now); and it is an excellent insurance policy of sorts to do things like leave water around the house or apartment in bowls in case your sitter is struck by lightning or loses your house key. (A dehydration disaster is a far greater worry than death from starvation.)

If you are driving with your cat or dog, be sure that he or she is secure whenever a door is open. A sudden bang from a backfire, and a dog who is not leashed or a cat who is out of the carrier may never be seen again. I shall spare you the stories of all the lost animals whose people said "pshaw!" to that bit of advice. Please be sure all collars fit properly (two fingers comfortably under the collar) to avoid someone slipping out of them at a crucial moment, and splurge on a cat carrier that is very sturdy, in case of accident and to avoid discovering the hard way that your cat could have been Houdini's understudy.

If you are thinking of flying an animal, never put her in the hold of the plane if she can fit under the seat. Despite the assurances of the airlines, many a dog or cat has gone missing or ended up injured or dead. Tabitha, a tabby who got lost aboard a flight from Los Angeles to New York, is one of the very rare animals whose story has a happy ending, but it took great expense and trauma, and the grounding of a jet and peeling back of its metal side panels, to achieve that reunion. Again, make sure any carrier used is very sturdy and properly locked.

If you absolutely cannot fly the animal in the passenger compartment or drive your animal to your destination, always pick a *direct, nonstop* flight in weather that is neither too hot nor too cold. You may be told that holds are pressurized, but tell that to the one-in-a-million pilot—my hero—who made the extraordinary decision to divert an entire planeload of passengers because he saw that the temperature in the hold was rising too high and knew the Labrador below would be cooked alive. Also, be there or have someone there to meet the plane so that if the animal does not arrive, immediate steps can be taken to try to find him or her.

The happy news is that pulling in for the night with a dog or cat has never been easier. Many hotels and motels allow or even cater to animals in rooms, from economy chains like Motel 6 and Super 8 to the Four Seasons Hotels and Hotel Pierre in Manhattan. Loews L'Enfant Plaza Hotel in Washington even donates 5 percent of the room charge to the local humane society. Be sure that if you go out, you put the "Do Not Disturb" sign on and that you tell the desk there is an animal in the room and that you want no one to enter in case the pet exits! See below for a handy guide that should make trips easy to manage.

Bon voyage!

RESOURCES

Travel With or Without Pets: 25,000 Pets-R-Permitted Accomodations, Pet-sitters, Kennels, and More. Torrance, Calif.: Annenburg Communications Institute, 1997.

Ignore the boarding kennels, vet clinics, and pet-sitters, but this book does list more than twenty thousand animal-friendly hotels and motels across the USA, Canada, and Mexico, from budget stops to posh resorts like the exclusive San Ysidro Ranch in Santa Barbara.

Barish, Eileen. *Vacationing with Your Pet: Eileen's Directory of Pet-Friendly Lodging: U.S. and Canada.* Gardena, Calif.: SCB Distributors, 2001. As with all guides, it is useful to double-check to make sure hotel/motel policies haven't changed since publication. This guide lists twenty-three thousand places where animals are welcome and includes helpful travel tips and even a dog biscuit recipe.

Four Seasons Hotels worldwide, including the Hotel Pierre in Manhattan

800-332-3442
www.fourseasons.com

Loews Hotels

www.loewshotels.com

Motel 6

www.motel6.com
Most motel 6 hotels allow one animal per room.

Super 8 motels

www.super8.com

Vari-Kennels

www.epetpals.com
Hard plastic travel carriers, airline ready.

32.

Being Ready for Animal Emergencies on the Road

My only solution for the problem of accidents . . . is to stay in bed all day. Even then, there is always the chance that you will fall out.

—THE BISHOP OF DURHAM, 1920

I could not have slept tonight if I had left that helpless little creature to perish on the ground.

—ABRAHAM LINCOLN (TO FRIENDS WHO CHIDED HIM FOR STOPPING TO PICK UP AN INJURED BIRD)

In addition to the jack, a can of Fix-A-Flat, and those other odds and ends floating about in the trunk of my car, I've found that keeping a kit for animal emergencies handy is essential.

Perhaps to compensate for my deteriorating eyesight, I seem to have developed a sort of animal radar. I'm forever spotting a lost dog stranded on a median strip, discovering an injured seagull in a parking lot, or turning back to see if that squirrel by the side of the road is really dead. Sometimes he's not, and I must get him suitably confined and into my car quickly so I can rush to the vet or wildlife worker. (Squirrels, who are the dearest of animals, can break your heart by lying very still and covering their eyes with their tails when they are hurt, in an attempt to hide.)

One afternoon, when dashing for an appointment, I almost didn't stop. Then a little voice, my conscience no doubt, forced me to turn around and find my way back to that tuft of fluff I had passed a mile or so back. The fur had moved as I drove by, but it was unclear whether that was just the wind caused by traffic zipping by on the busy highway. I parked my car on the shoulder, got out, and walked over. A part of the fluff itself raised up and looked at me.

She was someone's cat, a beautiful little tabby, and very much alive—although so hurt she was unable to crawl far from the edge of the road. That would be the last time I'd tell myself it was all right to "keep on keeping on" unless I was absolutely sure!

Some people are quite squeamish or afraid when it comes to touching, moving, or handling animals found in distress, let alone getting them into the car. Having a small animal emergency kit in your trunk can make your kind act a lot easier to perform.

Animals, whether wild or not, are usually very afraid of human intervention when they are hurt or dying. They may be uncertain whether you are friend or foe, so be reasonably cautious in your approach not only to avoid being bitten but to avoid frightening and hurting them even more (and should you be bitten or scratched, just as an extra precaution, check in by phone with your local health authority). It will help to remember the four rules of approach:

1. Be as quiet and deliberately slow moving as possible.
2. Avoid eye contact, which can be taken as a challenge.
3. Talk very softly.
4. Try to take with you on that first approach whatever you might need to use so that you won't have to go back to the car for something and approach yet again.

My first recommendation is to make the container for the kit useful in and of itself. Use a cat carrier, for instance, either a cardboard one (available from any veterinarian or pet supply store) or, better yet, a sturdy plastic cat carrier that can be used later if you take any small animal on a longer trip or on a plane. Having a proper, sturdy carrier will mean you will be ready to safely and appropriately transport an injured animal, such as a raccoon, squirrel, owl, or cat, without worrying that the animal will escape and get trapped under the seat or otherwise run amok while you are driving.

With the animal safely confined, here are the usual options:

For nonwildlife species: If you are willing to pay for treatment, head to the nearest veterinarian and insist on being seen right away. Some veterinarians will not charge for strays, but don't count on it. Try to call first, as some will refuse to treat an animal you do not own, even in an emergency! Another option is to drive the animal to the nearest humane society, shelter, or SPCA, usually listed in the telephone directory under the county you are in.

Wildlife: I do not feel it fair to put a wild animal through the trauma of being handled by humans and suffering the pain of surgery and recovery in an alien environment, especially when most do not pull through. Those that do are doomed either to live in a cage in captivity for the rest of their lives or to be released, but this time they will have a physical disadvantage as they attempt to fend for themselves again in Nature. I would suggest paying for euthanasia at the veterinary office, heading for the animal shelter and staying with the animal to ensure immediate euthanasia. Few experiences can be more traumatic for wild beings than to find themselves trapped in a cage in a facility where they can smell and hear predators (dogs and cats) all around them.

If the animal is only stunned or if injuries are minor, you may wish to find the nearest wildlife rehabilitator by calling the local humane society, SPCA, Animal Control, or a veterinary office and making inquiries.

It is wise to take the time now to research the telephone numbers and addresses of your local humane society, wildlife rehabilitator, and some well recommended veterinarians. Write this information on a couple of cards and put it in both your wallet and the glove compartment. There is nothing worse than having to scramble for information when an emergency arises.

What to Put in the Basic Kit

- A nylon lead
- A towel
- Names, addresses, and phone numbers you might need, such as your local wildlife rescue/rehabilitation center, humane society, veterinarians, and twenty-four-hour emergency veterinary services
- A pop-top can of smelly cat food, like mackerel
- A gauze bandage to stanch bleeding or to use to make a muzzle

RESOURCES

The PETA Rescue Kit

The kit is available for purchase on www.peta.org. The Rescue Kit contains a cardboard carrier, a nylon lead, a towel, and a "Be an Angel for Animals" packet full of information on how you can help animals in your community.

33.

Preserving the Beach—Its Life and Coral Reefs

In the Philippines, there are lovely screens
To protect you from the glare:
In the Malay states, they have hats like plates
Which the Britishers won't wear.

—NOEL COWARD, "MAD DOGS AND ENGLISHMEN"

The beach is most people's idea of a perfect vacation spot, but it is also the permanent everyday home to all manner of animal life, from the tiny crabs in their burrows to mother turtles laying their eggs to all the fishes and other forms of sea life who thrive in the waters, rocks, and reefs. I have spent many an hour half dozing yet mesmerized by the sandpipers' industry and fascinated by the almost invisible little sand-colored crustacean going about his chores next to my chaise longue.

There are many things we can do (and avoid doing) that will preserve the beaches and oceans and make us polite guests in this fragile ecosystem. If "your" beach is one where turtles come ashore, having a campfire after dark can scare turtles away from laying their eggs and disorient their young. If you are staying at a hotel in an area indigenous to sea turtles or birds who nest on the beach at night, please discourage them from using bright lights at the oceanfront. Look for "Sea Turtle Nesting Area" signs or ask locally.

There are even considerations in choosing whether or not to use a suntan lotion or oil! That is because coral reefs are under threat not only from warming waters, strong storms, and gas and oil from pleasure and commercial boats but also from bathers whose suntan preparations and insect repellants erode the colonies of sea creatures (polyps) whose industry and bodies form the reefs.

Humans and human activities have already killed 10 percent of the world's coral reefs, so it is vital to wash off any such preparations before entering the water (as well as to be careful while snorkeling or diving not to stand or lean against living corals). It takes seconds to destroy what has taken years to develop.

Here's how to do it: Apply your sunblock early in the morning, allowing it to soak into your skin rather than immediately rub off in the water. This will increase the effectiveness of your sunblock and prevent damage to coral reefs.

Friends of the Reef also asks that even when fishing is permitted, people not fish in the reefs because it can disturb the fragile balance that exists in those ecosystems. Of course, fishing itself is an ugly, violent pastime, so skipping it entirely is best.

For Virginia Bollinger, going on vacation to a sunny spot on the beach—and the choice of what to put on her skin for the occasion—will never be the quite the same for a very different reason. Virginia is the courageous woman who blew the whistle on suntan lotion experiments of all things, at a laboratory in Philadelphia, Pennsylvania.

One day Virginia went to work and saw a peculiar and disturbing sight: A dozen white mice, looking for everything in the world like little sugar mice, were being taped to a board with thick packing tape. The mice had been laid on their backs and the tape pulled over their stretched-out legs onto the board.

Experimenters then brought out some UV filter suntan lotion and smeared it onto the mice's little pink, exposed stomachs and turned on a heat lamp.

Virginia says that whenever she wants to get up from her towel on the sands and head for a cool dip in the ocean or put up her beach umbrella, she thinks of those mice, struggling frantically but with no hope of escape as the heat from the lamp burned into their skin.

Suntan product companies do not need to test on animals in such a crude way. In fact, they didn't have to test on animals at all. Many brands use human skin patch tests and known safe ingredients, as well as assays of ingredient and property combinations. So if we do use a suntan oil or lotion, we can reward those companies who are kind not only to our skin but to animals as well.

Even if we use kindly produced products, we must be sure to wash them off our skin before stepping into the ocean. And, of course, be careful never to break off any piece of the reef or collect living shellfish or starfish for souvenirs, never encourage the trade in dead sea horses (more will be killed to take their place), and never buy any jewelry made from black coral because removing coral destroys the reefs and harms all forms of life dependent upon them.

The fish who make reefs their home would thank us if they could.

RESOURCES

Tanning Products

Banana Boat
800-723-3786
www.bananaboat.com

PETA

www.peta.com
Provides a free list of companies that do and don't test on animals.

Reef Protection

Friends of the Reef
www.friendsofthereef.com

Project Aware

www.livingreef.org

Diving guidelines for reef excursions.

Eco- and Animal-Friendly Beaches

Coral Sea National Nature Reserves, Australia

Fishing is not permitted in these reserves and divers are cautioned not to disturb shells, coral, and other sea life. Nesting turtles and birds are protected.

Buck Island Reef Monument National Park, Virgin Islands

Camping is not permitted, the Marine Garden is closed to all fishing, and plants and animals here are protected.

National Marine Park, Had Mae Had, Thailand

Cozumel, Mexico

34.

The Benefits of Beachcombing

Oh, what a wondrous bird is the pelican!
His beak holds more than his belican.
He takes in his beak
People's trash for the week.
And I'll be darned if I know how the helican.

—ADAPTED FROM DIXON LANIER MERRITT, *NASHVILLE BANNER*

I caught the glint of metal in the sun's fading rays and bent to pick up my find. Partially obscured in the sand lay a complicated fishing set of four-pronged hooks, complete with flashy metal lure and about five feet of filament. My stroll that evening had brought me under the Sand Bridge pier on the Virginia shore, and I was lucky that my eye had caught the glint of steel before my foot had found the hooks.

Of course, I was at an advantage: I was looking. I'm a beachcomber, and looking for anything out of the ordinary is what I do when walking along the ocean shore or, for that matter, along a lakeside, pond, or river. My treasures bear me out, and the trash I find means lives will be saved.

In Atlantic City, New Jersey, after a particularly rough winter storm, I found not only the usual flotsam and jetsam on the sands but two perfectly preserved . . . dinosaurs! Well, they were modern ones made of plastic, but I still have them (and I love them). I also have a collection of the most unusual small floats from a beach in the south of France, a beautiful plastic mat decorated with colorful fishes (now used under the visiting cat's dishes on the kitchen floor), and a selection of yellow and white children's "sand shapers" that, after a careful bleaching, serve both as decorative sunroom conversation pieces or wall decorations for a child's room and large star- and starfish-shaped cookie molds.

The fact is that you won't find only amusing treasures if you beachcomb, but equipped with a plastic bag or two, you can do a world of good by ridding the beach of dangerous fishing gear and trash, like jagged tin cans, that are likely to maim and kill sea animals of all sorts if left lying around.

Wildlife rehabilitators report that the number one cause of waterbirds' injuries is . . . fishing gear. In fact, the National Academy of Sciences estimates that a stunning 350 million pounds of packaging and fishing gear are lost or dumped by the commercial fishing industry each year. That doesn't count any of the individuals who are out on or by the waterways, casting, and snagging, their lines and nets.

The Alabama Wildlife Rehabilitation Center, one of hundreds of wonderfully helpful wildlife rescue facilities, cares for nearly three thousand animals annually, just in its own region. Among that number are eagles, hawks, owls, songbirds, and water- and shore-birds. One of the center's successful rescues involved Perry, a hawk.

Perry was flying near a lake when he became tangled in fishing line that had been left behind in a bush near the water. He hung there helplessly for several hours before someone spotted him, clinging to his life, the struggle having caused the fishing line to become deeply embedded in the flesh of his leg and one of his wings. Although the wounds caused by the ordeal have healed, say his rescuers, the damage to his muscles and nerves seems permanent and Perry is grounded for life.

Fishing line, kite string, and other "stringy bits" act as invisible traps for animals, including birds, and especially waders like egrets, cranes, and herons. The birds can't see fishing line, so they walk or fly into it, even pick up something it has become attached to, and suddenly find themselves in deep trouble. The harder the animals struggle, the more entangled they become and the greater the damage to their delicate legs and wings. It is estimated that one in five pelicans will become entangled in fishing line during the course of his or her life! A whopping 85 percent of pelicans brought to the Suncoast Seabird Sanctuary in Florida are there because of close encounters with fishing line.

Once you start keeping—pun intended—an eagle eye out for the stuff, you will find filament, lead weights (which slowly poison swans, geese, and other birds who swallow them), and some pretty nasty hooks, often with barbs intact. Those barbs get caught in animals' throats and just won't budge, making swallowing impossible and resulting in starvation and infection.

There are other hazards, too. For instance, once you start looking along a seashore, you will probably be surprised at the seemingly ubiquitous supply of balloons that have come ashore tied to long colored ribbons, all left over from parties on cruise ships, yachts, and tour boats. Among other animals, leatherback turtles and even sperm whales have been found with Mylar balloon fragments clogging their intestines. Then there are plastic six-pack rings: Even the ones that eventually disintegrate can be insidious animal traps. Another hazard is posed by the bits of (swallowable) hard plastic mesh, which are impossible for any tiny creature to break apart and which so many seaside stores thoughtlessly use to encase children's spades, buckets, and other beach paraphernalia.

You may be incredulous at how much risky rubbish you can pick up in just one half-hour stroll. I have a photograph of my fellow beach collector and cleanup pal, Dawn Carr, standing with what looks like a massive odd sculpture of intertwined beach debris that is almost as big as she is. That lot was collected in just two hours and weighed in at over sixteen pounds!

It is incredibly easy to organize a cleanup party or simply to do it yourself. You can have terrific fun by turning your beach bum holiday into a cleanathon and going away from your holiday haven knowing you have likely saved many lives.

If you live near a pond, lake, or river, may I suggest planning an outing that involves a spot of spot cleaning? It is even possible to advertise for helpers by calling a local radio station and asking them to announce the cleanup on the air. What a great way to discover new friendships that may last a lifetime!

Tips

Clumps of seaweed can hide hooks and other dangerous bits and pieces, like plastic O-rings through which fish may swim only to find they cannot back out of them or extricate themselves. Avoid walking on them; just gently pick up a clump and shake it to see what you can see when the sand falls off.

Wear sensible shoes, and carry a rag to wipe your hands in case you come in contact with oil, tar, or something else you would like to remove.

Enlist others and raise awareness by contacting your local press. Some local newspaper or TV reporters may wish to come along with you as you clean; if not, be sure to take a picture of your finds and the volume of material you collect so that you can submit it to the press with a description of where, when, and why. One little story in the paper will certainly make other beach- or lake-goers, even anglers, more conscientious.

RESOURCES

The Alabama Wildlife Rehabilitation Center, Birmingham
205-663-7930
www.alawildliferehab.org

Suncoast Seabird Sanctuary, Indian Shores, Florida
727-391-6211
www.seabirdsanctuary.org

35.

Making Sure Sports and Sports Equipment Are Truly Sporting

The most vigorous sport I ever mastered was backgammon.

—WILLIAM JERROD

The Devil floats up to see St. Peter at the Gates of Heaven and says,
"Hey, let's have a baseball game—my people against your people."
"Sure," replies St. Pete, "but I should warn you,
I have all the Hall of Famers!"
"No worries," says the Devil. "I have all the umpires!"

—ANONYMOUS

I was sitting at the desk at the Washington Humane Society one Sunday afternoon, doing my volunteer stint by answering the phones, when Bianca Berry, then its president, burst through the door, a pig in her arms. She was looking very happy, but the pig wasn't too sure.

It turned out that the Georgetown Hoyas had been about to have some fun by staging a greased-pig contest when Ms. Berry drove by the field and spotted a "wiggling, pink animal where he shouldn't have been." If you've ever met Ms. Berry, you would know that that was the end of that: Apologies all around, the pig was handed over.

The pig shouldn't have worried. Courtesy of Ms. Berry's interaction with the basketball players, he would soon be on a vegetarian farm outside the capital, sharing Oreo cookies with another rescued pig who had learned to come to the kitchen and knock his large snout on the door until someone forked over the handout.

Greased-pig contests are like lots of silly sports that aren't sporting at all in that they involve an unwilling participant who gets abused—overgrown boys kicking donkeys around school gymnasiums, bullfights, rodeos, fishing, and . . . kangaroo boxing.

In Virginia, many years back, there was a humane society officer who was extremely frustrated. A boxing-kangaroo act was heading her way and she knew the kangaroo had no life to speak of. He was kept in a cage on a circus bus and dragged out into the ring by a neck chain, only to be hit by men fixing for a fight. The 'roo would be goaded to the point where he'd hit back, but then the next contender would have a go, and sooner or later the kangaroo would probably get "droopy jaw," a syndrome that is often fatal and is caused by repeated blows to the chin. Try as she might, the officer was unable to stop the act on the ground of cruelty to animals, because the law in that state required visible signs of broken bones or suffering.

Then she had a flash of genius. She read the boxing regulations and discovered that it was illegal in Virginia to put on a fight unless the contestants were over the age of seventeen and wore regulation shorts and shoes, that no contestant could have facial hair, and that the participants must pass an IQ test. The match was a no-go. Or, to put it another way, the kangaroo won!

Back to pigs—well, "pigskins" anyway. As you probably know, footballs aren't really made of pigs; they are made of cows.

It takes about three thousand cows to supply the National Football League (NFL) with a year's supply of them. Needless to say, spearheaded by PETA, there is a "moove" afoot to get the NFL to switch to synthetic ball material. The British soccer ball manufacturer Mitre, which supplies balls to soccer clubs worldwide, switched to synthetic balls in the midnineties when it discovered that synthetic balls perform much better, are more flexible, last longer, and repel water better than leather ones.

The National Basketball Association (NBA) still sticks to the old leather ball as its Official Game Ball, which PETA terms "a true foul ball," but the good news is that the NBA has "passed" on leather for its Official Indoor/Outdoor Ball, Official All-Surface Ball, and Official Outdoor Ball, all of which are made from synthetics. And the National Collegiate Athletic Association (NCAA) has also switched to better-performing synthetic basketballs, which most colleges and universities use anyway.

"We're always looking for new ways to prevent cruelty to animals," says PETA's Dan Shannon, the author of "Good Sports" in *Animal Times.* "The NCAA brought this issue to their supplier and Wilson told them you can get the same performance out of a composite. I think that was pretty key in their decision."

Considering dehorning, castration without painkillers, and the rest of the horrors cows endure on the way to the "processing line," how nice to know you can score one for the cows whenever you play ball!

RESOURCES

www.cowsarecool.com
For information on alternatives to leather in sports, including synthetic bicycle seats, baseball mitts, golf shoes, and ballet slippers, and to obtain a free copy of the PETA *Guide to Nonleather Products*.

Balls

Spalding
www.spalding.com
Makes synthetic basketballs, volleyballs, softballs, soccer balls, and footballs.

Baseball Gloves

Heartland Products, Ltd.
800-441-4692
www.trvnet.net~hrtlndp/

Biking Gloves

REI
800-426-4840
www.rei.com

Bowling Shoes

Dexter Shoes
207-924-5471
www.dextershoe.com

Boots for Hiking, Work, and Play

Lacrosse Footwear
503-766-1010
www.lacrosse-outdoors.com

Ice and Hockey Skates

L. L. Bean
800-441-5713
www.llbean.com

Horseback Riding Equipment

Thorowgood
44 1922 711 676
www.thorowgood.com

Vegan Wares
44 1273 691 913
www.veganwares.com

Motorcycle Apparel

Aerostitch/Rider
Warehouse
800-222-1994
www.aerostitch.com

Alpine Stars
310-891-0222
www.alpinestars.com

Competition Accessories
800-543-8208
www.compacc.com

Cycleport
800-777-6499
www.cycleport.com

Dennis Kirk
800-328-9290
www.denniskirk.com

Draggin Jeans
828-327-2644
www.dragginjeans.com

Ethical Wares
44 (0) 1570 471 155
www.ethicalwares.com

Giali USA
866-527-6987
www.motorcycle-uk.com

Harley-Davidson
800-258-2464
www.harley-davidson.com

Heartland Products, Ltd.
800-441-4692
www.trvnet.net~hrtlndp/

Joe Rocket Sports Gear
800-635-6103
www.kneedraggers.com

Marsee Products
800-293-2400
www.marseeproducts.com

MotoLiberty
800-214-RACE
www.motoliberty.com

Motonation
877-789-4940
www.motonation.com

Olympia Sports
800-521-2832
www.olympiasports.com

Road Gear
800-854-4327
www.roadgear.com

Teknic
616-866-3722
www.teknicgear.com

Tour Master
www.tourmaster.com

Vegetarian Shoes
44 (0) 1273 691 913
www.vegetarianshoes.co.uk.com

Willie & Max
www.willieandmax.com

Yamaha Motor Corporation
800-962-7926
www.yamaha-motor.com

Skateboarding Shoes

Circa
www.circafootwear.com

Emerica
www.emericaskate.com

És Footwear
www.esfootwear.com

Etnies
949-460-2020
www.etnies.com

Globe
888-4GLOBES
www.globeshoes.com

Hawk Footwear
www.hawkshoes.com

IPath
www.ipath.com

Macbeth Shoes
www.macbethshoes.com

Osiris
858-874-4970
www.osirisshoes.com

Snowboarding Boots

Airwalk
www.airwalk.com

Snow Boots

Payless Shoe Source
877-474-6379
www.payless.com

Weight-lifting Gloves

NewGrip.com
800-213-0450
www.newgrip.com

To help get the NBA to switch to a synthetic ball, write:
NBA Commissioner
c/o National Basketball Association
Olympic Tower, 645 Fifth Avenue
New York, NY 10022

36.

Alternatives to Catching Fish (and Even to "Catch and Release")

I too once was a sportsman. But I grew up.

—EDWARD ABBEY, AMERICAN ESSAYIST AND AUTHOR

I wouldn't eat a grouper any more than I'd eat a cocker spaniel. They're so good-natured, so curious. You know, fish really are sensitive, they have personalities, they hurt when they're wounded.

—SYLVIA EARLE, FORMER CHIEF SCIENTIST OF NATIONAL OCEANIC AND ATMOSPHERIC ADMINISTRATION

Whenever people say "We mustn't be sentimental," you can take it they are about to do something cruel.

—BRIGID BROPHY, AUTHOR

Enjoy thy stream, O harmless fish;
And when an angler for his dish,
Through gluttony's vile sin,
Attempts, a wretch, to pull thee out,
God give thee strength, O gentle trout,
To pull the rascal in!

—JOHN WOLCOT

In 2003 several studies about fish came out that should have shaken the angling world to its core. None of the results were ones that anyone who enjoyed fishing wished to hear about. What research observers on two continents found was that fish choose shoalmates, fish chums they like to hang out with; use words to communicate fairly complex messages to each other; enjoy "stable cultural traditions" and understand "social prestige"; use tools (something only primates and, more recently, birds were thought to do); build complex nests; cooperate to find food; and have long-term memories. Fish, it turns out, also have personalities, although I could have told the researchers that from my experience with a captive fish some twenty-five years earlier.

That fish, a banded severum, used to hover in the water, staring at the living room door, waiting for my husband to come home from the office. When the door opened and in stepped the object of his patient vigil, the fish would race up to the top of the tank, roll over in the water, and present his side to be petted. My husband would oblige.

The fish would also lurk behind a plastic plant and, timing his surprise attack just right, leap up and nip the cat on the nose when she bent her head to drink from the tank. No matter how cautiously the cat approached, for the cat was used to this treatment, it was rare for the fish not to outfox the cat and win the game.

Three fish experts from the journal *Fish and Fisheries,* biologists Calum Brown, Keven Laland, and Jens Krause, have rendered their shared opinion that fish are indeed intelligent and should be "compared favorably to non-human primates."

Quite impossible, then, to justify dragging them up out of the water on a hook while they gasp for air, even if "only" to mess about with them and let them go again, just for fun. The comedian Ellen DeGeneres performs a skit in which she compares "catch and release" fishing to hitting pedestrians with your car. She suggests that after you've mowed them down, you wait for them to stand up and brush the dirt from their clothes, then roll down your car window, wave at them gaily, and say, "Okay, you can go now. Just wanted to see if I could hit you!"

For reasons other than that fish are intelligent, a longtime friend of mine has reluctantly reached the conclusion that there are better ways to spend time than fishing after taking his nine-year-old son to the lake one summer. The experience changed both of them, and for an unexpected reason. Here's what happened:

"Our car drew up to our cottage," Mike says, "and a tired, hot nine-year-old already wearing a bathing suit saw little wisdom in formalities like unpacking. To the lake!

"But we couldn't ignore a commotion in the car park. A local kid was using a rubber band to fire paper clips at a little frog in a puddle of mud. Someone had called the police.

"The cop arrived, rescued the frog, put the youngster in the patrol car, and explained to the crowd that the boy was often in trouble. One more trip to the station and another stern lecture for the bad boy.

"Soon my son and I arrived at the edge of the lake and eventually found an opening between anglers where we could swim without getting entangled in their lines, or hooked and reeled in. There were scores of people with rods pointing toward the lake. Some were hardened, leathery types with coolers of beer. But many of them were just families with children, fishing and unwinding and bonding.

"Shrieks and applause greeted the animals yanked from the water and dangled by hooks jabbing through their mouths, full body weight tugging away. Some people pulled the hooks out and threw the fish into buckets until dinnertime. Many other people pulled the hooks out and just tossed their fish back into the water, for humane or ecological reasons no doubt. These were not bad people.

"Most would probably have joined the mob against the frog child. But the obvious was not lost on my child. He asked me to call the police.

"Youngsters say strange things. After all, there had to be some perfectly logical reason why torturing a frog for sport is considered an act of cruelty to animals, yet torturing a fish for sport is not only legal but widely regarded as an uplifting and wholesome recreation for the entire family.

"For better or worse, the images from the lakeside had changed us. We spent our last afternoon scrawling giant antifishing messages in the sand.

"Personally, I think 'Angling Is Cruel' would have been preferable to 'Fishing Sucks,' but at least my son's heart was in the right place.

"A millennium or two ago, gladiators and cockfights symbolized 'the good life.' Fifty years ago, it was fur and hunting and cigarettes. My son and I hereby jointly nominate angling to that same hall of fate."

RESOURCES

NoFishing.net (PETA)

www.nofishing.net

Information on angling and handy fish facts.

Pisces

An offshoot of the Campaign for the Abolition of Angling, this organization is dedicated to fish welfare and banning fishing. Pisces is focused on youth work, education, and informing people of the welfare needs of fish in all situations.

www.pisces.demon.co.uk

The PETA Catalog

www.petacatalog.com

Bass Avenger Computer Game

Did you ever want to get back at "sport" fishers? Well, here's your chance! You're the fish and the tables are turned on the humans who normally abuse you. Works with Windows or Mac. Available from Amazon Video Games at www.amazon.com.

37.

Helping Elephants and Whales by Staying Clear of Circuses and Marine Parks

[The god Apollo] saw the smallest whale, the dolphin, as the embodiment of peaceful virtue, undisguised joy, and . . . founded the oracle at Delphi, named in the dolphin's honour. There, the god hoped, Man might be guided by a sense of other-worldiness.

—HEATHCOTE WILLIAMS, *WHALE NATION*

So they loaded up their trunks and they moved to Tennessee.

—FROM *THE ELEPHANT SANCTUARY* NEWSLETTER

When you enter the big top at an "animal-free" circus like the Cirque du Soleil, it is not just the brilliant choreography, the jaw-dropping costumes, the music, and the skills of the talented acrobats, trapeze artists, and clowns that impress you. It is the absence of sawdust. Only when you realize it is not there does it occur to you that circuses use it to disguise animal "accidents," and suddenly you sense that something else is missing: There are no sad animals. Everyone in the animal-free circus is a willing performer, everyone is paid, and everyone can head off home at the end of the show.

There are at least twenty North American circuses, including Cirque du Soleil, the New Pickle Circus, Circus Oz, Cirque d'Hiver, and the Flying Fruit Fly Circus, that showcase fantastic clowns, jugglers, fire-eaters, and other exclusively *human* performers. If you wonder why they are *the* circuses to go to, you only have to ask Jenny.

While she communicates subsonically with her friends—in rumbles that travel several miles and at frequencies so low that humans can't hear them without instrumentation—or through trumpeting noises that humans have yet to interpret, Jenny's personal story is a strong endorsement of those "alternative" but more and more popular circuses.

Jenny, aka "Jenny Jelly Bean," eats 130 pounds of hay or vegetation a day, plus 20 pounds of hand-mixed whole grains, 2 pounds of ground corn, 2 pounds of soaked wheat bran, and 10 to 20 pounds of fruits and vegetables. Her favorite food is potatoes.

Jenny now lives at the Elephant Sanctuary in Hohenwald, Tennessee, but her life certainly didn't start there. She was born in Sumatra in 1969, captured from the wild, and taken away from her loving mother and family. She was shipped to the United States and put in chains. She has spent most of her life here in captivity, performing in circuses.

In 1992, after repeatedly running away from her trainers at the Carson and Barnes circus (presumably the sorts of people who were caught on videotape using sharp metal sticks to dig into another elephant's thighs and behind its knees and ears), she was sent away to a breeding facility, where she sustained an injury to her hind leg. No one treated her for it, but she was put on butazone, a drug that would have masked her pain so that she could still work—being exposed daily to a bull elephant in the hope that she would become pregnant.

Jenny's leg did not get better nor did she get pregnant and so, a year after her injury, she was declared "useless" and sold to a small traveling show. Competing for food with other elephants and trying to balance herself in a moving trailer took its toll on her fragile condition. She deteriorated to the point where her owner could do nothing profitable with her and left her at an animal shelter near Las Vegas, insisting that Jenny would get the care she needed. But there, in winter, she was exposed to freezing temperatures, suffering from injury and foot rot, chained and wasting away.

Amazingly, Jenny's owners then contacted the Elephant Sanctuary and asked the sanctuary to take her where, through a series of miracles, Jenny was finally taken. She is one of only a handful of elephants who got away while thousands of their sisters still pick up their chains in their trunks and jangle them against the ground, creating the plaintive sound made by slaves in another time. When she arrived, a ghost of an elephant, she was shy and scared. Tarra, the sanctuary's first elephant resident, gently stroked Jenny's head and coaxed her to entwine trunks. Everyone watched through tears of relief and joy at this display of comfort and love.

In the forest or on the plains, when herds of related wild elephants meet, there is an intense emotional exchange, both vocal and physical. This contrasts to their lives in the circus, where each lonely elephant is shackled separately: the one over here who was forcibly separated from her herd in India as a baby and shipped by sea in a crate; the one over there who was taken from her loving mother on a Florida breeding farm and put in chains even before she was weaned.

Capturing elephants for the circus has never been a pleasant endeavor, but it has gone on for centuries. Pliny the Elder reported: "Africa captures elephants by means of pits; when an elephant straying from the herd falls into one of those, all the rest at once collect branches of trees and roll down rocks and construct ramps, exerting every effort in an attempt to get [the family member] out." Today, dart guns are used by wranglers who stampede and separate the frightened herd by buzzing them with helicopters while capture teams on the ground lasso the babies.

Carol Buckley, who founded and runs the Elephant Sanctuary, points out that in their homelands, free elephants walk thirty to fifty miles a day. That's how they exercise, look for food, and interact with their large families. Not so elephant captives. In the circus, these highly social, playful, and intelligent beasts usually spend eighteen hours a day or more chained up like bicycles on a rack. As a result, they often become sick and some die. Lack of exercise, wet floors, and hard concrete floors cause many of them to live in chronic and excruciating leg pain. When they are trained, it is not with sugar cubes but with electric shock prods, bull hooks, and whips.

Tom Rider, a former Ringling Brothers circus employee, says, "After working with elephants, I can tell you that they live in confinement and they are beaten all the time when they don't perform properly." Indeed, some of the beatings elephants endure when they are first learning or when they do not wish to obey later, perhaps from illness, fatigue, or rebellion, are so horrifying that watching them captured on videotape takes a very strong stomach.

The public desire to see elephants up close and personal is what has caused this disaster and is the reason we must stay away from circuses and ask others to stay away too.

Marine parks are the watery version of the land circus and should be avoided. Many kids today are so sophisticated about animal-protection issues that they know that cheering for the trainer holding a fish in her mouth as the dolphins leap for their supper isn't fun for bright dolphins, who want to play in the real waves and have a real life. The more people patronize the marine parks, of course, the more animals will be captured from their homes in the great oceans, and the more their rarely born babies will be taken away from their captive mothers and sold to other tourist attractions, there to live out their lives in a space that can be no more than a bathtub to them.

Children did cheer (didn't we all?) for the orca, the "killer whale," in the 1992 hit movie *Free Willy,* when he was reunited with his family in the sea. Children know intuitively that in real life animals love and grieve and, when separated from all that is precious to them, suffer what Jacques Cousteau once called "a great emptiness of spirit."

Animals kept in captivity and servitude, whether on land or in water, teach us only that human domination still prevails, that human ignorance of other life-forms is rampant, and that we have a long way to go until we respect animals enough to leave them in their natural environment, where they belong. To make the dolphin's smile more than a facial feature, but a true expression of his or her feelings, he or she must be free!

Happily, in some states and countries progress is being made and laws are being passed to prohibit marine exhibits and the display of wild animals, and private organizations are reconsidering their relationships with such outfits. When Toronto, Canada, passed a prohibition on performing wild animals, the Garden Brothers Circus and others ran shows without animals. The Moscow Circus has traditionally toured Great Britain without performing animals. The Shrine organization of British Columbia announced an end to the use of wild animals in its circuses. In the U.S., a New York Elks Club recently decided to end its fund-raising activities using circuses.

The dramatic success of "all-human" shows clearly demonstrates that circuses don't need animals to be financially successful. There are now a substantial number of such acts performing without a single wild animal, including, in addition to the ones mentioned above, Cirque Eloize, Circus Smirkus, China's Beijing Circus, Cirque de Tonnere, and the Peking Acrobats. At circuses like these, there are no whips, bull hooks, electric shock prods, or muzzles. Truly *everyone* can enjoy the show!

RESOURCES

Organizations

The Elephant Sanctuary
Hohenwald, Tennessee
931-796-6500
www.elephants.com
You can visit and see the rescued elephants roaming free on hundreds of acres of land; you donate enough to feed a rescued elephant for a day ($30). Or you can help Acres of Elephants, a fund to buy additional land to house the rescued "herd."

Captive Animals Protection Society
www.captiveanimals.org

Zoocheck
www.zoocheck.com
Works on captive animals in circuses and zoos internationally.

Books

Johnson, William. *The Rose-Tinted Menagerie.* London: Heretic Books, 1990. This book is out of print and hard to find, but worth the search.

Videos

Elephant-beating video
www.circuses.com

Movies

Free Willy
Dumbo

Animal-Free Circuses

The New Pickle Family Circus
San Francisco, California
415-759-8123
laurafraenza@yahoo.com

Cirque du Soleil
www.cirquedusoleil.com

Circus Oz
www.circusoz.com

Cirque d'Hiver
www.cirque-dhiver.nl

Cirque Eloize
www.cirque-eloize.com/en

38.

Packing a Picnic

Fresh fruit was looked upon as dangerous

and salads were only for the very rich.

—FRANK MUIR, *FOOD AND DRINK IN THE MIDDLE AGES*

Summer afternoon—summer afternoon; to me these have always

been the two most beautiful words in the English language.

—HENRY JAMES IN A LETTER TO EDITH WHARTON

You can't get rid of the ants: After all, if you are going to sit on the grass, that's *their* home, although if you are in Costa Rica, here's a tip: don't spread out your blanket under a cecropia tree. Ants live in the hollow stem! And if ants bother you, remember they are sociable and have no idea you don't want them joining in. In fact, they are so innocuous that in a wonderful article called "Ants Create United Europe," you can read all about how Spanish and Italian ants, or ants from all over the Atlantic and Mediterranean coasts, form "supercolonies," all ants getting along with each other even though they are not related at all.

So forget the ants, and let's do something instead about the ubiquitous chicken salad and the boiled egg or egg salad that seem to lurk, most predictably, in almost every picnic basket. They are as easy to get rid of as it is to find outdoor fare that will please vegans, vegetarians, those watching their weight, and those just plain not paying attention.

One reason to ditch the egg is that we presumably enjoy the company of those invited to the picnic and the whopping 213 grams of cholesterol a single egg contains (before anyone adds mayonnaise!) won't help guarantee that we'll be enjoying their company for as long as we might if they ate healthily. There are about 25 milligrams of cholesterol in just one ounce of chicken, too, and that's nothing to crow about. So for human health reasons alone, I have some alternative suggestions.

Another reason to skip the eggs is because chickens are devoted mothers who will go without food and water, if necessary, just to have a private nest in which to lay their eggs; yet in today's egg factories, they are forced to lay eggs in a cage the size of a piece of typing paper, and in the company of five or more other hens. In nature, a careful mother hen will turn her eggs as many as five times an hour and cluck to her unborn chicks, who will chirp back to her and to one another from within their shells! Studies have shown what common sense tells us: Like us, chickens form strong family ties and mourn when they lose a loved one, if allowed to do so.

Kim Sturla, who runs Animal Place, a sanctuary for abused and discarded farmed animals, sees exactly how chickens empathize and show affection for one another. She recalls an endearing story about two elderly chickens who had been rescued from a city dump. "Mary" and "Notorious Boy" bonded and would roost on a picnic table together. One stormy night when the rain was really pelting down, Sturla went to put Mary and Notorious Boy in the barn and saw that "the rooster had his wing extended over the hen protecting her."

I say, let's leave chickens to be chickens and leave eggs on the shelf while we pack our wonderful picnic!

First, pack some fresh seasonal fruit (ripe mangoes and soft peaches smell especially wonderful). Cucumbers are easy travelers, and it's best to slice them on the spot for maximum freshness. (Save two slices to cover your eyes with later, when you lie in the sun.) They go well with cherry tomatoes that can be washed in advance and then simply popped into waiting mouths.

Now for the prepared dishes:

I suggest an easy chilled gazpacho and some simple finger sandwiches prepared with nondairy cream cheese, green olives and cucumber, and some faux lunch meats. Keep the gazpacho in a Thermos and the sandwiches in a cooler with a few ice packs on the sides. Then, if you fancy the taste of egg and chicken, try the delectable "Save the Chickens" Salad and the easy Excellent Eggless Egg Salad recipes below:

"SAVE THE CHICKENS" SALAD

1 pound of your favorite chicken substitute (Chic-Ketts or Cheatin' Chicken Chunks, available at many supermarkets and most health food stores)
½ cup diced green and red pepper, celery, and/or red onion
Pinch of parsley
Pinch of chives
¾ cup vegan mayonnaise (like Nayonnaise)

Dice the Chic-Ketts or use a food processor, and add the diced veggies, parsley, and chives. Mix well. Add the vegan mayonnaise and stir well. Chill. Serve in sandwiches or with crackers.

EXCELLENT EGGLESS EGG SALAD

1½ pounds firm tofu, mashed
½ cup vegan mayonnaise
½ cup chopped fresh parsley
¼ cup sweet pickle relish
½ medium onion, chopped
2 stalks celery, chopped
1½ teaspoons garlic powder
1½ teaspoons salt
¼ teaspoon turmeric
1½ tablespoons prepared mustard

Combine all the ingredients in a large bowl. Spread on sandwiches or crackers.

Makes 6 servings.

RESOURCES

Chic-Ketts

www.worthingtonfoods.com

Available at many supermarkets and most health food stores.

Contain wheat and soy and are kosher.

Recipes

Mediterranean Picnic Pie

www.pastrywiz.com

Tangy olives and hearty potatoes make this a satisfying peasant pie served cold for picnics.

Bean and Soy Cheese Stuffed Picnic Loaf

www.mexicanfood.about.com

Look under the vegetarian/vegan section and use any sharp vegan cheese to make a great spicy picnic roll.

Corn and Black Bean Salad and More

www.healthy.lifetips.com

39.

Looking Out for Stolen Souvenirs

Leave only footprints, take only photographs.

—ANONYMOUS

She seemed very anxious to get rid of me as fast as possible.

—*SIR CECIL BEATON, WONDERING IF QUEEN ELIZABETH WAS UPSET WITH HIM BECAUSE HE HAD STOLEN THE QUEEN MOTHER'S HANDKERCHIEF AS A SOUVENIR WHILE SHE WAS SITTING FOR HER PORTRAIT*

When I was six, my favorite shoes were a pair of beaded moccasins from an Indian reservation in Canada, which were about five sizes too large for my tiny feet, not that this stopped me from flopping about the house in them, and my favorite doll wore a butterfly-patterned kimono. I would hold her on my lap and read to her about a little boy who ran as fast as he could to escape a tidal wave, a story in the big book my father had brought back from Japan.

My father traveled all over the world, and as a consequence, I was the recipient of many oddball things from exotic places. I remember a train of three wooden camels that was stamped "Made from the Wood of Christ's Cross" and a golden metal tiger with a long tail that was actually a primitive lock.

Some of my presents were definitely not politically correct, but that term and concept was unknown then, and no one realized that hunting, export, and industry were taking a heavy toll on wildlife. It was a time when my own father, kind man though he was, a man who loved dogs with all his heart and despised cruelty to animals, thought it perfectly natural to tether giant Pacific island sea turtles to a stake by boring a hole in their shells and passing a rope through the shell to anchor the turtles in place until he and his party were ready to cook them!

One of the most bizarre gifts I received was a little statue of a mother seal and her cub he bought in Newfoundland. The seals were made of *real* seal fur! Then there was the bright orange and almost iridescent bird of paradise feather plume from New Guinea, a mother-of-pearl box from Tahiti, and a collection of dried sea horses from southern France.

Thanks to the campaigning work of the Royal Society for the Protection of Birds in England and the Audubon Society in the U.S., as well as local governments, in 1990 the Indonesian government passed a law banning trade in bird of paradise feathers. Clubbing seals to death still goes on but is no longer considered an endearing or necessary local custom, what with Europe banning the import of sealskins outright. And as for the sea horses, unscrupulous catchers are in trouble from environmentalists and animal protectionists for using cyanide to catch fishes and bombs to blow up their undersea habitat and flush them out into the nets.

Today, I suppose, I would choose that ubiquitous souvenir shop gift with the slogan "My father went to Borneo and all I got was this lousy T-shirt."

Those gift shops, and the vendors waiting for you on the beaches and boardwalks beside the Sphinx and the Eiffel Tower, still try to press contraband into your hands. No matter what we are told about their age or source, the fact is that objects made of tortoiseshell, coral, snakeskin, ivory, peacock feathers, fur, and bone are often from illegal trade. Even when they are not, they can represent big problems for animals and the environment.

Take the dear little hermit crabs, crammed into wire cages along the boardwalks these days, their shells crudely painted, sold for a song. These sea creatures have care needs their purchasers cannot meet or even know about and must change their shells as they grow, something few people realize. Treated as toys or trinkets, they are destined to die in their tiny aquariums. Discouraging others from buying them helps, as do letters to the beach press that visitors may read.

Kim Washock of the Coastal Discovery Museum on Hilton Island, South Carolina, might well be talking about any animal-derived purchase when he says, "Leave sand dollars and shells where they are. Pretty shells with pretty markings are a hard temptation to pass by, but they are often someone's home." In that neck of the woods, as in many other resorts, there is a five hundred dollar fine per conch shell removed.

My rule of thumb is this: If it comes from, or is, an animal, it is not ours to buy or take.

RESOURCES

Traffic

www.traffic.org

Fighting the trade in endangered species.

Beauty Without Cruelty

http://members.tripod.com/~bwcindia/history.htm

40.

Holiday Rescues: Helping Animals While Traveling

Fish cannot live without water,
Flowers cannot bloom in the sand—
and we cannot live without freedom

—OLD GREEK FOLK SONG

I've been things and seen places.

—MAE WEST

Where there's a will, there's a way.

—ENGLISH PROVERB

Greg and Jane Sidwell met at a dance club in a small town in Georgia. Jane was from an even smaller town about forty miles away. A friend of hers had asked her to go out that night, but she didn't want to go—she was in college and wanted to get serious about studying.

Studying took a nosedive that night. She and Greg fell in love on the dance floor and got married a year later.

Every year the Sidwells combine a vacation with their wedding anniversary, and on their sixteenth wedding anniversary, they decided to take a cruise to Greece.

One of the stops along the way was Kavála. A bus met the ship and off they went to visit the ruins. That's when they saw the puppy.

"When we got off the tour bus," Greg remembers, "we saw this little puppy with a twisted back leg, living in a hole she had dug and living out of garbage cans. All the people were shying away from her because she was looking grubby. We had a bottle of water, so we were able to give her water to drink."

Greg says, "She was willing to come up to people, but you could tell that she'd been swatted at. I'm sure she was hungry and thirsty. But she was very timid. She was in bad shape. She looked pretty rough. It was evident that she didn't belong to anyone."

After the Sidwells had given the puppy the water, everyone had to get back on the bus and leave.

As soon as they turned the corner, Jane looked at Greg and said, "We shouldn't have left that dog there; we should have done something." She kept talking about it during the hour-and-a-half ride back to the boat. Greg told his wife there was nothing they could do. "We're on this trip," he said, "and we're leaving soon."

Then his wife said something to him that he will never forget. She said, "If it was something that was important that was work related, you would have found some way to do something about it; you would have found some way to fix it. Well, this is just as important, even more important."

Back at the ship, Greg told the cruise director about the puppy and asked him to hire someone to go back there and get the puppy. The cruise director called the local travel agency and instructed them to send someone to look for the dog, but days passed without result, and every time the Sidwells asked for news, there was none. Finally, Greg called the travel agency himself.

"The owner's name was Irene," Greg remembers. "I got her on the phone and told her what I was after and that our vacation time was running out. She said, 'I'm sorry, we haven't done anything about it. We thought the cruise director was just pulling our leg. Who would want to rescue a dog and take it back to the States?' "

Greg gave Irene his credit card number and asked her to hire someone to search for the dog. But still nothing happened.

When the time came to catch their plane back to the States, they left Greece despondent and without any news.

"Then, two weeks after we got back, we got a call at four a.m. The puppy had been found."

Greg flew to Athens, met Irene at the airport, spent the night in Greece, and flew back on Sunday with their puppy, Cherry. Cherry was just five or six months old, a red and white dog that looked part springer spaniel with little tufts of hair sticking out of her body.

Greg knows how close this pup came to death. Twice a year they poison the stray dogs in Greece to keep the population under control. "We found her six weeks away from the time they would have poisoned the dogs," he says.

Cherry had to have part of her leg amputated right away, but these days she has no trouble jumping on the bed. Not that she will if the sun is out and she can sit by the pool and enjoy the fresh air. When Greg goes away on business, Cherry sits by the garage twenty-four hours a day, waiting for her hero and rescuer to return.

Greg and Jane did what almost anyone could do if he or she had a mind to. All it took was the decision to make it happen. They showed how important it is not to leave a starving, sick, or injured stray, indeed any stray, to scavenge. Strays will always come to a bad end.

If there is a good animal shelter nearby, where you can see the workers are gentle to the animals, the facility is clean and does not allow animals from their shelter to be sent to laboratories, and if the shelter's adoption policies are good (i.e., they do not allow animals to be kept chained up as guard dogs), that can also be an option. But one must be careful.

There is a Chinese saying that if you save a life, you are responsible for that life forever. A peaceful sleep forever is better than a thrown rock that blinds you, a car that makes you lame, mange sores that tear at your body so you cannot sleep, and a stomach that aches for the food your nose can smell but that no one will give you. If you absolutely cannot bring the animal back home, it is kinder to take the animal to a local veterinarian and have him or her euthanized. But be sure to be there when it is done or you will never know what really became of the dog or cat who trusted you to make sure that, at the very least, he or she left this cruel world peacefully.

Greg's final advice? "If it's important to you, you'll do something about it. There are always things you can do. There's some type of agency, or someone who can work with you. It's a lot of trouble, and even more trouble when you're in a foreign country. But it's a poor, helpless animal in need, and if it's important, you'll do something." Cherry agrees!

RESOURCES

PETA
www.peta.org

World Society for the Protection of Animals
www.wspa.org

41.

How Never to Be Tempted to Attend Bullfights, Rodeos, or Other "Animal Acts"

I can never see animals kept in captivity in the same way again.

—JOHN CERCIPIO AFTER RETURNING FROM IRAQ, WHERE HE WAS HELD AS A POW DURING OPERATION DESERT STORM

No one likes an eight-second ride.

—BONNIE-JILL LAFLIN, FORMER DALLAS COWBOYS CHEERLEADER, WHO PROTESTS THE RODEO

When in Rome . . ." Actually, for me, the light came on when in Spain. I must have been about six or so. I remember that I was happily eating popcorn out of a fancy paper cornet, when we pulled up outside a bullfighting arena plastered with posters of matadors doing what matadors do. I think we had missed a turn and stopped so that my father could study the map.

As we sat there, I studied the poster and realized that the red on the bull's back was blood and that the man in the silly pants with the cape was holding a dagger in his hand. In horror, I asked my mother to explain what was going on, and she did.

According to studies by antibullfighting groups, most tourists casually buy a ticket to this bloody spectacle, waltz in, take a seat, but are disgusted and nauseated by the time they leave, never to return again. I knew, then and there, as much as I knew I loved popcorn, that I would never, ever set foot in a ring in my life. Of course, that was years before I learned that the poor bulls are reportedly given laxatives to weaken them, and have Vaseline put in their eyes to blur their vision, before they enter the ring to be stabbed to death. It was years before I realized that firecrackers are used to stampede the bulls through the cobbled streets of Pamplona and that these magnificent beasts are killed in the ring that same night.

That said, in my life I have ridden a donkey on the English coast, had my picture taken with a parrot on a chain in Mexico, been to an aquarium in Provincetown and even to a roadside zoo in Tennessee, only to say, in each case, as the bullfight visitors have said after their own shocking experience, "I should not have patronized this cruelty!"

The bottom line is this: If there's an animal in the act, the answer to the question "Are the animals there voluntarily and do they like it?" is invariably "Not likely!" no matter what the person selling the tickets—not the most reliable, unbiased source of information on the subject—is likely to tell us.

The interesting thing about tourists going to events like the bullfight, which are illegal in the U.S., is that their judgment can be suspended simply because a tour guide says, "This is our tradition." Were we to look closely, we might find that there is a strong movement to get rid of this old atrocity and that bullfighting is kept alive mostly by the tourist trade.

Think of rodeo here in the States.

Former Dallas Cowboys cheerleader Bonnie-Jill Laflin put on her denim Daisy Dukes to pose for a provocative antirodeo ad that declares, "Nobody Likes an Eight-Second Ride—Buck the Rodeo." As a former bronco rider herself, she is determined to let the world know that while these events are promoted as rough and tough exercises of human skill and courage in conquering the fierce, untamed beasts of the Wild West, they are, in reality, manipulative displays of human domination over animals.

Bonnie-Jill, who competed in rodeo barrel-racing events in the fourth grade and who used to sign her posters for Rodeo Cold beer and Cowboy Up western apparel at rodeos, decided to spurn the rodeo because of the cruelty involved in many events. "Founding the West may have included tormenting animals," she says, "but there's no reason in the twenty-first century to keep glorifying that violence."

Standard rodeo events include calf roping, steer wrestling, bareback horse and bull riding, saddle bronco riding, steer wrestling, steer roping, and barrel racing. The animals are relatively tame yet distrustful of human beings because of the harsh treatment that they have received. Many of them are not aggressive; they are physically provoked through the use of electric prods, spurs, and "bucking" straps into displaying "wild" behavior to make the cowboys look brave.

The flank or bucking strap or rope used to make horses and bulls buck is tightly cinched around their abdomens, which causes the animals to buck vigorously to try to rid themselves of the torment, thus putting on a good show for the crowd. The flank strap, when paired with spurring, causes the animals to buck even more violently, often resulting in injuries, and sometimes burrs and other irritants are placed under the strap.

Cows and horses are often prodded with an electrical "hotshot" while in the chute to rile them, causing them a jolt of intense pain. Dr. Peggy Larson, a veterinarian who in her youth was a bareback bronc rider, said, "Bovines are more susceptible to electrical current than other animals. Perhaps because they have a huge 'electrolyte' vat, the rumen [one of their stomachs]."

Bonnie-Jill loves sports but says, "I don't consider beating up on helpless animals to be a sport. If rodeo riders took a few jolts from a nine-thousand-volt hotshot and had straps cinched around their groins, they'd be singing a different tune—mostly high notes.

"What began in the 1800s as a skill contest among cowboys with nothing else to do with themselves out in the corral has become a debasing show."

Dr. C. G. Haber, a veterinarian who spent thirty years as a federal meat inspector, worked in slaughterhouses and saw many animals discarded from rodeos and sold for slaughter. He described the animals as being so extensively bruised that the only areas in which the skin was attached to the flesh were the head, neck, legs, and belly, and seeing animals "with six to eight ribs broken from the spine, and at times puncturing the lungs." These injuries are a result of animals being thrown in calf-roping events or being jumped on from atop horses during steer wrestling.

There is one way to go to the bullfight or the rodeo. That is to stand outside the place, armed with brochures, and hand them to others to help turn them away!

RESOURCES

PETA

www.peta.org
For free brochures to use to educate others in your hometown or while traveling.

PART FIVE

Animals in the Home

42.

Understanding and Dealing with Your Dog's Barking and Digging

Dogs are deeply suspicious of anybody using a door. Even if, when the door is opened, it turns out that the people standing there know the dogs, and in fact live in the house, the dogs will sometimes continue barking at them in case it's some kind of trick.

—DAVE BARRY

Do not leave your mother alone with your dog.
The unruliness of mothers is great.

—DUB'IBN AL-HARITH AL-BURJUMI, ARAB POET, ON SOME PEOPLE TO WHOM HE HAD REFUSED TO RETURN A BORROWED DOG

Dogs bark and dig and do other things for a reason, and since getting annoyed at their behavior doesn't help stop it, by learning about it we can find ways to cope with and modify it. Basil Service, a ski instructor who inherited Deo, a stray taken in by his mother, realized that the reason Deo steals food and hides it under couch covers and even in the laundry basket is that he had to eat from Dumpsters as a pup and was so thin when he was found that the vet didn't think he would make it. How can you scold a dog for that?

Author, comedy writer, and "dog man" Dave Barry knows from

personal experience that it is unwise to assume that a growling or barking dog doesn't know something we don't.

One night after dinner at a friend's house, everyone, including the dog, who had been told to be quiet when he growled at the kitchen window earlier, went into another room to have dessert and watch the Miami Heat play basketball.

Barry says, "Actually, the women watched the game; the men actively controlled the outcome by shouting at the screen. The dogs watched the dessert."

When the game ended, the women discovered that their purses had been stolen from the kitchen table. The burglar had obviously been watching the group through the window. Said Dave Barry, "The growling dog had been telling us this all along!"

Worse than just dismissing those barks and growls is silencing them indiscriminately. A *Washington Post* writer once startled me by writing that my beloved old dog, Bea, must have had the last name "Quiet!" Bea was a very talkative dog, and when the reporter had been talking to me—and I to him—he noticed that I spent a lot of time asking her to put a sock in it! An independent sort, Bea had stalwartly ignored the advice.

After Bea died, I thought about her barking almost as much as I did when she was alive, which is really saying something. I realized that it must have seemed unfathomable and unfair to her that I was allowed to talk as much as I wanted to, and that the same applied to all other humans, visitors or residents. If we were talking, why shouldn't she be talking too? But when she tried to chime in, or even alert me to someone at the door, she was told, and quite sharply, to silence herself. Oh dear!

Perhaps if she'd been a chicken, I would have gone easier on her. There was a chicken who grew up in one PETA member's house who used to reduce everyone to laughter at the dinner table by joining in loudly if ever the family began to argue. She didn't understand exactly what was being said, but she obviously realized that people were distressed and she didn't like that, so she found a way to break the fights up.

Now, how can dogs get through to us if we don't let them bark? They haven't the necessary vocal construct to make human sounds, any more than we can learn to speak "wasp," and they weren't born with the opposable thumbs a creature needs to write us a note. However, they can certainly "outsense" us, sometimes realizing pending perils like fires, earthquakes, volcanic eruptions, and storms, as well as the approach of strangers and friends. They are kind enough to alert us, even to warn us, even when we make no sense in our own behavior and keep yelling at them to keep quiet and calm down.

All in all, it's unfair when you think about it. Dogs spend most of their lives watching and listening to us and trying to figure out how they are expected to fit into our alien lifestyle. They are expected to wait patiently to eat and drink until *we* think it is the right time, to eat what *we* choose for them, to keep their legs crossed until *we* think they should go outside. They can go nowhere without permission, and sometimes they are not even permitted to stop and sniff and say hello to a fellow dog when they are being pulled along on their "walk."

On top of this, we expect them to understand human language spoken at all speeds and in all tones and any accent. It's a bit much.

Dogs need to bark, just as much as birds need to chirp and we need to speak to people—it's just a question of the how and why of it; and punishment should never be delivered to them for doing what comes naturally. So perhaps you can find a time and place for your dog to bark his heart out. And remember always to praise and thank him for alerting you to that squirrel or car going by before respectfully asking him to please be quiet. Of course, any request for quiet should be delivered not as an admonishment, but through the use of diversions and a loving touch.

The same goes for digging. Dogs are born to dig. That's how a good dog provides a home for her family, underground, where it is neither too hot nor too cold. And a comfortable place for a dog to lie down means a dip in the earth, not a flat surface. A nicely dug hole, a dog knows, is also far cooler on a hot summer day than sitting, plonk, at the top on the hot ground. On top of all that, so to speak, is the possibility that a dog, with his or her superior hearing, can detect an animal moving about down there, and is dying to take a look.

Can something be done about it? Yes, but ask yourself if you cannot really tolerate a hole in the ground and consider it the equivalent of a child's sandbox and even a great conversation piece for outdoor parties.

Chances are, chewing and digging, if done in the home, indicate that your dog is upset, panicked, or has a lively mind that is not sufficiently stimulated. One of the saddest cases of rejection I can recall involves a couple who returned a "shelter adoption" back to the pound. The dog tore everything to shreds every time they left the apartment and no amount of scolding had fixed the problem.

A little investigation revealed that the dog had once been in an apartment fire that had broken out while his first family was at work. The dog had lived but suffered from smoke inhalation. Ever since, he panicked when left by himself, something his people had feared to tell the shelter workers in case it hurt his chances of adoption! One just never knows what traumas, real or imagined, spark "bad behavior."

RESOURCES

The Sense-ation Harness

www.softouchconcepts.com

For dogs who pull on the leash, this terrific harness doesn't hurt the neck and really works. It has the ring where you attach the leash in the front of the chest, so that if the dog lunges, he or she instantly gets turned back around to face you so that you can redirect that energy.

Miller, Pat. *Positive Perspectives: Love Your Dog, Train Your Dog.* Wenatchee, Wash: Dogwise Publishing, 2003. Miller is commited to safe, effective, dog-friendly training methods that work without *ever* compromising the all-important relationship between dogs and their human(s). Easy to understand, with a friendly and encouraging tone.

McConnell, Patricia B., Ph.D., and Karen B. London, Ph.D. *Feisty Fido.* Black Earth, Wisc.: Dog's Best Friend Ltd. (608-767-2345; www.dogsbestfriendtraining.com), 2003.
The technique described in this book is for dogs who "freak out" at birds, at other small dogs, and so on while on the leash. It involves getting the dogs, through treats and other rewards, to concentrate on the walker's face for cues as to what to do. The PETA librarian swears by it.

McConnell, Patricia B. *How to Be the Leader of the Pack . . . and Have Your Dog Love You for It.* Black Earth, Wisc.: Dog's Best Friend, Ltd., 1996.

43.

Cats and Their Claws

Spare the sofa, spare the drapes

But spare my claws, for goodness' sake!

—FROM "A SIAMESE LAMENT,"
AUTHOR UNKNOWN

Ginger, the world's cutest overgrown kitten, is up against the fabric wallpaper again, stretching like a yoga teacher, her back arched, her legs thrust as far up the wall as she can reach. I know she'd have that wall looking like frayed jean bottoms if I hadn't clipped her nails this week, but I did, so I don't have to bite *my* nails over her wild (and healthy) calisthenics!

Cats have to scratch as surely as birds gotta fly, for reasons buried deep in their psyches, like marking territory, as well as for play, exercise, and nail conditioning. However, rather than take a hatchet to a hangnail and remove kitty's claws (and ligaments, muscle, and bone, for that is what happens in "de*claw*ing" surgery), there are simple, noninvasive solutions to worries about the furnishings. Those solutions, unlike declawing, do not lead to "out of litter box" experiences, neuroses, and spinal problems. Of course, if everything must be pristine and perfect, a house isn't a home for any living being!

Kind veterinarians will not declaw. As Dr. Nichols Dodman of the Tufts University School of Veterinary Medicine says, "Declawing is abhorrent and inhumane," and as Dr. Louis J. Camuti, who has practiced veterinary medicine for forty years, puts it, "I wouldn't declaw a cat if you paid me $1,000 a nail." Declawing is illegal in England because it is cruel, and it should be here, too, but commerce sometimes gets the better of compassion.

The reasons not to declaw are too numerous to count on one paw. It can make cats who were once full of life lifeless, withdrawn, and upset, and you will not be able to turn back the clock. Also, cats naturally walk like ballerinas on their "points," but declawing throws them off balance, forcing them to learn to walk in a very different way, which can cause irreparable and painful damage to the spine.

Some cats become so shell-shocked by the experience, and upset by the pain in their feet or memories of it postsurgery, that they will no longer use the litter box, a problem that far outdoes any damage they can do to a curtain. They can also feel betrayed by the realization that the person they thought loved them has removed a vital part of their very being. There are other problems that arise from declawing, but suffice it to say that alternatives to declawing are the only things acceptable to a kind cat companion.

Here's how to avoid tatters:

It is the little hook on the end of your cat's nails that is responsible for pulling threads and tearing at things, so that hook has to be worn down or snipped off. Then, bingo, the problem is solved.

1. Get as many scratching posts as you can (the horizontal ones work as well as the vertical), trying different surfaces and styles. Put catnip on them once in a while to make them superinviting. Don't just buy ones at the store; try to pick up the occasional log, the taller the better, or a large fallen branch. Shake it out well to dislodge insect life, then leave it outside, in the sun if possible, and up off the ground on a piece of newspaper for a couple of days, just to be extra sure. Make sure any log you bring home is anchored so that it can't fall on your cat while being used.

2. Smear a little cologne or flea dip on any fabric area where you do not want your cat to scratch. Sometimes covering a piece of furniture temporarily with contact paper or something else that's slippery will stop the behavior.

3. If you have a steady hand and good eyesight, buy a pair of cat nail clippers and use them. Gently squeeze each nail out, look for the quick (this is vital), and snip off the hook *only*, just above the quick. If you are unsure, go to a *gentle* veterinarian or groomer and insist on staying with your cat while his or her nails are clipped.

RESOURCES

PETA

www.petamall.com

Scratching posts and nail clippers.

Books

Newkirk, Ingrid. *250 Things You Can Do to Make Your Cat Adore You.* New York: Fireside, Simon and Schuster, 1998.

44.

How Adopting Beats the Pet Shop Approach

To his dog, every man is Napoleon—hence the popularity of dogs.

—ALDOUS HUXLEY

I love my dogs, because when I come home it's like the Beatles just walked through the door!

—BILL MAHER, HOST OF *POLITICALLY INCORRECT*

Friendship is seen through the heart, not the eyes.

—HELEN KELLER

I wonder if other dogs think poodles are members of a weird religious cult.

—RITA RUDNER

Are you thinking of getting a dog? Perhaps a golden retriever or Labrador because they have a reputation for being good with children? Or a shih tzu because you love the look of that long-haired little lapdog? If you have your sights on a "purebred" (an odd term really, since all purebreds are man-made mixes of natural breeds—"fighting dogs" bred for stocky bodies, strong jaws, and massive chests; "hunting dogs" for sleekness and their ability to smell out prey; and so on), there are "breed rescue organizations" to contact who allow you to save a rescued dog's life in an overpopulated dog world. These marvelous groups put their own money and time into trying to give unlucky dogs a second chance at a decent life. But first, there is another option to consider.

Let me introduce Ambeka Gandhi, a beautiful and elegant woman of the world whose home is in Delhi, India. Ambeka jets to Paris and London, buys couturier clothes, and charms everyone she meets with her looks, wit, and wisdom. But I admire her because of something different, something quite revolutionary. Just as Mahatma Gandhi reached out to India's "untouchable" "lowest-caste" citizens, Ambeka has made it her mission to popularize and make desirable, even in the most affluent circles, the once poorest of poor dogs, the Indian street dog.

People used to turn their noses up at these wise and dear—almost always yellowish red (called *lal* in Hindi), ring-tailed—street dogs. In fact, they'd have the dish water thrown at them, and worse. But Ambeka has taken several into her home, as has her famous sister Maneka Gandhi, member of the Indian parliament and daughter-in-law of the Indian prime minister Indira Gandhi. Now, every visiting statesman and socialite wants an "Indian dog." Sadly, there are more than enough to go around.

The dog and cat overpopulation crisis isn't limited to India. You could have knocked my socks off when I went to the very first "dog pound" I had ever seen. It was in Silver Spring, Maryland. The place was bursting at the seams, and it was staggering to see the number of homeless animals who needed a loving place to rest and caring people to play with. The pound consisted of a low, ugly cinder-block building you would never find unless you were determined to find it. It was on the wrong side of the railroad tracks, next to a stinky leaf mulch dump where the county stored the salt to sprinkle on icy roads come wintertime.

The din was deafening when I entered the kennels. Every sort of dog imaginable looked back at me from a line of pens that seemed a mile long. Except for the few withdrawn and sorry souls who sat huddled in the corner, their backs to visitors, as if to say, "I've seen it all; I know you won't stop and pick me," each one of them jumped and howled and begged frantically for my attention, often getting so excited they overturned their water dishes.

The dog pound or animal shelter is a terribly sad place. Since that first visit I've worked in them and even run them. If I had a magic wand, I would wave it and give us the ability to explain what is going on to the animals who end up there, for most of them are frantic with worry. I would like to say, "Look, that family you thought you had? They moved, so you must stop looking up the walkway for them—they aren't coming back." Or, "The lovely lady you lived with who went to the hospital—she's in a nursing home now. Please stop thinking you just have to bark loudly enough and someone will take you back to her. It isn't possible." Not knowing is one of the worst conditions for any human or other animal.

Until I saw what the overpopulation crisis meant to homeless animals, my family and I had always had a "purebred" dog. An Irish setter called Seanie was my constant companion until I was eight. He and I did everything together except go to school. I'd lie in his big wicker basket with him on sunny days, and in the winter we both wore Fair Isle sweaters hand knitted by my mother. Both of us would disgrace ourselves by being carsick when my parents took us on the long drive to see my grandmother at the seaside.

Later, when my family moved to India, we had a wirehaired dachshund called Daisy. Come to think of it, my parents used to joke that Daisy was not a dachshund at all, but a pedigree "counter and hoarder." Every evening without fail, she would race outdoors to bury a portion of her supper, and if the door failed to yield to her little body being slammed into it with some force, she would kick up such a terrible racket that someone would be forced to leave the dinner table to let her out. As for the counting, we had inherited Daisy from a British diplomat who had returned to England from India after his two-year overseas posting. He had raised Daisy from puppyhood, but when he, his wife, and two daughters set off home, the decision was made to leave Daisy behind. They thought it unfair to force Daisy to live in a cold climate after the Indian sunshine and to confine her to a barren kennel for the first time in her life (the quarantine laws then required kenneling for six months). Shattered at the unexplained and, to her, sudden loss of her beloved family, Daisy was determined to keep a very close eye on the whereabouts of her new people. Should any of us leave the others for more than a few minutes, she'd jump up and race from room to room or up the mountain path we were hiking until she could account for every member of her family.

It is often said that the most physically and psychologically stable dog in the world is a "Heinz 57," that wonderful mix whose parentage is a complete or near-complete puzzle. My very first mixed breed was the wonderful Ms. Bea. When she came to live with me, Ms. Bea's given name was Princess Buttons, but that seemed absurd for a dog who looked like a cross between a German shepherd and a couch and who almost took my arm off the first time I said hello! She was a grump until the day she died, about fourteen years later at the ripe old age of seventeen and a half, but I quickly came to love her and her peculiarities, including her penchant for the hottest curries I brought home, her aversion to joggers and gas station attendants, and her uncanny ability to put any sad or scared being at ease.

But will a mutt be a good dog? That question could easily be answered by looking through the other end of the looking glass. One of PETA's investigators spent some months on one of the puppy mills in the Midwest that supply pet shops, and he will tell you, "Many purebreds are bred in a factory, their stress levels are high, they are inbred, and they are not fit or easily able to be socialized." Why? He goes on, "Because they have not been touched by human hands very much, their mothers live in raised pens off the ground but exposed to the elements, and they get little to no medical care and eat the cheapest of food their masters can buy." These poor little tykes are shipped to pet stores across the nation. If we buy one, we perpetuate a bad business that will breed another pup or, really, another litter. All the while, the mutts on death row at the pound are crying out for homes.

If you are dead set on a purebred—and remember, a purebred is really just a man-made concoction of various kinds of dogs bred for certain characteristics, usually to do with hunting or other blood sports—many humane societies keep lists of breed clubs who have dogs who are being fostered in the hope of a permanent home. They must not be bred, naturally, or that would defeat the purpose of the groups' rescue work, but they are particular breeds nonetheless.

RESOURCES

Your Local Animal Shelter

Look for them (there is probably more than one) under "Animal Control" in your Blue Pages, the name of your city SPCA and the name of your county SPCA, and the name of your city and county animal shelter or animal control. Also look in the Yellow Pages under "Animal Shelters" and "Humane Societies." And remember, if you can provide the love, patience, attention, veterinary care, and all else that is needed for a lifetime, save two animals, not one, from death row. They will keep each other company while you are at work, not a small consideration.

American Kennel Club

Look on their Web site, www.akc.org, under "Clubs" for a national directory of breed rescue groups to find compassionate fanciers of every dog from affenpinschers to Yorkshire terriers.

Greyhound Rescue

www.greyhoundrescue.com and www.greyhoundrescue.org for two of many affiliates. To save dogs from going from arduous racing life at the track to laboratories for heart and other research, this organization's affiliates rescue "retired" track greyhounds and find them loving homes. The dogs are gentle companions but do love to have room to run.

45.

Why It Pays to Cook for Cats and Dogs

We don't want no dry dog food 'round here!

—JOHN BARTLES, *DOG COLLECTION* RECORD

You can't use the snooze button on a cat who wants her breakfast.

—ANONYMOUS

Cats are considered very polite indeed if they wait patiently until after dawn to stick a claw up your nostril—as my associate Lisa Lange's cat, Camilla, does—or to push a paw with increasing pressure into your eye socket—as does Rita, one of the cats I "babysit" for—so as to let you know that it's time to eat!

As for dogs, perhaps only their old age can save us from those most graceless, determined leaps on the bed and scratching at the door that say, "I'm desperate for that prebreakfast walk—what's keeping you?"

While the can opener may be "a dog's and cat's best friend," there are two key points to know about the fancy, often expensive food that comes in those cans, and in the bags of dry commercial kibble, too. First, some dog and cat foods are tested in laboratories on animals just like your friends at home, and sometimes in shockingly cruel ways. For example, an undercover PETA investigation found dogs at a laboratory contracted by IAMS had apparently been kept for six years or longer on cement, in what amount to cells, with some of them having chunks of their leg muscle removed for testing and some even having their vocal cords cut so that their cries would go unheard. (While IAMS still justifies animal testing, it made the wise public relations choice to stop working with this particular lab when PETA went public with what it had found.) And, happily, many companion animals foods are not tested in laboratories at all but, are "home tested," or use trials of veterinary patients with diagnosed special needs.

The second thing to know is that some veterinarians suspect that those little cancerous bumps, as well as an increasing rate of certain heart diseases and other diseases in cats and dogs, may be caused by ingredients in many commercial foods—not only the chemicals added to this food but also a common ingredient (often called "meat by-product" on the hard-to-decipher labels) that sometimes comes from a rather ugly source: the so-called "4 D bins" at slaughterhouses. Yes, even the fanciest of foods in the prettiest-labeled cans come from bins into which the dead, dying, diseased, and disabled animals, considered "unfit for human consumption," are tossed.

I have looked into those bins and even rescued dying chickens from them, and would bet that most people wouldn't pay a plugged nickel for commercial cat and dog food if they saw what's in it. It is a bit like the brew in the cauldron stirred by the witches of Macbeth:

Eye of newt and toe of frog.
Wool of bat and tongue of dog.
Adders fork and blind-worm's sting,
Lizard's leg and howlet's wing,
For a charm of powerful trouble,
Like a hell-broth boil and bubble.

Another troublesome ingredient to look out for when you're checking the label of commercial pet food is sugar. Dr. R. Geoffrey

Broderick, D.V.M., warns, "Every time an animal companion eats another bowl of high-sugar 'pet food,' he is being brought that much closer to diabetes, hypoglycemia, overweight, nervousness, cataracts, allergies, and worse."

Of course, each species has its own special nutritional needs. For example, cats need amino acids like taurine, a deficiency of which can lead to blindness, and it is believed that cats prone to urinary tract infections should be kept away from whole grains. Adding vitamin C to food can help prevent infection and acidify the urine. Vets who know something about nutrition, not just about how to talk to pet food salespeople and promoters, recommend supplements for all dogs and cats. I've listed some good ones below.

You may be surprised, once you start home-cooking for your animal companions, how much they relish variety in their diet and how some familiar (to us) foods appeal to them. Steamed broccoli is a huge favorite with many dogs; lots of cats like foods like chickpeas, as long as they are moist from the can, and many animals love beans and peas, rice, and spaghetti. Stay away from tomato sauces and cow's milk (even for cats!), however, as these can cause digestive disturbances and discomfort.

Bon appétit, or should that be bone appétit?!

HOMEMADE VEGAN KIBBLE

⅓ cup yeast powder
2 tablespoons Vegedog
4 teaspoons baking powder
¾ teaspoon lecithin granules
⅔ teaspoon salt or 1½ tablespoons soy sauce
6½ cups whole-wheat flour
1⅓ cups wheat gluten flour
⅓ cup oil
4 cups water (as necessary)

Preheat oven to 325°F.

Thoroughly mix the yeast powder, Vegedog, baking powder, lecithin granules, and salt (if not using soy sauce). Then add the whole-wheat flour and wheat gluten flour mixing all ingredients together.

To the dry ingredients add the oil and water and soy sauce (if not using salt).

Stir with a large spoon to form soft dough.

Flour your hands and counter. Knead the dough well until smooth and elastic. Divide the dough into two halves. Roll out each half to fit a large cookie sheet (12" × 17"). Work the dough into the corners and prick with a fork to prevent bubbles. Bake for 20 minutes.

Remove from oven and flip each half-baked piece over by putting an empty cookie sheet on top, holding them both together with pot holders, and turning. Bake for 20 more minutes (don't brown the edges). Remove from oven.

With a large chef's knife cut each slab into 9 to 12 parts on a cutting board by cutting horizontally into three strips and then each vertically two or three times. Cut each resulting rectangle into kibble-sized pieces (like a miniature checkerboard) by cutting first in one direction and then the other.

Place kibble pieces on cookie sheets, breaking apart pieces that stick together. Dry the kibble in a warm oven set at its lowest temperature. Or set the kibble out in the hot sun if you can. The pieces should be brittle and not yield to finger pressure.

Refrigeration is not necessary for properly dried kibble. Store in covered containers for convenience.

For more flavor, substitute a sugar-free prepared pasta sauce for the water or add tomato paste along with any necessary water.

Some dogs may prefer kibble slightly coated with mashed vegetables, sauces, and yeast.

This recipe yields 3½ days' worth of kibble.

HOMEMADE SOY VEGAN KIBBLE

Dry ingredients:
5⅓ cups whole-wheat flour
2¼ cups whole soy flour
½ cup cornmeal

Wet ingredients for all dogs:
¼ cup oil
3 cups water as necessary
Soy sauce if not using salt (see measurements above)

For puppies:
⅛ cup Vegedog
1¼ teaspoon salt (or 3 tablespoons soy sauce added with wet ingredients)

For adult dogs:
4 teaspoons Vegedog
¼ teaspoon salt (or ½ tablespoon soy sauce added with wet ingredients)

Preheat oven to 325°F.

Combine whole-wheat flour, whole soy flour, cornmeal, Vegedog, and salt (if not using soy sauce).

Add the oil, water, and soy sauce (if not using salt). Stir with a large spoon to form soft dough.

Flour your hands and counter. Knead the dough well until smooth and elastic. Divide the dough into two halves. Roll out each half to fit a large cookie sheet (12" × 17"). Work the dough into the corners and prick with a fork to prevent bubbles. Bake for 20 minutes.

Remove from oven and flip each half-baked piece over by putting an empty cookie sheet on top, holding them both together with pot holders, and turning. Bake for 20 more minutes (don't brown the edges). Remove from oven.

With a large chef's knife cut each slab into 9 to 12 parts on a cutting board by cutting horizontally into three strips and then each vertically two or three times. Cut each resulting rectangle into kibble-sized pieces (like a miniature checkerboard) by cutting first in one direction and then the other.

Place kibble pieces on cookie sheets, breaking apart pieces that stick together. Dry the kibble in a warm oven set at its lowest temperature. Or set the kibble out in the hot sun if you can. The pieces should be brittle and not yield to finger pressure.

Refrigeration is not necessary for properly dried kibble. Store in covered containers for convenience.

For more flavor, substitute a sugar-free prepared pasta sauce for the water or add tomato paste along with any necessary water.

Some dogs may prefer kibble slightly coated with mashed vegetables, sauces, and yeast.

This recipe yields 2½ days' worth of kibble.

GREAT GARBANZO DISH FOR CATS AND DOGS

6 cups canned chickpeas
1⅓ cups crumbled veggie burger and 2 cups tofu
⅞ cup nutritional yeast powder
⅓ cup oil
1 teaspoon salt or 4 teaspoons soy sauce
¼ cup Vegecat
Seasonings

Cook chickpeas until just soft, then crush them with a potato masher. Stir in other ingredients. Let soften before serving. You can cover bite-size pieces with nutritional yeast. This is excellent served on cooked rice or noodles, and you may like it yourself!

RESOURCES

Commercial Vegan Dog and Cat Food

Below is a list of companies that sell vegan dog and/or cat food.

Boss Bars
PO Box 517
Patagonia, AZ 85624
888-207-9114
100 percent certified organic dog biscuits, 4 flavors, including wheat- and corn-free.

Evolution
287 E. 6th St., Suite 70
St. Paul, MN 55101
800-659-0104
Dog and cat kibble and canned food, ferret kibble, fish food.

Harbingers of a New Age
717 E. Missoula Ave.
Troy, MT 59935
406-295-4944
Vegecat, Vegekit, and Vegedog supplements, recipes for homemade vegan dog, cat, and kitten food, digestive enzymes, and acidifying nutritional yeast.

Natural Life Pet Products
1601 W. McKay
Frontenac, KS 66763
800-367-2391
Canned and kibble dog food.

Nature's Recipe
341 Bonnie Circle
Corona, CA 91720
800-843-4008
Canned and kibble dog food—call for closest distributor.

Pet Guard
PO Box 728
Orange Park, FL 32067-0728
800-874-3221
Canned dog food and biscuits, digestive enzymes.

Wow-Bow Distributors
13-B Lucon Dr.
Deer Park, NY 11729
516-254-6064
Canned and kibble dog food and biscuits, nutritional supplements.

Wysong Corporation
1880 N. Eastman Rd.
Midland, MI 48642
800-748-0188
Dog and cat kibble.

Supplements

Try adding small amounts (¼ of a teaspoon or less) of sprinkles of nutritional yeast, crushed Vitamin C, marmite, vegemite, alfalfa, rosehips powder, garlic, and crushed vitamins to food, and check to be sure your dog or cat still finds these health-boosted dishes palatable. Use a little bit of oil like olive, high-oleic (not regular) safflower, peanut, and sunflower or sesame for dry coats.

Seameal

Solid Gold Health Products
El Cajon, California

1-800-364-4863
www.solidgoldhealth.com
Great sea vegetable powder to add to food.

Vegecat and Vegedog

Troy, Montana
1-800-884-6262
www.veggiepet.com
This company provides excellent nutritional advice as well as products and recipes for puppies, kittens, and for adult, geriatric, and nursing dogs and cats.

Books

Pedan, James A. *Vegetarian Cats and Dogs.* Troy, Mont.: Harbingers of a New Age, 1995.

46.

The Importance of Sterilization

Please don't litter!

—POSTER FOR THE PROGRESSIVE ANIMAL WELFARE SOCIETY, SEATTLE

Most people who haven't been exposed to the overpopulation crisis for dogs and cats in America think that they are not part of it, even if they "only" allow their dog or cat to have one litter. "After all," they think, "we can find good homes for all of the puppies/kittens and our dog/cat is *so* wonderful she *should* have a litter."

To those of us who are trying desperately to place a sea of animals as vast as the Atlantic Ocean, them's fightin' words—like telling a member of Mothers Against Drunk Driving that it is okay to have just a shot or two of vodka before taking the wheel.

Anyone who cares about dogs and cats must know, if only deep in his or her heart, that far better than creating more dogs and cats is helping rescue the wonderful lonely and abandoned ones sitting on death row in every shelter, all through no fault of their own. Every one of those angels putting a paw through the cage at you wants and deserves a home.

If you have five friends who will take a puppy or kitten into their lives, what could be a greater testament to your sense of responsibility and community caring than to put your arm in theirs and go off to the shelter with them and save a life—or five!

In nature, dogs and cats did not "come into heat" as often as they do now that they are domesticated. Nor did they yammer and howl when they were in heat, as mates were close by and available. Tomcats did not get beaten up and have their jowls and ears ulcerated by rivals, because they had lots of turf to share.

Spaying and neutering does not make animals fat and lazy, as some people mistakenly believe. What does that is their owners' failure to get them out to run and exercise (or to play with them in the house, in the case of cats). Also, eating fatty foods, rather than adding steamed broccoli and carrots to food or offering a more natural and healthy diet, contributes to the problem (see chapter 45: "Why It Pays to Cook for Cats and Dogs," page 234).

Spaying and neutering merely remove the desire to wander off looking for a mate, the mess of "coming in heat," and the problems inherent in having and coping with litters. Happily, it is possible to get dogs and cats surgically sterilized before they reach puberty, in fact as early as at eight weeks of age, eliminating the possibility of any "accidental" litters; but if you wait longer, it is still wise to get them "fixed" as early as you can. Neutering is a relatively simple procedure, and spaying is an ovario-hysterectomy. In most cases, animals can go home the same day, and despite some discomfort on the part of males, they don't look back, while females need to take it easy for a few days. Stitches come out in ten days and that's the end of that.

Now it's just you and your wonderful animal. If you decide there's room, and that two is company, you can save yet another life by heading down to your local animal shelter.

RESOURCES

Call your veterinarian, or if you need to find a low-priced service, call your local humane society or SPCA and ask if there are any spay/neuter clinics available to you.

Spay U.S.A.

www.spayusa.com

Referrals to low-cost spay programs nationally.

47.

Incorporating Dog- and Cat-Friendly Elements into Your (and Their) Home

Dogs have owners; cats have staff.

—ANONYMOUS

We give dogs time we can spare, space we can spare, and love we can spare. And, in return, they give us their all. It's the best deal anyone ever made.

—M. FACKLAM

When Loretta and Bob Hirsch built their modern home high above Rock Creek Park in Washington, D.C., they had lots of good ideas, but the very first instruction to their architects was to make all the windows throughout the house have glass from floor to ceiling. That way, their dear dog, Trixie, a pup rescued by the Washington Humane Society, would be able to watch (and bark at) the squirrels and birds without having to stand up.

As Loretta said, "It's easy to arrange furniture so that cats can sit and look out, but not so with dogs. I wanted her to have a more interesting experience than just staring at the wall when we go out gallivanting and have to leave her behind."

All dogs need comfy places to sit, of course. Old dogs with creaky joints and small and short-haired dogs need a bed that has corners to it, so they can snuggle down and keep warm, one that is up off the floor by at least two inches to prevent drafts that can aggravate arthritis and make small beasts shiver.

Dog and cat doors are useful too, putting an end to one of the worst debasements: having to beg to go outside for important reasons! Or just to enjoy the day. If a cut door isn't possible, a reliable dog walker is as vital as any babysitter. In some cities, there is doggy day care, which can be a godsend for working dog people, as long as the place is as open as a book—no hidden corners, no "by appointment only" peeks behind the scenes, no "insurance regulations forbid your visit."

Chances are that you come and go from your home daily. And chances are, your dog and cat spend most of their lives inside without much to do when you are gone, i.e., most of the time. One cannot underestimate the dangers of letting any animal out unsupervised unless the yard is fenced (and for cats, that means a full enclosure or a fence that is angled outward at 45 degrees at the top), but dogs need more than evenings and weekends at the dog park ("dog socials" with chances to meet and greet one's own familiars). Dogs need to smell the great outdoors and "read the news" on lampposts as often as possible, and cats can go out on a harness or on a supervised romp in the yard.

If you have a shut-in cat, modifications can be made to liven up her life and keep her mind from going numb. First, do be sure she can look out of the window, even if that simply means pushing a piece of furniture, like a heavy bureau, up to it and putting a piece of bedding on top of it for her to lounge on while enjoying the view. For added joy, hanging a bird feeder out there in winter allows her to watch "cat TV." There are cat window perches available for purchase, and I wouldn't count on a cat's bottom being thin enough to fit a windowsill without one.

Bob Walker, a San Diego architect, has constructed a 110-foot carpeted, elevated catwalk in his house, but no one has to go that far to bring happiness to a cat (details below). A few nesting boxes, scratching posts, a place or two to jump up and get a different view, some peekaboo cutouts into cupboards or, at floor level, into an adjoining room are all possibilities to consider.

Finally, a few moments looking for home hazards can be time well spent. Many a dog or cat has been hurt and even killed by being caught in a recliner chair or folding bed, or from curling up in the warmth of a dryer, among the clothes, when the door was left open (always check before turning the clothes dryer on, and never, ever ignore thumping noises). Commercial oven cleaners and fabric protectors, conventional antifreeze, and other unexpected poisons are to be avoided, and it's always good to check before bringing home a new plant that it is not toxic if eaten. Like children, animals must, of course, be kept away from the stove, and burners should be dutifully turned off and covered (I use a pan of water) while they cool.

Here's to the little things that make our homes as comfortable and pleasant to our dogs and cats as to us.

RESOURCES

The Walker Catwalk

www.thecatshouse.com

Plans for this elaborate cat walk are available, with proceeds from their sale going to the National Cat Protection Society.

Flexi-Mat Corporation

773-376-5500

www.flexi-mat.com

Orthopedic beds for dogs, cat perches to attach to your windowsill.

Coolpetstuff.com

"Canine cooler" thermoregulating bed.

Happypaw.com

Dog beds, pillows, blankets, and travel accessories.

Doggie Day Care

www.petplace.com

National Animal Poison Control Center

Run by the University of Illinois, Champaign, a twenty-four-hour-a-day emergency advice center.

Calls billed to a credit card: 800-548-2423

Calls billed to a telephone number: 900-680-0000

48.

Letting Animals Open Your Eyes and Heart to What's Important in Life

He is very imprudent a dog is; he never makes it his business to inquire whether you are in the right or the wrong, never asks whether you are rich or poor, silly or wise, sinner or saint. You are his pal. That is enough for him.

—JEROME K. JEROME

Maybe this dog didn't come to us to learn, but to teach.

—THOMAS D. MURRAY, AMERICAN WRITER

One of the most moving stories I have ever read about the relationship between a caring soul and his dog is in an editorial entitled "What George Taught Us" by Thomas D. Murray. When Mr. Murray, a writer, lost his dog to old age, he began to think back on what joy his dog had brought into his life and what he had not noticed about his dog while George was still alive. I have kept a copy of that article in my files. I know the truth of it, for when my dogs had died, I began to wish I had been more patient and considerate.

When the Murray family got George, they had to teach him to go up and down stairs, as he'd lived his life on one floor.

Murray said this was about the only thing the family ever taught him in thirteen years. He says, "It was mostly desperation that made me finally give up and conclude that maybe this dog didn't come to us to learn, but to teach, though it took me a while to understand the lessons."

Murray started out trying to teach George by using a rolled-up newspaper to stop his barking and dancing through the house every time the doorbell rang or he heard a car in the driveway. "I think he was trying to make me understand," concludes Murray, "that a friend at the door, even a stranger or the mailman, can be a nice little diversion on a humdrum day, and something to celebrate with a little excitement."

George was impatient whenever his food was being fixed, prancing around the kitchen, standing on his rear legs, and then gulping down a full bowl almost before it was set in front of him on the floor. No matter what was said or done to calm him down, George never stopped this excitement, probably, as Murray decided, "to remind me of the pure joy of wanting and waiting for something, and, by always wagging his tail the entire time he was eating, demonstrating that gratefulness is a priceless part of good manners and doesn't cost a thing."

Early on, Murray had tried to get George to hurry up and finish his business in the yard and come back inside. "In time," he says, "he taught me the joy of a much longer sunrise walk to see the new day, even in winter, and another after dinner to help put the day's work and worries in perspective. I think I grew to look forward to those walks as much as George did."

There are many more lessons George taught the family over time, but my favorite is about Christmas celebrations. The Murrays thought that they would make Christmastime special by putting a red bow on George's collar and giving him some extra treats but realized that on all the days that weren't Christmas, George was trying to show them that it was possible to spread that feeling of anticipation and happiness over the whole year, not just when the holly decorations and the tree were put up. In other words, George's lesson was "that the only presents that meant much of anything to him were those that were waiting for him, not just on Christmas, but every morning of the year—his family, his friends, his freedom, and not too many baths."

Murray's lesson is the lesson each of us can and should bear in mind if we have the joy of an animal in our lives and homes. His biggest regret is that "I'm a little ashamed that right up until the end, I was still trying to teach him things."

RESOURCES

Your animal companion!
www.helpinganimals.com

PART SIX

Children and Family

49.

A Most Beautiful Wedding Reflecting Beautiful Values

Whenever I hear geese flying overhead, making their way south, their gentle honks comforting each other in their careful formation, I count them. Geese mate for life and when I find they are of an even number, my heart calms, for I know that these couples have survived the guns and stand to enjoy another year of peace together.

—REFORMED HUNTER

Life has taught us that love does not consist in gazing at each other but in looking outward together in the same direction.

—ANTOINE DE SAINT-EXUPÉRY

Christian and Dawn Pilosi met when she was a freshman and he was a senior in high school in Moosic, Pennsylvania. Moosic is a small town near Scranton and lies in a heavily wooded valley, and from the Pilosi family home you can see the mountains.

Christian had hunted deer with his grandfather every season since he could carry a gun, although once when he shot a doe he had been disturbed to see, from his perch in a tree stand, a young deer walk out of the wooded area and come up to the dead deer. He realized that he had just taken this fawn's mother away from him and started questioning what he was doing shooting animals. Neither he nor Dawn knew a vegetarian or had heard the word "vegan."

Eight years after they first met, Dawn picked up a copy of PETA's *Animal Times* in the library at Penn State University and read an article about an Indiana factory farm. She brought it home for Chris to read.

It was later that week, they recall, that things changed. Chris was sitting at the dinner table, getting ready to cut a piece of chicken. Keesha, their nine-year-old dog, sat beside him. Keesha, who was about seven years old then, was born with a congenital heart defect, and both Chris and Dawn are very protective of her. Suddenly, Chris remembered the article he had read. He looked at his plate and thought, "I can't believe I'm eating this chicken's leg. It could as well be Keesha's leg!"

Chris and Dawn decided to become vegetarians and to stop any other use and abuse of animals they could identify. Christian stopped hunting, much to his grandfather's initial disappointment, although today his granddad even picks up soy milk at the corner store.

When they decided to get married, Dawn and Chris knew from the very start that their wedding would need to reflect their values as well as please their guests and extended families. Says Dawn, "What kind of people would we be if we were untrue to our beliefs on our wedding day? And our friends are coming to wish us well, not to make us do things we don't approve of just for old time's sake."

It turned out that the planning alone was great fun and everyone they spoke to seemed to move from skepticism to enthusiasm very quickly, getting in the swing of it all.

Dawn chose a traditional white wedding gown by Jasmine of satin, embroidered net, and other nonanimal fabric. It sparkled with a fretwork of gorgeous hand-sewn beads and crystals, was fitted at the waist, and had a magnificent train and cotton lace veil. The four bridesmaids wore silver A-line skirts in metallic cotton knit and each chose a top from the same material to suit her personality. The three flower girls also wore satin A-line dresses.

It took a bit of work at first to find nonwool tuxedos for the groom, the best man, the groom's party, and the ring bearer, but a local store, Sarno and Son, which at first tried hard to talk them out of synthetic ones, came up with them when the groom insisted.

Nonleather shoes were easy to find, and the Pilosis took it a step further, asking their guests not to wear leather either.

The only hitch was finding a limousine without leather seats. They simply couldn't! In the end, Dawn thinks that turned out for the best. "We had to improvise, so we rented a party bus, which meant that the entire wedding party could go together rather than be split into separate cars.. It was a great hit and I recommend it!"

The rehearsal dinner was held at the East Mountain Inn, a local hotel in Wilkes-Barre, Pennsylvania. The chef was at first rattled by their needs, as she'd been in the restaurant business forever and had never heard of such particularity. But she took on the challenge, right down to the rolls and the margarine. It all turned out fine.

Chris and Dawn rushed home with the photographer before the ceremony and again after the wedding to have wedding pictures taken with their best friend, Keesha.

As for the wedding feast, Chris and Dawn think it couldn't have been more attractive and delicious. When you walked into the foyer, there was a table with a spectacular display of hors d'oeuvres and tapas piled high, with tumbling grapes and natural greens. Guests could sample marinated wild mushroom and spinach pâté, spicy Louisiana-style tofu, marinated teriyaki mock children, Mexican rice salad, mock oysters, Polish potato salad, garden crudités, grape leaves with couscous, squash vinaigrette, and mousse of legumes, to name only some of the dishes.

"I don't know what people were expecting," says Dawn, "but there was something for everyone, and everyone raved about the food, including some of the older people who, I'm sure, went home none the wiser that it was all vegan!"

The caterers, Everybody's Café and Caterer in Stoudsburg, had catered vegetarian weddings before, but never vegan ones, but they had worked out every detail without a fault.

Chris's favorite eggplant parmesan, made with soy cheese, was on the lavish buffet, together with "Mock Chicken Scaloppine Marsala," "Mock Boeuf and Onions in Gravy," "Rigatoni Mezza à la Calabrese," roasted vegetables, parsleyed potatoes, and signature salads of different kinds, including one with broccoli and walnuts and one with tomato and tofu.

For dessert there were "petite confections," fresh fruit salad, nut coffees, and a four-tier banana spice cake with vanilla "butter cream" filling and white icing specially commissioned from Lotus Cake Studio in Philadelphia.

Last, as the guests were leaving, they were given gold-foiled heart-shaped dark (nondairy) chocolates from Krön chocolatier or, if allergic to chocolate or not fond of it, banana chips!

RESOURCES

Vegetarian Weddings Online

Donna Zeigfinger
7 Froude Circle
Cabin John, MD 20818
301-320-2892
www.vegetarianwedding.net
For all of your vegetarian wedding needs.

Bridal Dresses

Jasmine wedding gowns are available in most major department stores.

Morilee by Madeline Garner
www.morilee.com

Caterers

Everybody's Café and Caterer
905 Main St.
Stroudsburg, PA 18360
570-424-0896
Vegetarian and vegan catering in eastern Pennsylvania and New Jersey.

Chocolates

Krön Chocolatier
5300 Wisconsin Ave. NW
Washington, D.C. 20015
202-966-4946
www.krondc.com
Dark chocolates in many amazing shapes and sizes.

Chris's Reception Grace

With this food before us, we honor all of Your Creation;
We thank you for that which You have so generously provided.
In return, we promise to always keep Your Word and follow Your Way.
We only ask that You light it. Amen.

Party Buses

Northeast Transit Inc.,
Scranton, Pennsylvania
570-347-8877
Party buses without leather seats for all occasions.

Shoes

Payless
877-474-6379
www.payless.com

This store is fantastic and has outlets everywhere. A myriad of styles from hiking boots to dancing shoes, and it offers bargains and discount deals all the time.

Mudd shoes
Available at many major stores, and discount Mudd shoes can be found at:
www.zappo.com

Tuxedos

Erik Lawrence Classics Polyester one-button notch.
www.4atux.com
This company sells single-breasted, 100 percent synthetic "Chaplin" tuxedos (with a satin stripe and satin-covered buttons) as well, on the Web for $159.
sales@4atux.com

Sarno & Son Tuxedos

800-233-1404
For the store nearest you:
www.sarnotux.com

Vows

Christian and Dawn chose readings and Gospel that showed their faith as an all-encompassing, all-inclusive one.

Wedding Cakes

Lotus Cake Studio
PO Box 44292
Philadelphia, PA 19144
215-848-8770
Delivers to New York, Pennsylvania, and New Jersey.

50.

Why Your Vegan Baby Will Smile All the Time

It is unnatural for a dog to nurse from a giraffe; a child drinking the milk of a mother cow is just as strange.

—DR. MICHAEL KLAPER

Some children have respiratory problems, skin conditions, chronic ear infections, or digestive upsets that clear up when they avoid cow's milk. In addition, cow's milk tends to interfere with iron absorption and has virtually no iron of its own.

—DR. BENJAMIN SPOCK, AUTHOR OF THE BEST-SELLING BABY CARE BOOK IN THE WORLD, *DR. SPOCK'S BABY AND CHILD CARE*

At a conference in the Catskill Mountains recently, I listened to vegetarian and vegan mothers comparing notes as their children ran around the trees and over the grass, chasing each other, tumbling, and giggling.

The vegetarian mothers whose children were drinking cow's milk or who had breast-fed their babies while drinking cow's milk themselves reported that their babies' problems with colic, ear infections, and gastrointestinal disturbances were common. The vegan mothers reported that their babies slept soundly, rarely cried, and did not suffer from the problems that usually come with consuming cow's milk.

"When Jilly was a baby," one of the vegan mothers, Kathy

Guillermo, said, "she was almost the *only* baby I knew who didn't have ear infections or colic. My friends thought I was just lucky, but the truth is that I knew what I ate would be passed on to her when I nursed, and there was no meat or milk in my diet."

The funniest remark was from an Indian man who was singing the praises of his vegan grandchild.

"He is so healthy," he said, "and his droppings are like those of a baby goat!" No one knew exactly what that meant—or wanted to inquire too deeply—but the grandfather said the words with such pride that it had to be something good!

I should not have been surprised by the difference in the health of the infants given cow's milk and those who weren't. I myself had been plagued with chronic bronchitis until I stopped drinking milk, and my friend's pediatrician had warned her to get her children off milk pronto because of the potential risk of respiratory problems and the risk of anemia. Cow's milk has been shown to cause or exacerbate a host of health problems in infants, and is not desirable for or needed by toddlers or older children, either.

Just as many adults are lactose intolerant, many babies cannot digest cow's milk. Why should they? Every species' own mother's breast milk is best for the young of that species, and cow's milk is, of course, designed for calves. It is chock-full of the proteins needed for *bovine* growth and development, not for that of a human infant. While many doctors and others in the scientific community still discount the apparent risks associated with dairy consumption, it seems only logical that giving children a set of nutrients, meant for another species and depriving them of the immune system protection that only their mothers can give them, can lead to health problems in the short term, just as the mothers at the conference were describing. In the case of cow's milk—especially whole milk—it can cause problems like heart disease, cancer, and high blood pressure in the long term.

As children grow, many mothers, used to seeing and believing the ads put out by the dairy industry, are fearful that their offspring *need* cow's milk. Kathy Guillermo says, "My family was scandalized that I wasn't going to feed my kids milk!"

"They'll be sickly and scrawny," they warned. Kathy showed her relatives that they had nothing to worry about.

"I went to a nutrition consultant after Jilly was born," she says. "The consultant said, 'Kids not only don't need animal products, they're much better off without them.' She gave my parents extra confidence and she gave me easy instructions."

What those cute dairy ads touting the benefits of calcium neglect to say is that drinking cow's milk is certainly not the only and may not be the most efficient way to get calcium. Most green, leafy vegetables, like broccoli, and also tofu, almonds, and beans are almost equal in being good forms of calcium that the body can easily absorb. Along with the calcium from such healthy sources come many vitamins, complex carbohydrates, and fiber, all of which are lacking in cow's milk, as well as iron, for which cow's milk is a poor source. What *is* in cow's milk is often what kids don't need, for example, antibiotics fed to the cow to prevent infections common in crowded, "modern" dairy operations, and when it comes to whole milk artery-clogging saturated fat and cholesterol.

Another reason to skip the dairy is the news from medical studies that the rate of insulin-dependent diabetes in children under the age of five is rising dramatically. According to a recent study, milk may be the culprit in children's being predisposed to developing insulin-dependent diabetes.

To make life even easier, there are excellent books on nutrition for the vegan mother-to-be, the vegan baby, and the vegan child. I've listed those the vegan mothers I know have relied upon.

Tips for Growing Bodies

For babies, I advise that only mother's breast milk or specially fortified soy formula are appropriate, but when children have moved on to solid foods, they often enjoy black beans, cornbread, kale, fortified orange juice, tofu, and dried figs (all excellent sources of calcium), and raisins, broccoli, squash, lentils, pumpkin seeds, and blackstrap molasses (all great sources of iron); and of course soy milk on their breakfast cereal. Even the pickiest children will drink chocolate-flavored soy beverages and eat dairy-free frozen treats!

Always be sure your child has a source of vitamin B_{12}, which is found in fortified cereal or any common multivitamin.

RESOURCES

The Vegan Society
www.vegansociety.com

Veg Family
www.vegfamily.com

Physicians Committee for Responsible Medicine
www.pcrm.org

Veg Source
www.vegsource.com

Books

Attwood, Charles, M.D. *Dr. Attwood's Low-Fat Prescription for Kids.* New York: Penguin USA, 1995.

Klaper, Michael, M.D. *Pregnancy, Children, and the Vegan Diet.* Gentle World, 1988.

Pavlina, Erin. *Raising Vegan Children in a Non-Vegan World.* Vegfamily.com, 2003. This is a handy book that answers parents' many questions, such as "What will you say to your pediatrician when he insists you feed your child milk?" and "How will you handle family members who insist upon offering your child meat at family events?"

Physicians Committee for Responsible Medicine. *Healthy Eating for Children.* Canada: Wiley Publishing, 2002.

Spock, Benjamin, M.D., and Steven J. Parker, M.D. *Dr. Spock's Baby and Child Care.* Pocket, 1985.

51.

The Perfect Baby Shower Gift

"I have no name;
I am but two days old."
What shall I call thee?
"I happy am,
Joy is my name."
Sweet Joy befall thee!

—WILLIAM BLAKE, "INFANT JOY"

Where did you come from, baby dear?
Out of the everywhere into the here.

—GEORGE MACDONALD,
AT THE BACK OF THE NORTH WIND

Jack came into the world bang on time, much to the delight of Tracy and Dale, his mother and father. A happy little baby who sleeps through most nights without a peep, Jack is the child who has everything that's important: a doting mother with a strong sense of right and wrong, a doting father with a great sense of humor, and doting grandparents nearby. What else counts?

Jack's parents also have longtime friends who were delighted to see them get together and pleased for them when they announced that the baby was on his way. Everyone seemed to be involved in planning the baby shower. Jack would be born to a world filled with baby bootees, baby clothes, cuddly toys, twirling cot mobiles, strollers, bottles, and blankets.

Of course, Jack will outgrow the clothes and his cot, but he also received a few gifts that will, with a little luck, grow as he does. It doesn't have to be an expensive purchase, but giving a baby one or more shares in a company you can feel good about is a great idea for a gift that will give the child, over the years, a fun reason to learn about and be interested in the stock market, as well as teaching the value of saving and planning, and giving a boost to a business that builds the kind of society we all want.

For Jack's birthday, Tracy's friends at work chose two of his family's favorite companies, Hain Celestial, a natural foods and herbal tea company, and Tofutti Brands, maker of the soy ice cream sandwiches Tofutti Cuties, as well as a host of other products like soy "cream cheese," egg substitute, pizza, and more. Then, because they couldn't resist, they threw in Duncan, a plush pink piggie from the Right Squeak who, when tickled or squeezed, says, "Pigs are friends, not food."

There are, of course, lots of green and animal-friendly stocks to choose from (see chapter 58: "Investing in Green and Animal-Friendly Companies," page 295) for every little Jack you will watch grow tall as a beanstalk.

RESOURCES

Tofutti Brands Inc.
50 Jackson Dr.
Cranford, NJ 07016
908-272-2400
www.tofutti.com

Hain Celestial
734 Franklin Ave. #444
Garden City, NY 11530
www.hain-celestial.com

The PETA Catalog
www.petamall.com
Duncan the pink pig (and his friend Simon the cow).

52.

Cultivating Kind Kids

I am working at the roots. If you teach a child to be kind to a caterpillar, you do as much for the child as you do for the caterpillar.

—GEORGE ANGELL, FOUNDER OF THE MASSACHUSETTS SOCIETY FOR THE PREVENTION OF CRUELTY TO ANIMALS, WHEN ASKED, "WHY DON'T YOU HELP CHILDREN?"

Kindness is the important thing. Kids and animals are our responsibility.

—MINNIE PEARL, SINGER-ENTERTAINER

A little learning makes the whole world kin.

—MARK TWAIN

If you have a child in school or are a teacher, or perhaps simply wish to do your part to make sure today's children grow up with a caring attitude, there is a free program you might care to know about. It is called *Share the World.* It comes as a kit in many languages, and it is in use from Bangladesh to Barcelona, and from New South Wales to New York City. It is also free for the asking.

What it teaches, to elementary- through young middle-school children, is the age-old lesson of putting yourself in the other "guy's" shoes, a lesson as vital today as at any time in history. What it brings into the classroom is a simple tenet: the Golden Rule of "Do unto others as you would have them do unto you."

In times of uncertainty and strife, of violence, war, and disrespect, there may be nothing as important and as useful to a growing mind as being able to relate well to others. From everything we know, the children who were involved in the school shootings in Colorado, Oregon, and Michigan could have benefited to see similarities rather than differences in the "others" around them, to curb their aggression instead of acting upon it. Rather, they shot and tortured animals, and as studies show, children who hurt and take little lives often do not stop there.

Sociologists recognize cruelty to animals as a red flag. One does not have to look far from the pages of the daily papers or the nightly news to confirm that. Lee Malvo, the "Washington sniper," and Jeffrey Dahmer, the serial murderer of young men, for example, both killed cats when they were young.

But there is hope and opportunity. If you would like to play an active part in molding future generations, it is as easy as ABC.

Share the World is designed to increase students' understanding that animals are living, feeling beings to be treated with respect and compassion. It helps them see that animals often experience the same needs and feelings that we do, like pain and fear, love and joy; enables them to appreciate the amazing characteristics and abilities of animals, such as an albatross's ability to navigate around the world without a map or a compass, or a penguin's ability to guard an egg on the ice for forty-five days without eating even a morsel of food; and it helps students understand how human regard for animals has changed and developed as our knowledge of animals has increased.

The program invites children to see how the once-pervasive use of animals is being replaced, for example, from carrier pigeons and the Pony Express, thanks to increased understanding and technological developments, and it asks them to challenge themselves to think of more alternatives to animal use.

The author Roger Lewin once wrote, "Too often we give our children answers to remember rather than problems to solve." *Share the World* gives children a chance to practice not only their reading and writing skills but also their critical thinking skills. Its creators let little minds wonder and ponder.

Most important, perhaps, the kit encourages children to put themselves in the place of animals in a variety of settings, at a zoo, for instance, or when a boy is seen throwing rocks at a bird, and to figure out how to react and what should be done.

Teachers love the program wherever they are; but in some classrooms, where resources are scarce and teachers pitch in to buy students books and pens, the pretty poster of children and animals, the practical lesson plans, the reading materials from the classics, and the exciting video of the natural world and our obligations toward it are all extra special. Perhaps you would like to place *Share the World* in a teacher's hands in your neighborhood or send it to your first school. Or get it shown on cable TV in your city. Future generations will owe you a debt of gratitude for helping to shape kinder, more understanding citizens, who will in turn shape the world.

RESOURCES

Share the World
www.sharetheworld.com

53.

Retirement Income Planning with an Annuity

Do not resist growing old—many are denied the privilege.

—ANONYMOUS

Here's to:
A little health, a little wealth;
A little house and freedom;
With some few friends for certain ends
But little cause to need 'em.

—TOAST

Wrinkles merely indicate where smiles have been.

—MARK TWAIN

Retirement income needs vary from person to person, but one thing retirees seem to agree on is that finding the right annuity can be the foundation of a comforting and productive income partnership.

Dr. Ronald Baumbarten is a case in point. He lives near the shores of Lake Michigan now, but for thirty-five years he was a down-to-earth professor of chemistry at the University of Illinois in Chicago. There he considered his pre-med students his children and talked to them about not only chemistry but also ethics and personal responsibility.

Dr. Baumbarten became politically aware during the Vietnam

War, and at one point in his life he even packed up and left the United States in disgust, taking up residency in Holland. He did so because, he says, "I was on the periphery when Mayor Daley unleashed the police at the 1968 Democratic Convention. It was like something out of a Nazi movie and I thought, 'I won't live in a Fascist state.'" When he returned, he remained politically active, although he is quick to say, "I don't consider myself Gandhi. I wouldn't do well in a loincloth!"

Just as Chicago has changed, so, over the years, has Dr. Baumbarten's diet. When one of his students challenged him about holding pacifist views, which, the student argued, were contrary to his "taking a bit of chicken or turkey now and then," he found himself unable to argue the point. At first, he says, he missed the sausage pizzas they made in Bloomington, Indiana, but now, if someone offers him meat, "it takes a lot for me not to make a face." He can be found in the kitchen on any evening, cooking up pasta with lots of veggies, olive oil, garlic, and onions.

Dr. Baumbarten's retirement gives him plenty of time to walk along the water, to read fiction and mysteries, and to contemplate the state of the world. He has a circle of friends with whom he goes out to the theater and to concerts, and he has recently been on a whale-watching cruise to Alaska.

Not long after he retired in 2000, he read about annuities and did some research into them. He found out that through a charitable gift annuity he could make a gift to a charitable interest of his and receive fixed annual payments for life. The payment amount is based on the amount given, the age of the payment recipient or recipients at the time the gift is made (with the older recipient[s] receiving larger payments), the number of payment recipients, and when the annuity begins.

Dr. Baumbarten found out that he can take an income tax deduction for a portion of the amount transferred to the charity and for a period of years only part of the payments will be taxed as income. If stocks or other property that has been owned for more than one year and that has risen in value is given for a gift annuity that pays income to the donor, a portion of the capital gain is never taxed and the remainder may be reported gradually over time. If the donor and/or spouse is the only payment beneficiary, the amount he or she has used to fund the gift is generally not subject to estate taxes that might otherwise be due upon his or her death. Moreover, the donated asset is removed from the donor's estate, which may help reduce potential estate taxes.

Dr. Baumbarten liked what he read and ended up taking out two annuities with different organizations. At first, he put some funds into the Nature Conservancy, then realized they approved of hunting in certain situations and decided not to do that again. He chose other organizations instead.

Both annuities provide a little bit of extra income, and, he says, "organizations I believe in and who do good works that I want to support get money in return." Dr. Baumbarten laments that "with inflation getting bad, the retirement story isn't as great as I thought it was, so I'm lucky I have this supplement from my annuity."

RESOURCES

As you consider the suggestions offered in this chapter (and throughout this book), keep in mind that no investment is without risk—and charitable gift annuities are no exception. The information being provided is designed to give you ideas to consider. Before following any suggestions on matters that call for expert assistance, you should get the advice of a competent financial professional.

You can also find out about charitable giving and investments from PETA and other organizations.

PETA offers free information about gift annuities, including minimum distribution tables, as well as other booklets on charitable remainder trusts and living trusts and life insurance. Contact PETA's Development Department, 501 Front Street,

Norfolk, VA 23510, or call Planned Gifts at 757-622-7382, or contact the charities you favor.

PETA Guide to Health Charities
www.caringconsumer.com
Dame Judi Dench introduces this guide with the words: "Instead of hurting animals, cruelty-free health charities are helping people by funding programs that focus on direct care, clinical studies, community education, and prevention. They truly deserve our support."

54.

Making a Will: Leaving a Lasting Legacy

Excuse my dust.

—DOROTHY PARKER'S PROPOSAL FOR HER GRAVESTONE INSCRIPTION

I told you I was sick!

—HYPOCHONDRIAC'S EPITAPH

I once read a story about a fantastical wristwatch that allowed the wearer to glance down and see precisely how much time he or she had left in the world. When we are young, most of us think of ourselves as immortal. I know I did. I careened about, first on my skates and bicycle, then in my car, in all weathers, immersed in all manner of distractions, and often at foolhardy speeds.

As we age, however, our mortality seems to become more real by the minute. Still, many of us fail to make a will or fail to update our wills to reflect what we would like to see happen when we are no longer around to oversee matters in person.

I think of my will as an insurance policy of sorts. It allows me to hop on a plane to an international trouble spot or cross the street and know that should something unexpected happen to me, I've tied up the things I can control and that I find important.

The Augustus Club is an honorary club recognizing those who have made a lasting gift to PETA, and the animals PETA serves, through their wills. Membership costs nothing and is open to anyone who includes PETA in a will, trust, life insurance policy, or retirement plan or who makes an irrevocable life-income gift. The club is named after Augustus, one of the famous "Silver Spring monkeys" purchased in the late 1970s by an experimenter who used them in nerve experiments.

Augustus was seized, together with eighteen other monkeys in the experiment, when police, acting on information painstakingly gathered by PETA, raided the laboratory. His rescue was part of a historic event: It was the first time in U.S. history that a laboratory had been served with a search warrant, and the experimenter charged and convicted under the cruelty to animals laws (although subsequently acquitted on a technicality). Later, the Silver Spring monkeys case became the first animal protection case to go all the way to the U.S. Supreme Court.

During the legal battle, which went on for years, PETA was successful in getting most of the monkeys out of experimenters' hands, although they tried mighty hard to thwart those efforts, and the courts ultimately denied PETA's efforts to get custody of the animals. Augustus was not one of the few lucky monkeys. He was killed by experimenters in July 1990.

Augustus Club members are moved by the image and documentation of Augustus's noble nature, his dignity, his innocence, and his suffering to ensure that after their own deaths, funds will be available to PETA to fight animal abuse.

Maru Vigo, a professional translator in Tucson, Arizona, is an Augustus Club member who moved to the U.S. from Peru. She is the only person I know of who made out her first will when she was twelve years old.

She says, "Whenever you bring a new idea to me, I go home and really think about it. I had an elderly French friend in the neighborhood, a Holocaust survivor. And at one point, she said that she was going to make her will. I asked her about it.

"I just had my stuffed animals and my books, but I asked my mom, 'If I die, what would you do with them?' And she said, 'Your sister would get them.' And I said, 'But what about all my friends?' So I wrote myself a will and just hoped that people would grant my wishes."

When Maru was twenty-five years old, a friend showed her a pamphlet about Britches, a little monkey who was used in experiments, another about cosmetics tests on rabbits and rats, and one on cruelty in the meat industry. The whole concept of animal rights was foreign to her. Maru says, "I had rescued strays from the streets in Peru, but I had never thought that the cosmetics industry and animals had anything to do with each other. Then I read about lethal dose testing in which they let fifty percent of the animals die in these tests. It upset me greatly."

Maru says, "I tend to be skeptical, so I went to a slaughterhouse in Lima. Even though I had read about it, I couldn't believe it. To get in, I borrowed my sister's school ID and said I was writing a report. It was really, really traumatic. Those images are still with me. I was taken to the killing floor. I have seen it myself. It was awful. That night I became a vegetarian. My mother thought I was going to get sick and die. I survived on pizza for months, because my mom wouldn't fix anything for me."

Maru revises her will whenever she wants to. She believes: "You have to be prepared, especially when you're by yourself. My family is still all in Peru."

Another Augustus member, Diana Artemis, a systems analyst in Washington, D.C., also believes that making out a will is vital.

She realized that she had been working and saving all her life, but if she was hit by a car and died in Virginia, where she lives, and didn't have a will, the state would dictate who would get her property. "I took that really seriously. I thought it was important that my estate go to causes that I believe in."

One cause Diana believes in is fighting needless animal experiments. She worked at a hospital to help pay for college, and it was there that she first saw animals used in research and "scattered about in cages."

She describes one particularly chilling experiment in which holes were drilled into cats' skulls to embed pipes and wires. "One cat I remember in particular was being caged to test effects on his emotions by passing electrical current into different sections of his brain. His one eye was very enlarged and his brain was stimulated with wires to make him feel perpetually angry and frothing at the mouth. I suppose this was some sort of stress test."

Diana managed to adopt one of the cats and take her home. She named the black and white "tuxedo" cat Gillian. In time, Gillian overcame her fear of human beings to some extent but would never allow herself to be picked up, even by Diane.

She says, "There are pictures of me when I was little, petting deer and holding butterflies. I've never thought of animals as inferior beings—they're pals and friends. I could always emotionally connect to them."

Later, Diana had several near-death experiences: She was a captain at the U.S. Air Force headquarters in Germany when it was bombed by terrorists, and she was shot at in an attack against American tourists while on vacation in Peru. Perhaps that's why she says: "Most people don't think about their will, but it is really important to me."

Of course, making PETA a beneficiary in your will, as Diana Artemis has done, is just one option. The important thing is to find the charity or charities you wish to remember beyond your lifetime and, while you are of sound mind, to formalize your ability to live on through your good works, now.

RESOURCES

Consult with an attorney who will listen to what you want to do and give you advice fitting your particular situation. The following words can generally be used to make a bequest:

I give, devise, and bequeath to People for the Ethical Treatment of Animals, Inc., federal tax identification number 52-1218336, with the permanent address of PO Box 42516, Washington, DC 20015 (or other charity you wish to name), the sum of $ ____________ (or describe the real or personal property or portion of the estate) to be used for its general purposes.

Books

Warda, Mark. *How to Make Your Own Will* (Legal Survival Guides). Naperville Ill.: Sphinx Publishing, 2000.

PART SEVEN

Business and Education

55.

Respecting Life's Lessons in Class: Choosing a Superior Alternative to Dissection

---

What a wonderful bird the frog are!
When he walk, he fly almost;
When he sing, he cry almost.
He ain't got no tail hardly, either:
He sit on what he ain't got almost.

—FRENCH CANADIAN POEM

The clever men at Oxford
Know all that there is to be knowed.
But they none of them know one half as much
As intelligent Mr. Toad.

—KENNETH GRAHAME, *THE WIND IN THE WILLOWS*

My high school biology class was great fun at first. My school was in the mountains and we would go out hiking with our teacher, singing along the paths, stopping at streams, collecting leaves, and drawing flowers. We would sit outside, breathing the oxygen the forest flora gave us, and talk and learn about the workings of the plant world in all its wonder.

Then one day everything changed, and I never wanted to set foot in biology class again.

Our teacher arrived that morning with two mice in a cardboard shoe box under her arm, and a bottle of chloroform in her hand. She put the box down on our lab table and allowed us to look inside. The mice peered up at us great alien beings. I am sure they could only have been worried. Then their heads were stuck in a ball soaked in chloroform and we watched them struggle to stay alive, then stop struggling. My enthusiasm and interest in biology died with them.

If only educational consultant Patricia Trostle had been my teacher. She would never take a scalpel to a mouse or any other animal, thinking it barbaric and needless, and she well knows the importance of nurturing, not destroying, sensitivity in the students she counsels. Like all of us, she is opposed to violence in schools and has amassed chilling evidence that teaching children that life is cheap can be, for some, a precursor to an escalating interest in mutilation. Although these are extreme cases indeed, sociological studies have shown that incarcerated serial killers report enjoying "practicing" by cutting up animals; and Jeffrey Dahmer, the infamous dissector of young men, admitted that dissecting animals in class led him to explore cutting up human beings. We can only wonder what effects, glaring or unseen, these "lessons" have on countless impressionable school kids every day.

Some of the students who call on Patricia are seeking arguments as to why they need not dissect; they want to present their teachers with better options than dissection. "That's a snap," says Patricia, who equips them with everything they need to make their case. Others are upset. They feel weird, "uncool," and alone. Not realizing what would happen in class, some have been traumatized when bits of bloody frog spleen were deliberately wiggled in front of their faces, revolted when the stench of formaldehyde hit their nostrils, or demoralized when their teacher told them to "stop being a sissy" and "dig in" to the corpse on the slab.

Patricia gives students the courage and the encouragement

they need not to go along with classroom cutups in any sense of the term.

"Feeling that dissection is wrong has nothing to do with being afraid or squeamish; for many students, it is a violation of deeply held principles. It is also okay to feel squeamish about doing something you find morally offensive," she says. "We need to teach students to respect the ecosystem and all the diverse forms of life who live in it, not to be bullies who seize and cut up animals simply to see how they tick."

If she shows any impatience, it is with the excuse that "animals are already dead when they arrive in the classroom." Animals used for dissection come from sources such as animal shelters, and most are killed by the crudest and cheapest methods. Frogs are pulled from their ponds and drowned in chemicals; rabbits and cats may have been crammed into a crude gas chamber. None of them had a pleasant death.

For very young students, Patricia uses the lessons of Hope Buyukmihci, whose wildlife advocacy and creation of the very first beaver sanctuary in the U.S. is deeply respected. She says, "Go out into the woods and imagine what it must be like to dig a home for yourself with only your hands; to find food for your family from just what you see around you. Imagine life with no tap to turn on, no refrigerator to open, no supermarket to drive to, no tools, no roof over your head, and no car or bicycle to use. Not even a school or library. Then ask yourself if animals deserve your respect."

Perhaps her favorite freebie for kids is an alternatives-to-dissection video starring movie and TV star Alicia Silverstone. Silverstone, like Patricia, has a way with kids and knows they can never be talked down to no matter how young they are. She leads them through a journey from the moment an animal is chosen to be killed to the wide array of options available to students looking for a kinder approach to science and biology. These include books, CD-ROMs, computer software that shows human anatomy and virtual dissections, and truly enlightening observational studies of wildlife that can be carried out without encroachment.

"Kids are so open," says Patricia. "They want to know everything. They're like sponges."

Children in grades kindergarten through 12 who attend public school in the following states can just say no to dissection: Pennsylvania, Maryland, Florida, New York, Illinois, Rhode Island, California, and Louisiana. These states have dissection choice laws in place. Private schools, colleges, and universities are not covered by those laws, but students can still get an alternative. They simply have to ask for it the right way.

Regardless, whether a student or a teacher wishes to change from dissection to a superior learning and teaching method, all it usually takes is a request. There have been exceptions. For instance, sixth-grade student Laurie Wolff was told that if she didn't cut up an earthworm in class, her grade would plummet from A to C.

Laurie wrote letters to her principal and the superintendent and to school board members. She made phone calls and talked to teachers and students. Her work paid off when the Clark County, Nevada, School District—one of the largest in the country, with 277 schools—passed a "student choice" policy. From then on, students have been able to decide for themselves whether or not to dissect.

So, should there be resistance—from teachers, administrators, or even from a parent—kind and knowledgeable professionals like Patricia Trostle are waiting to lend a guiding hand. As Patricia is happy to note, "There has never been a case where kindness didn't win the day."

RESOURCES

Guide to Animals and the Dissection Industry
www.peta.org
Patricia Trostle
patriciat@peta.org
757-622-7382

Classroom Cutups, narrated by Alicia Silverstone
available from peta.org

The Alternatives in Education Database

From the Association of Veterinarians for Animal Rights and the Norwegian Inventory of Audiovisuals (NORINA), contains thousands of alternatives to animal use in education.

American Anti-Vivisection Society

AAVS's educational division is Animalearn.
800-729-2287
www.aavs.org

Humane Society of the United States

Balcombe, Jonathan, Ph.D. *Animals in Higher Education: Problems, Alternatives, and Recommendations.* An in-depth overview of the entire issue.

National Anti-Vivisection Society

800-888-6287
www.navs.org

New England Anti-Vivisection Society

The NEAVS's educational division is the Ethical Science and Education Coalition (ESEC).
617-367-9143
www.neavs.org

56.

Getting Through Medical School with a Clear Conscience

The only thing a student can do in a dog lab that we don't cover in the operating room is kill the animal.

—DR. MICHAEL D'AMBRA, THE CARDIAC ANESTHESIOLOGIST WHO DIRECTS HARVARD'S OPERATING ROOM PROGRAM

Some years back, a young man stood on the beach in Mexico, dressed in shorts and a T-shirt. He was looking into the calm turquoise waters, watching the antics of the cigar fish swimming near the surface. When he turned around, the American strolling in his direction along the waterline saw that he was wearing a T-shirt with an animal rights slogan on it.

"I like your shirt!" the stroller said. "Wish I could wear one of those."

"Why can't you?"

"Oh, I'm a doctor back in the States," said the man. "I'd be hung, drawn, and quartered."

"But I'm a doctor back in the States too," said the man in the T-shirt. "I bet I know some of your colleagues who feel as you do about animals and you just don't know it."

The two men stood and chatted, and the stroller learned that they did indeed have mutual acquaintances, fellow doctors who were as interested in protecting animals as they were.

The man in the T-shirt was Dr. Neal Barnard, founder of the Physicians Committee for Responsible Medicine (PCRM), an organization dedicated to helping medical students get their training and doctors pursue research, all without violating the Hippocratic oath of "First, do not harm."

Since his medical training at George Washington University, when students were required to use dogs and pigs and other animals, things have changed drastically. Today, medical students all over the country are learning about medicine in the species they will ultimately diagnose and treat, the human being.

Harvard University Medical School made the switch because of a medical student named Rachel Freelund. Rachel went into medicine because she wanted to save lives, never dreaming that she would be asked to take them. Like all first-year medical students, Rachel was expected to participate in "dog lab." The purpose was to see firsthand how certain drugs affect the body. The students were to anesthetize a dog, slice open his chest, and watch the reaction of his beating heart as various drugs were given.

At the end of the "exercise," the healthy dog would be killed.

Horrified, and believing there had to be a better way, Rachel went to her instructor, who told her that she would definitely not be forced to do the lab if she thought it unethical. So Rachel went to the Physicians Committee for Responsible Medicine, and they worked with her to come up with a simple, inexpensive, and more effective way to learn about drugs and the heart.

Thanks to Rachel's perseverance, Harvard medical students can now go to Boston area hospitals and observe heart bypass surgeries on human patients. Dr. Michael D'Ambra, the cardiac anesthesiologist who directs Harvard's operating room program, was very open and understanding. He says that seeing human surgery helps students understand the human physiology they need to know.

The majority of medical schools in North America have now done away with animal labs (they are illegal in the UK), and many schools have computer models that even bleed and vomit. The best thing about them is that if a student inadvertently "kills" the patient, he or she can start all over again, something impossible in an animal lab.

Says Rachel, "It was such a privilege to be in the operating room where someone was being given life and being healed, compared to being in the dog lab where you were taking a life."

Rachel is surely the epitome of what a doctor should be: caring, compassionate, and innovative.

RESOURCES

Physicians Committee for Responsible Medicine

202-686-2210

www.pcrm.org

Directing medical students and medical schools to computer models, CD-ROMs, videos, interactive video discs, and more.

57.

Becoming a Kind Veterinarian

Kinship with all life must be expressed with action, since belief is no longer enough.

—MICHAEL W. FOX, PH.D., B.VET.MED., AUTHOR OF *BETWEEN ANIMAL AND MAN*

The veterinary school at the University of California at Davis sits on a huge, sprawling, flat campus in a rather ugly whitish-colored building. Believe it or not, it was, not long ago, quite a lonely place for any student who cared deeply about animals and wished to help, not hurt, them.

Some veterinarians who graduate from UC Davis's vet school end up as rodeo vets or catering to the cattle business. Others go into private practices that are run factory-line style, "processing" as many patients as quickly as possible, with the main goal being to make and keep the business profitable. Not so for one graduate: "Dr. Ned," who today runs a sanctuary for more than four hundred snow monkeys—all brought to the U.S. from Japan by researchers and then abandoned when their research funds ran out—as well as for rescued baboons and vervet monkeys.

Dr. Ned's full name is Nedim Buyukmihci, and he, perhaps more than any other person, has changed how veterinary students in the U.S. are trained. Of course, there were other veterinary students in other schools who had to put up their own fights for change, some who even sued their schools in order to receive an education without having to violate animal rights or their own ethical code. However, when Dr. Ned took a teaching post at UC Davis, he got a bit of a surprise, and so did the school. Nothing has been the same since.

Dr. Ned's attitude must, in part, be attributed to experiences in his childhood. He grew up on a six-hundred-acre refuge for beavers and other wildlife run by his mother, Hope. She was a naturalist and artist and spent hours in the woods, drawing and studying indigenous plants and animals. The refuge and its lively ponds meant everything to her, and by the time he reached high school, Ned had learned not only that beavers are immensely clever engineers and wonderful parents but that they enjoy listening to the flute. He had watched bluebirds build their nests in the spring and listened to his mother telling true tales of foxes, toads, and waterfowl to visiting groups of schoolchildren. Naturally, the family had become vegetarian.

Wanting to help animals, young Ned went to vet school. He was trained in what was then the traditional way, by killing dogs in practice surgeries and treatments. Yet a voice inside him told him there had to be a better way. And by the time Dr. Ned became a veterinary ophthalmology instructor, he had found it.

"They used to bring dogs over to our class from the vivarium [the central holding place for animals used in experiments]," he says. "Eye procedures were done on them and then they'd be returned, to be used again and again."

Appalled, Dr. Ned had students bring in their own animals and learn simple diagnostic tests on them. There was a lot of tail wagging, a lot of treats. The students enjoyed it.

Says Dr. Ned: "It was eye-opening for the students. They got to feel what their clients would feel as they were doing certain tests on their animals."

But when the school learned that Dr. Ned allowed his students an alternative to live animal experimentation, they dismissed him from the course, worried that he was setting a precedent and that the end of all terminal surgery would follow.

Dr. Ned persisted, refusing to perform any experiments on animals, risking ridicule and even being subjected to an attempt to fire him for being a "radical."

In the end, Dr. Ned won the day, as well as the abiding respect of every kind student. Having claimed initially that it was impossible to use alternatives to terminal surgery, the school now uses cadavers and even performs spay and neuter surgeries for the local dog pound rather than take dogs from that pound and kill them, as they once did.

His advice to students: "Get into school and, once you are there, don't compromise your values at all. Don't rationalize even for a second. That's what I did and I still have nightmares about what I did in vet school. Seek help from people like me who have been there before you. Fortunately, schools are much more enlightened today because good students have made for good teaching practices." What a wonderful role model!

RESOURCES

The API Primate Sanctuary

c/o Animal Protection Institute
PO Box 22505
Sacramento, CA 95822
916-447-3085
www.api4animals.org
Snow monkey sanctuary in Dilley, Texas.

Association of Veterinarians for Animal Rights

PO Box 208
Davis, CA 95617-0208

530-759-8106
www.avar.org
Publishes a useful newsletter; provides support for veterinary students and veterinarians who view animals as worthy of respect; promotes alternatives to animal experiments and practices such as declawing.

Unexpected Wildlife Refuge
PO Box 765
Newfield, NJ 08344-0765
856-697-3541
www.animalplace.org
Beaver and wildlife sanctuary of Dr. Ned's childhood. Books available, donations appreciated.

58.

Investing in Green and Animal-Friendly Companies

Money is better than poverty, if only for financial reasons.

—WOODY ALLEN

Money can't buy you friends, but you do get a better class of enemy.

—SPIKE MILLIGAN, ENGLISH RADIO ACTOR

Where does the money go? That age-old question takes on added meaning when we talk about not just spending it but doing something useful with what is left over, that is, investing.

Ethical investing usually means screening companies to see if they meet certain criteria, for example, are they "green," do they make armaments, do their products contribute to cruelty to animals or children, are they mixed up in sweatshops in developing countries or the rape of forests and habitat, or do they make unhealthy goods, the kinds that threaten people's lungs or lands?

Trillium Asset Management's Stephanie Leighton says ethical investors have many different criteria but the same bottom line. For example, one investor who runs a Doberman rescue group didn't want to invest in pharmaceutical companies, so Ms. Leighton guided her to HMOs to get health care exposure and growth without testing on animals. Another of her clients, Angela Warton, from Maine, switched to Trillium after "freaking out" when her previous investment managers bought Saks Fifth Avenue stock. Saks has a fur salon, and Angela is adamantly opposed to fur ranching and trapping.

"Clients tell us what issues concern them," Ms. Leighton says, "and we find the stocks that work. We have a social questionnaire that we ask people to fill out to identify their concerns."

Ms. Leighton says that if a client wishes to be fastidious on animal rights issues, that excludes only 5–7 percent of the S&P 500 list of companies from his or her consideration, companies like racetracks and drug-testing corporations, which is pretty good going.

Angela Warton says, "My friends, from the beginning, told me I was crazy, that I would never make money, that socially responsible stocks wouldn't produce. However, I have weathered the stock market storm better than some of my friends!"

Ms. Leighton substitutes "offensive" medical stocks with ones like Lifeline, the company that makes bracelets that contain your medical history and which some elderly people wear in case of an accident. Trillium not only surveys companies over their practices but seeks out corporations that are actively trying to protect animal rights and the environment, such as vegetarian food companies and growth hormone–free foods, and companies that are perfecting technologies to replace crude and cruel animal tests.

Trillium's specialists also introduce shareholder resolutions, for example, to keep corporations from developing the Arctic National Wildlife Refuge and to phase out the use of chlorine and chlorine-containing compounds used as bleaches. They ask companies to reduce their emission of greenhouse gasses and to step up their use of renewable energy too.

In 1993 Trillium became the first social investment firm to file a shareholder resolution on the issue of farm animal welfare. Working with Animal Rights International, the firm helped persuade McDonald's to adopt its very first policy regarding the humane treatment of farm animals. Now Trillium is also working with PETA to push McDonald's to apply these standards globally, instead of just in North America and the UK.

Trillium is not alone. Calvert Funds is one of the major brokerage firms and investment houses that cater to consumers who wish to do something with their money to contribute to positive growth in more than the traditional sense of the term, who want to see old-growth trees left standing, owls and all, and desire no role in helping strip-mine the valleys or pour pollutants from tanneries or canneries into someone's water source.

Rocky Mountain Humane Investment is one of the small companies devoted solely to such ethical investing. While you have to look carefully yourself to see if a particular company seems right to you, and offers the degree of screening and attention you want, RMHI pledges to offer only stocks that meet certain humane and environmental criteria, eliminating "offending industries" like nuclear, tobacco, and major oil and chemical industries. No stock is included if the business behind it tests on animals, uses animals in entertainment, or is linked to weaponry, fast food, factory farming, or the "extractive" industries, such as paper, oil, and gas drilling and refining.

Where we put our money *does* make a difference and can have a meaningful effect on what future generations of all species will inherit.

RESOURCES

Keep in mind that, as with any sort of investing, there are inherent risks in ethical investing—whatever the fund or other investment vehicle. The following are some additional resources for you to consider and explore as you determine whether this form of investment is appropriate for you.

Coop America's Socially Responsible Mutual Funds
www.coopamerica.org

Trillium Asset Management
www.trilliuminvest.com

The Calvert Fund

www.calvert.com

Calvert's environmental standards are not as stringent as some, but they bill their program as "multidimensional, covering both stated policies and actual performance." They do not invest in nuclear power plant operators, owners, or contractors because of concerns that the technology is not environmentally or economically viable. They also look for companies that have implemented innovative programs to prevent pollution and protect natural resources, with a view to sustainable development.

Rocky Mountain Humane Investment

800-962-1980

www.greeninvestment.com

Smith Barney

Socially responsible investment section.

800-345-3050

www.smithbarney.com

59.

Making Your Workplace a Healthy, Helping Place

A man is known by the company he organizes.

—AMBROSE BIERCE

We've learned how to make a living, but not a life.

—NEW AGE WISDOM

Every working person spends one-seventh of his or her life on Mondays.

—ANONYMOUS

If you own your own business, you can do what Jeanne Daniels did and insist on all the changes you want, but if you work for someone else, there's still a lot you can achieve. Ms. Daniels owns the Tarrytown Shopping Center in Austin, Texas, and, some years back, having come to realize how destructive some of our buying habits are, she decided to stop renewing leases and not to rent to anyone new unless the shop owners agreed not to sell anything that wasn't earth- and animal-friendly. Said Ms. Daniels, "I was always taught to live up to my convictions. I didn't want to have a wishbone where a backbone ought to be!"

No matter what our jobs, we spend much of our lives at work, so it is comforting to realize that there are opportunities galore to make that second home more progressive and humane. In chapter 65: "Selecting a Lifesaver Health Charity" (page 327), I mention how some companies like Jamba Juice and Sara Lee have made sure that no money they give to charity goes to hurt animals, but let me touch on four other areas in which small changes can have a big impact. Let's look at: what food is served in the cafeteria or at nearby favorite lunch spots; what paper goes into the copier; whether the company has a matching gifts program; and if it is involved in such community-oriented programs as blood drives or collecting dog and cat food for shut-ins and others who get charity meals delivered to their homes. We don't have to go over the top to make sure our company does at least one or two things that make it a better place to be, but it may well thank you for the improvements.

Everyone eats! And what our associates eat is important for their health and the output of the enterprise they work for. U.S. Department of Labor statistics show that, hazardous jobs aside, American industry loses $32 billion and 132 million workdays every year because of employees' premature deaths that are associated with cardiovascular disease (high blood pressure, heart attack, stroke, diabetes, and obesity). The amount of work time lost to doctor's appointments and illness due to these diseases is even higher. These are all diet-related diseases, so you can actually improve workplace attendance by revolutionizing the workplace cafeteria with healthy meals (see the Gold Plan for institutional kitchens, below).

If your workplace does not have a cafeteria, the managers of restaurants close by are likely to be pleased to hear from you (not in the time leading up to or during lunchtime, but when they're slowing down!) with a sensible suggestion of, say, which zero-cholesterol, low-fat veggie burgers, bean burritos, or sliced vegan lunch "meats" their business could carry. For example, they may not realize that all they have to do is keep a box of veggie "pockets"—like Dilberitos, those tasty Mexican, Italian, and other flavored ones (made by Scott Adams, creator of Dilbert, the ultimate office expert)—in the freezer, then simply zap them in the microwave upon demand.

It helps their business and it's good for their customers' arteries. The icing on the carrot cake can be that you volunteer to put the word out as soon as the health-conscious fare is on their specials board or printed menu.

Does your office recycle? It's simple enough to do, and the community is always looking to list which companies have joined in and will even publicize how many pounds (or tons) of recycling you achieve in a year. Tell the boss: using one ton of paper takes up 3.3 cubic yards of landfill space, 4,100 kilowatt-hours of electricity (enough to heat a home for six months), 3,700 pounds of lumber, and 24,000 gallons of water! One ton of *recycled* paper, on the other hand, uses 64 percent less energy and 50 percent less water, causes 74 percent less air pollution, saves seventeen trees, and creates five times more jobs than one ton of paper from virgin pulp wood. That's money in the bank.

New Leaf Paper (see below) leads the paper industry in the development and distribution of environmentally superior printing and office papers. They use high postconsumer recycled content, and most of their papers are whitened without chlorine or chlorine compounds.

Earth University recommends Banana and Coffee Paper notebooks and journals, made from, yes, bananas and coffee fibers, a natural by-product of Costa Rican Industry.

Lots of companies have matching-gift programs to encourage personnel to be generous to those in need. Your gift to save a forest or to feed a hungry child in Appalachia or closer to home can be doubled if you can persuade the company to follow in the footsteps of companies as different from each other as Avon and the *Washington Post.*

Another idea is to organize a blood drive, enlisting everyone to sponsor or participate in an activity for charity. Perhaps you can find out which SPCA or humane society is trying to alleviate the local homeless dog and cat problem by carrying out low-cost or free spay/neuter surgeries. Just print out a signup form and decide what you'll do to raise the money, for example, take a "polar plunge" during winter, or climb a local hill or a faraway peak. Corporations pay big money to develop a team spirit, but you can do it for them free of charge and in no time at all!

Another way to help is to link up with your local Meals on Wheels. Some of these excellent programs to feed the elderly and disabled, like the one in Tarrant County, Texas, have come to realize that an alarming number of their clients—who anxiously await that one daily meal—have an only friend in the world who shares it with them, their precious dog or cat. This meal sharing could have very serious consequences for both the primary clients and their animals, as their isn't much to go around from a little tray, delivered just once a day.

In many areas, there is no program to help, but in Tarrant County, Meals on Wheels linked up with Little Orphan Angels Animal Rescue, a local nonprofit animal welfare agency, and developed a new program, called Kibbles and Catnip, which supplies dog and cat food free of charge to Meals on Wheels clients who have animal companions and need assistance. Perhaps your company would like to do the same!

RESOURCES

New Leaf Paper

www.newleafpaper.com

The mission of New Leaf Paper is to be the leading national source for environmentally responsible, economically sound paper for business uses.

Roaring Spring Paper Products

800-441-1653

Distributors of Banana and Coffee Paper products.

Paper Recycling Online

www.recycle.cc/freepaper.htm

The Gold Plan

www.pcrm.org

Meals for institutions and workplace cafeterias.

Dilberito

www.dilberito.com

Healthy frozen fast "office" foods.

American Red Cross

www.pleasegiveblood.org

For help with organizing blood drives.

Meals on Wheels Inc. of Tarrant County

817-336-0912, ext. 14

Helping the hungry of all species.

Little Orphan Angels Animal Rescue

Keller, Texas

817-741-2386

www.littleorphanangels.org

PAWS

Seattle, Washington

516-364-PAWS

60.

Doing Good Business: Embracing Ethical Ideas in the Marketplace

The last stage of fitting the product to the market is fitting the market to the product.

—CLIVE JAMES, *THE OBSERVER*

Because you like nice things.

—SLOGAN OF THE CAROL HOUSE FURNITURE STORE, ST. LOUIS MISSOURI

This little business success story is just one among many, but it shows that where's there's an interest in helping a company change with the times while sticking with traditional values of honesty and integrity, there is a way.

Nathan Dubman came to the U.S. from Poland when he was ten years old. A born salesman, as soon as he was old enough to do so, he started walking door to door in Valley Park, Missouri, selling household wares. In time Nathan Dubman bought a truck and expanded his bailiwick. By 1964 he had enough money to open a real furniture store. Carol House, as it was called, was a tiny showroom back then, but by the time Nathan Dubman passed away in 2001, it was a household name in Missouri and a place where a customer might have to carry a compass so as not to get lost in its seventy-five thousand square feet of floor space.

When Amy Dubman and her brother Brook took over the business, they knew that they would make changes. Nathan Dubman's father had been a cattle rancher, and Nathan had never understood what Amy and Brook call "the animal thing." Their mother, however, had nurtured the kids' strong empathy toward all animals since they were born. When they decided to make the biggest change in Carol House ever by going leather free, she "thought it was wonderful!"

When Amy and Brook took inventory, they found that Carol House had over $3 million tied up in leather—sofas, love seats, desktops, dining room chairs—but no matter, they couldn't find it within themselves to continue to support the slaughter business. They added rugs to help compensate for the loss.

The Dubmans employ 140 people, part of whose take-home pay comes from commission. How would they take the switch?

Amy and Brook invited a PETA speaker to come and explain all the problems with leather (see chapter 16: "Shoe Shopping," page 75), including showing a heart-wrenching video. It was mandatory viewing for all employees.

Says Brook, "We were so happy to have the opportunity to show the staff what we were thinking, and we could see that watching what happens to animals, and the effect of leather on the environment, had an effect on them. They know we made our decision for ethical reasons, but we know it makes good business sense too. We felt so good giving them the whole story, and asking them to join us in seeing that today's synthetics have the feel and durability that consumers demand without costing the animals an arm and a leg."

Although the Dubman family shunned publicity, soon after the switch a columnist for the *St. Louis Post-Dispatch* picked up on the story. Then a couple of radio stations called. Amy says, "My dad was dearly loved. He treated people fairly and honestly and people enjoyed being around him. Even when people were irate, our dad would talk to them and they would melt like butter." How would his children fare in the public spotlight? The consensus of the community: "They're noble."

The Dubmans' example shows that people in business for themselves can make huge changes and incorporate ethical considerations into their companies. The rest of us can also participate in this positive trend by finding ways to tweak or change the practices, even the basis business, of the companies we work for. It just takes a desire to see an end to practices that, under scrutiny, should raise our eyebrows in the twenty-first century.

As Amy and Brook Dubman say, "We felt so strongly about not supporting factory farming, we would have done it sooner if we could have. Now, we wake people up every day to what is going on and the options they can choose from, simply by running our store. It's been terrific!"

RESOURCES

Carol House Furniture
Valley Park, MO 63088-1698
636-225-3666 or 529-0550

PART EIGHT

Health

61.

Trying to Keep Our Loved Ones Alive and Healthy a Little Longer

"I understand," said a member of a posh London club, objecting to the poet Thomas Moore's application for membership, "that your father was a shopkeeper. How very interesting. May I enquire why you didn't follow in his footsteps?"

"Because my talents were limited," said Moore, adding, "I have heard that your father was a gentleman. May I ask why you haven't followed in his footsteps?"

—THOMAS MOORE, FROM *LIFE OF SIR THOMAS MOORE* BY WILLIAM ROPER

An ounce of prevention is worth a pound of cure.

—*ANONYMOUS*

My father had the dry sense of humor of an English elder statesman and I rather think he would have enjoyed Moore's rebuttal. But my father has gone and I will never be able to read him those lines.

In my closet are my father's medals from World War II, when he fought with the Black Watch in France; the pictures of him, as a boy, playing with Mickey, the mixed beagle he loved; the wedding announcement of his marriage to my mother; and the notebooks that constitute his memoirs of the oil-exploration years he spent on a dhow in the Persian Gulf, and catching sea turtles in the weeks leading up to the big bomb test on Easter Island.

I think he sometimes didn't really know what to do with a daughter. I have a photograph of us sitting together on the running board of the family car when I was about seven years old. The two of us look like characters out of a Monty Python skit: We are wearing handkerchiefs on our heads to keep the sun from burning our scalps, and my father is teaching me to spit out cherry pits in a straight line. At other times, he took me clambering over the rocks in the south of England and taught me to pick mussels, how to remove their poisonous beards and how to steam them in vinegar over a camping stove. My father also tried to teach me to drive by instructing me on how to repair a crank shaft or some such mystery car part. I remember staring at the oil-covered diagrams, when all I wanted was to put the car in D and head for the beach.

This clever and fearless man who relished danger somehow survived typhoid, German gunners, the sinking sands of the Little Rann of Kachchh in India, and hurricane conditions at sea in his little boat off the Gulf Coast. Yet his downfall was that he lived dangerously at the table. He had been raised on meat and relished it all, from calves' liver to steak. He drank a glass of whole milk each night before he went to bed and always stopped the car if he spotted an ice cream parlor.

My father suffered an attack of gout; then came a stroke, then another. His arteries hardened and pain gripped his chest. In the end, he was a very frustrated man with a razor-sharp mind trapped inside a failed body. No amount of medication could open up the arteries to his heart and brain, the flow of blood to his feet. But that could have come from a diet like Dr. Dean Ornish's regimen of vegan food, moderate exercise, and stress reduction, a diet proven to reverse plaques and lower cholesterol to the 150 mark—the magic number at and below which no one has been known to die of a heart attack.

One day, I predict that the meat and dairy industries' alluring ads will be replaced with judgments against them and forced admissions that meat and milk are addictive, as many binge-eaters' experiences suggest. People acquire more than a casual taste for the stuff, a fact borne out when you see someone seemingly unable to break the habit, no matter that their bodies have become overweight and their health has deteriorated. They cannot miss the barrage of news stories about the ill-health consequences of the bacon and egg breakfast or the cheese pizza topping, and they turn a blind eye to the sight and plight of animals intensively farmed, inhumanely transported, and prodded to their deaths.

I know that some people resent having veganism "shoved down their throats," no matter how pleasantly one raises the issue. But I also know that if I could turn back the clock, I'd far rather have a dirty look than have lost my father.

If your father is heading down the same road mine trod, perhaps some dietary advice, sent with a loving note or simply left on his favorite chair, might help persuade him to stay around for a little longer.

RESOURCES

Dr. Dean Ornish's Lifestyle Program for Heart Disease Reversal

Preventive Medicine Research Institute
900 Bridgeway
Sausalito, CA 94965
415-332-2525
www.pmri.org

Dr. Ornish uses a regimen of diet, moderate exercise, stress management, and social support that allows patients to lose weight while eating more, to reduce or discontinue their medicines, and to diminish their chest pain.

The Physicians Committee for Responsible Medicine

5100 Wisconsin Ave. NW, Suite 400
Washington, DC 20016
202-686-2210
www.pcrm.org

Providing dietary information to reduce high blood pressure and the risk of various cancers, heart attack, and stroke, as well as to prevent and treat diabetes. A wide range of books and materials available on health issues.

Books and Video

Barnard, Neal, M.D. *Breaking the Food Seduction: The Hidden Reasons Behind Food Cravings . . . and 7 Steps to End Them Naturally.* New York: St. Martin's Press, 2003.

Barnard, Neal, M.D. *Eat Right, Live Longer: Using the Natural Power of Foods to Age-Proof Your Body.* New York: Harmony Books, 1995. Also available on videotape.

62.

Breast Cancer: Steps to Prevent It and Finding Friends and Support

I kept repeating their words . . . it will be okay, you will make it, be strong, we're here for you, right up to the moment the anesthesia took over.

—ELAINE KEEVE-SLOANE, BREAST CANCER SURVIVOR

Breast tumors are "fueled" by estrogens and on high-fat diets, estrogen levels increase.

—"FAT AND HORMONAL EFFECTS," PHYSICIANS COMMITTEE FOR RESPONSIBLE MEDICINE

Elaine Keeve-Sloane is one of the "short-straw gals"—the one in every nine women in the U.S. who are diagnosed with breast cancer. A busy advertising agency executive who lives in Manhattan, Elaine was diagnosed with breast cancer in 1992. She had resolved to go to a breast doctor every six months when, one day, she reports: "I'd made an appointment for a routine mammogram at lunchtime. When the radiologist came in and said, 'I think there's something there,' I felt absolutely sick and frightened beyond belief!"

Elaine underwent a radical mastectomy and radiation therapy. She found the radiation therapy easy to get through.

Elaine is an activist. She works to convince breast cancer charities to spend their funds on human-need programs and prevention and to persuade them to move away from old-fashioned reliance on animal tests. She has learned a lot in the course of her cancer experiences and has ridden the roller coaster of emotions that follow the first detection of an abnormality, moving from disbelief to shock to panic to having to make life-and-death decisions.

Elaine wanted to know how she could have reduced the odds and was surprised to learn that fatty foods contribute significantly to risk. She read about a study, published in the *Journal of the National Cancer Institute,* of more than 90,000 premenopausal women that found that consuming the animal fats in red meat and dairy dramatically increased a woman's chance of breast cancer. On the other hand, vegetable fats, such as olive oil, do not increase this risk, according to the study. The Harvard School of Public Health concluded in 1996, after distilling virtually the entire body of research into cancer's causes, that nearly 70 percent of cancers can be attributed to smoking, eating, and drinking habits and a sedentary lifestyle. Only 2 percent are traceable to environmental pollution and 10 percent to genetics.

According to Dr. John McDougall, who runs the Center for Wellness, "The Harvard report is an antidote to the fatalistic feeling people have that 'everything causes cancer.' Because there are no drawbacks or side effects from improving your diet and lifestyle, these changes should be made immediately, and to the greatest degree."

Dr. McDougall says: "Breast cancer serves as an enlightening example of how, with the right information, we can change our future health. The risk of breast cancer varies worldwide among populations of people who live and eat differently. The strongest contact we have with our environment is our food—we take in one to five pounds of it a day for breakfast, lunch, and dinner. Women living in Japan, eating a diet based on rice, have one-sixth the risk of cancer as women in the U.S. Women who change their diet to rich foods while living in Japan, or move to the U.S. and make that change, increase their risk of breast cancer dramatically. In the U.S. the highest rates of breast cancer are among affluent women, with a lifetime risk of one in seven."

Elaine believes strongly in lowering the odds by educating women not to eat fatty foods that unbalance the body's natural hormones, impair immunity, and accelerate cancer cell growth; and she advocates dealing with menopause naturally too, partly by eating soy—epidemiologists believe that the reason there is no Japanese word for "hot flashes" is because of all the soy in the low-fat Japanese diet—as well as yams and herbs rather than taking hormone replacement therapy, which she considers dangerous (see chapter 64: "Dealing with Menopause Without Hormone Replacement Therapy," page 321). She gets her beta-carotene not in pill form but in the best possible way, from carrots, kale, spinach, and whatever else nature packages it in. She also takes vitamins C and E and selenium to boost her immune system, and she gets rid of excess estrogen with a fibrous diet that includes beans and grains. Elaine's dog helps her get vigorous "lopes" through the park.

Elaine has come to treasure her life since her brush with cancer and believes that all living beings should be permitted to enjoy their lives too, rather than being ground up in breast cancer experiments. When Elaine heard that a university near her home was using mice in cancer research, she was livid. "They should be doing human epidemiological studies," she says.

Elaine feels that the National Cancer Institute recommendations are weak and that women need to take control of their bodies and do far more to prevent cancer than just reduce their fat to less than 30 percent of calories, the NCI's recommendation. She says adamantly, "That kind of advice leaves women thinking they're safe, and they're definitely not!"

Elaine works both independently and with the Physicians Committee for Responsible Medicine's Cancer Project to promote good health and to get cancer research funds channeled into women's health projects and away from animal tests. She is also indebted to support groups like the organization SHARE, the Self Help for

Women with Breast and Ovarian Cancer. Through SHARE women pool their experiences with others who are in, or have been in, the same boat. Elaine considers it a godsend that after her first surgery, she found cancer survivors through SHARE, women whose advice caused her to fire a physician who, having discovered more cancerous cells in her breast, told her not to worry about them, he'd "watch" them, something Elaine realizes meant they could have spread throughout her body!

As Elaine says, shared experiences are more than information exchanges: "When I meet women who've had breast cancer, I feel a certain connection. We know where we've been. There's an instant bond."

One other woman I must mention is Ruth E. Heidrich, Ph.D. Diagnosed with breast cancer at forty-seven, Ruth became a vegan that year. She also started a vigorous exercise program and has gone on to win at least four gold medals (it could be five by the time you read this!) in the sixty-plus group of the Senior Olympics. She looks great in a track suit!

Not only did she lick cancer, but she increased her bone density from 447, at age fifty, to 466 by the time she reached sixty.

Ruth has written a marvelous, inspiring book about her experience that makes great reading for anyone worried about cancer survival. So women unite: Ruth and Elaine have shown that cancer can be overcome with a positive and truly healthy approach to life!

RESOURCES

SHARE

1501 Broadway
New York, NY 10036
866-891-2392
www.sharecancersupport.org

The Cancer Project

Physicians Committee for Responsible Medicine
212-686-2210
www.pcrm.org

McDougall Wellness Center

800-941-7111
office@drmcdougall.com
A ten-day live-in program conducted at the Flamingo Hotel and Resort in Santa Rosa, California, by Dr. John McDougall and his staff.

Books

Barnard, Neal, M.D. *Healthy Eating to Prevent Cancer.* Wiley Publishing, 2002. Available from the Physicians Committee for Responsible Medicine, www.perm.org.

Goldberg, George, J.D. *Enough Already*. Goldberg is a former Harvard Law School professor who carefully researched the literature with his wife after her diagnosis.

Heidrich, Ruth E. *A Race for Life: A Diet and Exercise Program for Superfitness and Reversing the Aging Process* and *The Race for Life Cookbook.* Honolulu: Hawaii Health Publishers, 1990. Available from Hawaii Health Publishers, 1415 Victoria Street #11, Honolulu, HI 96822.

Keon, Joseph, Ph.D. *The Truth About Breast Cancer: A Seven-Step Prevention Plan.* Larkspur, Ca.: Parissound Publishing, 2001.

Guide to Charities

PETA's free "Guide to Charities That Do and Don't Test on Animals" is available from peta.org or by calling 757-622-7382.

63.

Three Little Steps That Can Make All the Difference If You Are a Diabetic

It may well be that avoiding cow's milk would prevent the vast majority of cases of insulin-dependent diabetes.

—NEAL BARNARD, M.D., *FOOD FOR LIFE*

Refuse to be ill.

—EDWARD BULWER-LYTTON

My colleague Mary Beth Sweetland is an insulin-dependent diabetic. As you may know, diabetes is, essentially, starvation. A diabetic's cells want, but can't get, glucose because normal insulin isn't there or isn't working properly.

When she turned twenty-five, Mary Beth had to start taking daily doses of insulin. Quite rapidly, her weight plummeted to just over ninety-five pounds, her vision became blurry, and if she cut herself, she found that she didn't heal well. She was usually hungry, thirsty, and tired, too, which wasn't useful, given her busy job at a brokerage firm in Baltimore.

The injections Mary Beth gave herself caused her to lose muscle mass from her thighs and stomach, and her blood sugar level was a mess. She worried what would ultimately become of her, especially because she had a son, a live-in sister, a widowed mother, and a virtual pack of dogs, her precious "Beagle Boys," who all depended on her to be the family anchor.

Dragging home at night and trying to make dinner while wanting to collapse into bed, Mary Beth would look at Puppy and the other beagles standing in the kitchen, wagging their tails at her, and know that other beagles were in cages in laboratories, being studied in the name of diabetes research. Although little has changed for diabetics since the 1920s other than the discovery of synthetic insulin—which does not cause the side effects of the old pork- and beef-based insulin—and although everything important we have ever learned about diabetes has come from human studies like those of the Pima Indians, beagles still suffer while the cure eludes diabetes patients.

Mary Beth credits three simple things with improving her health and, as she says with enthusiasm, "saving my life!" Today, she has cut her insulin dosage from 50 units a day to only 15. She easily checks her glucose level three to four times a day with a monitor and takes up to four low doses of Humulin, a synthetic, nonanimal insulin that has restored her muscle mass.

She credits the change with a change in her diet. First, she eats lots of beans, peas, green vegetables, and carbohydrates (in studies published in the *American Journal of Clinical Nutrition,* whole grains have been shown to improve insulin sensitivity). Second, she stays miles away from fat—one tiny bag of potato chips can send her glucose sky high! She never touches animal flesh, eggs, or dairy products, which are all riddled with fat, and even avoids vegetable oils. Last, she walks briskly with her dogs or does other exercises for at least thirty minutes a day.

Cheering her on is not only her physician but Matt Mullins, a certified prosthetist from Knoxville, Tennessee, who has countless clients with type 2 or "adult onset" diabetes. Matt makes artificial limbs for a living, and he believes that the most tragic amputees are diabetics who, as he puts it, "have cut off their own legs with a knife and fork" thanks to the traditional Western diet. He knows firsthand that diabetes not only causes heart disease, stroke, blindness, kidney failure, and pneumonia but leads to nerve damage and poor circulation in the feet and legs. About eighty-two thousand people undergo diabetes-related leg and foot amputations a year.

Matt isn't on hand only when the damage is done; he has made it his life's work to help spread the message of prevention. His article called "Would You Pay an Arm and a Leg for a Steak?," which focused on the risks of high-fat diets, has appeared in many publications, including *In Motion,* the Amputee Coalition of America's magazine. In it, he explains that his recipe for diabetes reversal is to shun old-fashioned diets that curbed sugar and starch consumption and switch to a healthful diet that is high in fiber and carbohydrates and low in fat. His favorite quote is from Dr. David Snowdon, chief research scientist of a twenty-one-year dietary study, who said, "In my years of practice, I have never treated a vegan diabetic!"

As for children, researchers theorize that their bodies may reject intact cow's milk protein as a foreign substance and the antibodies produced to destroy the alien invader may also destroy the cells that produce insulin. A study of children in forty countries found that the higher the consumption of cow's milk and other animal products, the greater the chance of developing diabetes. Moreover, a comprehensive review of clinical literature found that early exposure to cow's milk may increase the risk of diabetes 1.5 times. As early as 1994, the American Academy of Pediatrics condensed the information in more than ninety articles and concluded that avoiding cow's milk may delay or prevent diabetes in susceptible individuals.

So, where there is knowledge, there is hope and a chance to reverse or prevent the disease.

RESOURCES

Messina, Mark, and Virginia Messina. *The Dietitian's Guide to Vegetarian Diets*. Boston: Jones and Bartlett Publishers, 2004.
Available through the Physicians Committee for Responsible Medicine, www.pcrm.org.

64.

Dealing with Menopause Without Hormone Replacement Therapy

We are not spiritually unconnected from the drugs we take, or from the pain and suffering that goes into their making.

—ALICE WALKER, AUTHOR

Premarin is a natural hormone if your native food is hay!

—JOEL HARGROVE, M.D., DIRECTOR OF THE VANDERBILT MENOPAUSE CENTER

I don't have headaches anymore, and my energy has bounced back a hundredfold.

—DORIS THOMPSON, RELATING HOW SHE FELT WHEN SHE STOPPED TAKING PREMARIN

I hit menopause when I hit fifty, right on the nose.

Almost the moment I blew out the candles on my birthday cake—a fabulous surprise cake shaped like a Formula One racing car to celebrate my love for racing—I experienced my first hot flash.

Being a vegan reduced the "pits and pinnacles," those hormonal fluctuations that come with the "change of life," but the hot flashes were with me for many months.

I didn't find them too bothersome, although there were embarrassing moments when I suddenly turned red and began perspiring profusely during a meeting, feeling a bit like being caught in the Sahara in a winter sweater. At work, I controlled the thermostat in my office, so that was easy, although I couldn't help but pity the attorney in the next room. Poor man! For almost a year, I wouldn't let the temperature go above fifty degrees, and I discovered that he had covered his vents with cardboard to stop his teeth from chattering.

Other women aren't as lucky.

While I was simply tossing my wet sheets into the washing machine and longing for maid service, Doris Thompson was taking Premarin. The pills had been prescribed by her doctor when she had a hysterectomy, but she wondered why she constantly felt rundown, tired in the morning and tired all day at work, and why by the afternoon her feet had started to swell.

When Doris learned what I will describe below about the hidden ingredient in Premarin, she stopped taking if for ethical reasons and switched to estrogen "supplements" in the form of natural plant estrogens found in soy foods like tofu, tempeh, and soy milk, and in berries, and citrus fruits. She also started taking Pro-Gest, a cream derived from yams, which contain progesterone identical to that made naturally by the human body. Like countless other women, Doris experienced a huge and unexpected health boost. Her energy returned, she lost five pounds "right off the bat," and her headaches disappeared.

It was a few years later that the research reports came out linking hormone replacement therapy (HRT) to serious health problems, findings that rocked the research world and sent women fleeing from a pharmaceutical approach to menopause management. Physicians had to rethink their strategies too. They began exploring and discovering the benefits of plant-derived synthetics; herbs like black cohosh, which has been used for centuries; and vitamin E, and finding them superior to the old drugs, and with far fewer, if any, side effects.

When the National Institutes of Health abruptly pulled Prempro out of the Women's Health Initiative study because of disturbing information on the drug's link to heart attacks and breast cancer, it was also a huge blow to the pharmaceutical company that produces the drug, Wyeth Ayerst, and to its stockholders. It was, however, a great and overdue blessing to those who were taking the pills in the belief that they were doing something good for their bodies.

As Drs. Suzanne Fletcher and Graham Colditz of Harvard Medical School wrote: "The whole purpose of healthy women taking long-term estrogen/progestin therapy is to preserve health and prevent disease. The results of this study provide strong evidence that the opposite is happening."

Luckily, I had always known I would not take HRT, but not simply for reasons of my own health. As unlikely as it sounds, the most widely prescribed HRT drug in use is an estrogen "substitute" called Premarin, and Premarin is an abbreviation for *Pre*gnant *mar*es' ur*in*e! The same ingredient goes into Prempro, Premphrase, and Prempak-C. Some women who have crushed their pills in their hands report that you can smell the horse barn when you do. I don't know about that, but as the actress Dame Judi Dench exclaimed in a jaw-dropping ad for PETA, "I've heard that women do strange things during menopause, but swallow horse urine . . . never!"

The way the urine is collected is, like the ingredient itself, not very pleasant. Tens of thousands of mares are kept pregnant, confined by being tethered in small stalls, face forward, unable to take more than one or two steps, for six months at a clip without being allowed to exercise. The industry claims that on some farms, the mares are exercised every three to four days, but PETA's investigator found that even this anemic claim was untrue on the farm she visited. During this time the mares are also strapped into urine collection bags that often chafe their legs and prevent them from lying down comfortably.

One of the worst things—aside from the lack of movement, which results in swollen joints and other problems—is that the mares are deprived of the normal amount of water they crave during pregnancy. This is so that their collected urine will be concentrated and rich with estrogens.

What happens to the babies is also upsetting. Most of them go to auctions along the Canadian border when they are just a few months old, long-legged and newly separated from their mothers. They whinny in fright, unsure of what is ahead of them in the auction barn where men often poke at them with sharp sticks and electric shock prods as they move them into pens. While some are sold off as "pleasure horses," most are fattened up for slaughter and end up on tables in France and Japan or as dog food.

Few women know that horse urine goes into their pills, but a Zogby International poll showed that 75 percent of all respondents believed that Premarin should be labeled to say that it contains animal waste.

One woman who is trying to make a difference is Andrea Eastman of upstate New York. Andrea, a Hollywood agent, devotes herself to rescuing mares and foals caught up in Premarin production. She could not stop thinking about the plight of the horses after she read a story in PETA's *Animal Times,* and she used her contacts to recruit Robert Redford, Richard Gere, and Sylvester Stallone to take in equine refugees from the horse barns and give them permanent, loving homes on their ranches. Andrea herself has provided sanctuary to many mares and their foals. She will be the first to admit that it is just a drop in the bucket, whereas teaching women to adopt natural ways to deal with menopause is the real key to a healthier, more humane world.

On the other side of the country from Andrea, Marlene Wedin, a bartender and ceramicist, is one of those women. She was changed by menopause in more ways than one.

"I got a flyer about the horses and Premarin," she says. "I was on Premarin at the time, so I was pretty shocked and upset that my doctor didn't tell me about the cruelty of it and give me another choice. I gradually cut back and then stopped taking it. Now I'm drinking soy milk three times a day—chocolate soy milk, you can't tell the difference—and taking vitamins. The soy milk was what helped the hot flashes."

Marlene asks that every woman tell another. In other words, "Pass it on!" Here's what Monique Gilbert calls

A "GET-YOU-STARTED RECIPE FOR THOSE NEW TO TOFU"

Golden Tofu Strips from *Virtues of Soy: A Practical Health Guide and Cookbook* by Monique N. Gilbert (www.virtuesofsoy.com).

5.3 ounces of firm tofu
½ tablespoon of canola oil
¼ teaspoon of salt
¼ teaspoon of turmeric

Cut the tofu into strips about ¼ inch wide and 2 inches long. Heat the canola oil. Add the tofu strips, the salt, and turmeric. Stir to thoroughly coat all sides of the tofu. Cook the strips for about 5 minutes or until golden brown. Serve on top of a salad or on bread with lettuce.

Makes 1–2 servings.

RESOURCES

Books

Barnard, Neal, M.D. *Healthy Eating for Life for Women*. Hoboken, N.J.: Wiley Publications, 2002. Available from the Physicians Committee for Responsible Medicine, www.pcrm.org.

Dean, Carolyn, and Phyllis Herman. *Menopause Naturally*. New York: McGraw-Hill, 1999.

Gilbert, Monique N. *Virtues of Soy: A Practical Health Guide and Cookbook*. Boca Raton, Fla.: Universal Publishers, 2000. Available from www.virtuesofsoy.com.

Gilbert, Monique N., B.Sc. *Coping with Menopause Naturally*. Available from www.geocities.com/virtuesofsoy/book-ordering. This helpful book begins: "The first thing to remember is that menopause is not a disease" and goes on to explain exactly what is happening as hormone levels change and how to deal most comfortably with what is happening to your body.

Help Line

1-800-KNOW-PMU is a help line for women interested in menopause solutions.

Synthetic Estrogen Drugs

The following are some examples of the many FDA-approved synthetic estrogen drugs that are currently available. As with any drugs, there are risks and side effects associated with these, and this list is not intended to treat or serve as a prescription for menopause. When you speak with your physician about your concerns, you should ask whether these or other synthetic alternatives are appropriate for you:

Cenestrin

Estrace

Estraderm

65.

Selecting a Lifesaver Health Charity

Cruelty-free health charities are helping people by funding programs that focus on direct care, clinical studies, community education, and prevention. They truly deserve our support.

—DAME JUDI DENCH FOR PEOPLE FOR THE ETHICAL TREATMENT OF ANIMALS

Real progress is progress in charity, all other advances being secondary thereto.

—ALDOUS HUXLEY, *ENDS AND MEANS*

If the March of Dimes gets hold of her, she'll need all her nine lives.

—ANDREW BUTLER, PETA CAMPAIGNER, REFERRING TO A LOST CAT

Thank goodness for choices, even in the saddest of circumstances.

When my friend's father died, he asked that donations go to a particular charity doing cancer research. I looked that charity up on PETA's pocket reference "Guide to Charities That Do and Don't Test on Animals." It did not carry the "Humane Seal of Approval," so I chose to send a donation to another charity instead. It felt a bit awkward at the time, since I didn't want to broach the subject with him while he was grieving, but when he received the acknowledgment from the other cancer charity, he sent me a note of appreciation.

I was sure that later he would realize the reason I had chosen that organization.

Such choices are important, for some charities, like Easter Seals, Caring for Children and Families with AIDS, the Arthritis Trust of America, the Children's Burn Foundation, the Spinal Cord Injury Network International, the National Children's Cancer Society, the Cancer Project, and the American Association on Mental Retardation, to name just a few, use all their funds on direct care for people, prevention of disease, and finding cures and treatments *without hurting animals*. In my book, and in my checkbook, these are the true lifesavers.

On the other hand, there are "lifetaker" charities that have experimented on animals for years and continue to do so, despite an uproar from donors demanding reforms and a concentration on putting funds where they will do the most good.

When the actress Linda Blair's mother was ill, Linda did some homework and decided which health charities she would support and which not in the quest for a cure. Her conclusion? Says Linda, "If we have a prayer of beating disease, we must stop animal experimenters from siphoning funds from more productive programs and high-tech research."

Some well-known charities are among the worst offenders, sad to say. The March of Dimes, for example, has been under attack from parents, donors, and others for funding horrific experiments at the Oregon Regional Primate Research Center in which mother monkeys wear backpacks filled with instruments and are tethered into their barren steel cages for years, and other experiments in which cats have had their eyes sewn shut when researchers had the option, instead, of studying blind children in their homes.

Once caring people began to find out about the animal tests, donors began either to switch to other, more progressive charities or, as in the case of corporate donors Kmart, Jamba Juice, and Sara

Lee, to make sure, by earmarking donations, that their contributions go only to nonanimal programs and research.

As Debbie Chissell, mother of Brie, a bouncy, energetic toddler, has said, "The values I instill in my daughter, to love animals and respect life, are the same values I insist on when it comes to selecting a charity."

RESOURCES

For a handy pocket reference, "PETA's Guide to Charities that Do and Don't Test on Animals," call PETA at 757-622-7382 or go to www.peta.org.

American Association on Mental Retardation

www.aamr.org

As a strong advocate for people with intellectual disabilities, the AAMR promotes progressive policies, research, and universal human rights. Established in 1876, the AAMR is the oldest and largest organization of professionals and others concerned about mental retardation and related disabilities.

Arthritis Trust of America

www.arthritistrust.org

Arthritis Trust of America provides physician referrals and educational materials to people suffering from rheumatoid diseases, and funds alternative, holistic, nonanimal medical research.

The Cancer Project

www.cancerproject.org

An innovative approach to a medical challenge, this charity aims first to prevent cancer. When cancer has been diagnosed, it works to improve survival. The Cancer Project distributes lifesaving information on reducing cancer risk and, when cancer has been diagnosed, how diet and other factors may help improve survival.

Caring for Children and Families with AIDS

www.4ccfa.org

Caring for Children and Families with AIDS (formerly Caring for Babies with AIDS) provides services to children and families affected by HIV/AIDS and other life-threatening diseases. Established in 1987, the CCFA also promotes public education and advocacy.

Children's Burn Foundation

www.childburn.org

The Children's Burn Foundation provides educational programs and financial assistance to meet the needs of severely burned children and their families and caregivers, including therapeutic and psychological care, and specialized educational and recreational services.

Easter Seals

www.easter-seals.org

Easter Seals provides services to children and adults with disabilities and other special needs, and support to their families. They have been providing therapy, job training, day care, and other services for more than eighty years.

National Children's Cancer Society

www.children-cancer.com

The National Children's Cancer Society provides financial support to children with cancer and their families, as well as support services and education and prevention programs.

Spinal Cord Injury Network International

www.spinalcordinjury.org

The Spinal Cord Injury Network International provides referral services and information to individuals with spinal cord injuries and their families. SCINI facilitates access to quality health care by providing a vital link to organizations and agencies offering information, assistance, and services for those with spinal cord injuries.

PART NINE

Volunteering and Getting Active

66.

Joining the Animal Savings Club

We have multiplied our possessions, but reduced our values.

—ANONYMOUS

Dr. Alka Chandna was looking in a window at the McArthur Center Mall in Norfolk, Virginia, one day when she had a brainstorm. She was standing near a sign that announced the savings on store specials, and holding in her hand her car keys, which had attached to them a little plastic token that identified her as a "supersaver" on specials at a local grocery store.

Suddenly, Alka thought, "What if we create a club for people who shop and spend, which, after all, describes everyone, but a club you join to save *lives* instead of money? Imagine if you could make a difference for the animals every time you bought a shampoo or wrote a check?"

That is how the Animal Savings Club was born.

The reasoning behind Alka's idea is that, amazing though it seems, even the most compassionate people, who dutifully send what they can—a few dollars or a few thousand dollars—to groups fighting to help animals, invariably spend far more, unthinkingly and even unknowingly, on products, goods, and services, even on health charities, that hurt animals. How? By not remembering or realizing that they have shopping choices.

Saving animals can be as easy as swiping a credit card when you buy cruelty-free cosmetics and household items for yourself, your family, and friends.

And if you are preparing to donate to a charity, simply check to make sure it is a "human-helping," not "animal-hurting," organization. You can give your donation even more miles by rewarding cruelty-free organizations and helping compassionate charities flourish (see chapter 65: "Selecting a Lifesaver Health Charity," page 327).

Every dollar you spend can encourage kind treatment of animals and take a bite out of Stone Age companies that still test on animals. It's like voting for compassionate business policies—your dollar is your ballot! You can say yes to progress when you open your wallet.

Members of the Animal Savings Club simply take a pledge—to themselves—to use the "Four C's." They get an ASC tab to put on their key chain and stickers for their checkbooks that remind them of their wealth of choices and how important making the right ones are. They are philanthropic consumers!

The "Four C's" pledge:

1. Charities: I contribute only to those that do not test on animals.
2. Companion animals: I buy only home- or vet-tested "pet food," not brands that confine dogs and cats to laboratories for years.
3. Cosmetics and household products: I buy only those made with no animal ingredients and that are tested in humane nonanimal ways.
4. Colleges and universities: I give only to those that do not fund animal tests.

Dame Anita Roddick, super entrepreneur and famous founder of the Body Shop, says, "In my work and in my life, I have always tried to give people the tools they need to make a difference. My motivation for starting the Body Shop was to give everyday people a way to make change for the better. When we announced 'Against Animal Testing' in our window displays, on our materials, and on our labels, we knew we couldn't shut down laboratories that poisoned animals, but our customers could flex their muscles with their purchases. It turned out to be an incredibly powerful tool for compassion, and we managed to change the law to ban cosmetics tests on animals in England!"

Dame Roddick is a member of the Animal Savings Club. She says, "I am proud to endorse this wonderful, meaningful program. I hope everyone joins!"

Alka's dream is catching on like a house on fire. Animal Savings Club members get real value for every dollar spent, knowing that they are helping make the world a kinder place almost every time they buy or give. A habit like this becomes almost second nature once you get the hang of it. Now *that's* consumer muscle!

RESOURCES

Elsewhere in this book, you'll find chapters that describe the differences between life*saver* and life*taker* charities; give the lowdown on pet food tests and how important it is to train the companies to switch to nonlethal and nonhurtful test practices; describe which ingredients to be on the lookout for and how to get a handy list of companies that do not pour their products into rabbits' eyes, for instance; and finally, a chapter that offers a primer on how to persuade your institution of higher learning to take the moral high ground if it still funds animal research.

The Animal Savings Club

www.animalsavingsclub.com

67.

Sponsoring the Care of a Rescued Animal

Guess she figured on a different life for her child!

—CLYDE JOHNSON, MANAGER OF BLACK CREEK RANCH, A REFUGE FOR RESCUED COWS IN TEXAS, COMMENTING ON A THOUSAND-POUND PREGNANT COW WHO JUMPED THE FENCE TO GIVE BIRTH TO HER CALF ON SANCTUARY SOIL

Do you have time to help me unpack?
There is so much to carry,
So much to regret.
I pray that you do—I'm so tired you see,
But I do come with baggage—
Will you still want me?

—EVELYN COLBATH, "BAGGAGE"

Fred looks as if he were on his way to a costume party. His beak is black, his face is white with peculiar black stripes, his sideburns are bright orange, and his body is a deep azure blue. When he walks, his head bobs up and down as if to music. No one knows exactly how old he is, but Fred, a blue and yellow macaw, arrived at the New Life Parrot Rescue Centre in Cambridgeshire, England, on March 30, 1995. He had been chained by the leg to a small metal stand for nineteen years.

The last nine of those years, Fred and his stand had been moved into a bathroom, so Fred had stood on his twelve-inch perch with nothing to do for all those years. His right eye had developed a cataract from infection caused by his being hit with a newspaper when he cried out. When Fred arrived, he also had innumerable psychological problems from loneliness, boredom, and trauma and was suffering from a calcium and vitamin A deficiency, and his muscles had atrophied to almost nothing.

Can you imagine this, especially knowing that birds like Fred have so many abilities humans once liked to think were unique to our species, such as musical ability (not just singing but composition and appreciation), the ability to form abstract ideas, to figure out tricky problems, and to fall deeply in love?

Today, thanks to the center, and to the caring donors who support Fred, Corky, Pressy, Precious, and all the many other bird refugees—each with a heartbreaking story of his or her own—this highly intelligent, talkative, and social bird, who must hold so many memories of abuse, is healthy and active. Most important, he is safe.

It all started in the 1980s, when an animal protection organization followed the lead of a children's charity and wrote an appeal to anyone interested in whales to please pick a whale from a set of photographs of their unique tails, or flukes, and to "adopt" that whale, at least in name. The program was a huge hit.

Today, the need to sponsor animals in trouble is every bit as great.

People love pigs. Unfortunately, people also love ham. But some people have taken in the lucky pigs who ran from the knife. Among the famous refuge providers are George Clooney and the late Willem de Kooning's daughter, Lisa, who both fell for pigs and kept them in their homes. But you don't have to invite a pig, potbellied or otherwise, or a cow or chicken for that matter, into your home to enjoy their company. Sponsoring a rescued farm animal can bring all the delight, without having to housetrain him!

Poplar Springs farm animal sanctuary is one place to bear in mind. One spring I was giving a talk there, telling jokes and stories about animals, but I was distracted by the vivid colors that leaped to my eye. The lawns were bright green, the barns were bright red, the sky was deep blue, the clouds were white as white could be. Just as a farm might appear in a children's storybook, but nothing like how farms are today. For the way animals are raised by the billions for food, there is no color, there is no prettiness.

It couldn't have been a more perfect day. The guests were delightful, but the stars of the show were the animals, the "ones who got away." Each one seemed happy to be breathing fresh air, aware of the good humor around them, and full of a joie de vivre that must come from almost having your vivre taken away from you! The rescued chickens, many survivors from a farm that had been hit by a hurricane causing the sheds to collapse, were all happily doing "chicken things": preening for the rooster, gossiping among themselves, walking about, looking through the long grass, sunbathing, even flying into the low branches of trees and making comfy nests.

It's easy to sponsor a rescued chicken—and to know that those wattles have your name on them and that the cock crowing at dawn is singing freedom because of your generosity.

Another organization, Farm Sanctuary, runs two shelters, one in upstate New York, the other in California, and you can choose to "adopt" a rescued farm animal, one from a stockyard or a slaughterhouse or even frightened pigs or turkeys who have survived when the trucks in which they were traveling overturned on the highway. Each one is named and loved and looked after for his or her lifetime, an expensive proposition.

Take Alby. Please! He is a Holstein calf who was found abandoned. When the farmer moved away, he left behind a very neglected Alby chained to a small crate in which he was going to be raised for veal. Despite all he's been through, Alby likes being around people and is very sweet and gentle. He lives at Farm Sanctuary's New York shelter.

Opie lives with Alby. He is a much bigger fellow, but he was also abandoned when he was young because he was a "downer" calf, meaning he was so weak that he couldn't walk. Today Opie not only walks but dances to country music.

Farm Sanctuary provides a photo of your adopted cow or calf and an adoption certificate (perfect for a gift). The sanctuary has regular hoedowns at both its locations, and visitors are welcome to come and meet their adopted animals by making an appointment. The bonus is that all your adoptee's friends will be there to greet you too: chickens, turkeys, pigs, all of them living happy endings after being rescued from the meat label and sorry beginnings.

You can even adopt an elephant at the Tennessee Elephant Sanctuary, a special facility for a few of the old, sick, and cast-off elephants who made it out of the big top or the zoo alive. See chapter 37: "Helping Elephants and Whales by Staying Clear of Circuses and Marine Parks," page 198.

These are just a few fine examples of the many opportunities to bring absolute joy to rescued animals and keep hay or seed on their "tables." There are many more, as in this world the number and species of animal refugees is endless, but carefully check out any refuges you find and make sure they are approved by TAOS—The Association of Sanctuaries—by contacting TAOS at 972-485-5647 or www.taosanctuaries.org. Visit the facility, if possible, or ask a humane society official nearby to visit. Check with PETA to confirm accreditation. How lucky we are to be able to bring love and security to someone in the animal kingdom who started out by getting the short end of the stick.

RESOURCES

The Donkey Sanctuary

Sidmouth, Devon, EX10 0NU
United Kingdom
011 44 (0) 22 48398
www.thedonkeysanctuary.org.uk
This sanctuary has several facilities that take in rescued donkeys from work situations from several countries. Donkeys have a

marvelous life and extremely good care and are able to enjoy the companionship of other donkeys as well as visitors. There are many donkeys up for sponsorship.

The Elephant Sanctuary
Hoherwald, Tennessee
www.elephants.com

Farm Sanctuary
PO Box 150
Watkins Glen, NY 14891
607-583-2225
www.farmsanctuary.org
For a minimum $15 donation a year, you will receive a certificate and information on the progress and personality of your adopted cow or calf.

Humane Farming Associations—Suwanna Ranch
PO Box 3577
San Rafael, CA 94912
415-771-CALF
www.hfa.org
The HFA's Suwanna Ranch is the world's largest rescue facility created for abused farm animals.

New Life Parrot Rescue
PO Box 84
St. Neots
Huntingdon, Cambridgeshire, PE19 2LB
United Kingdom
011 44 (0) 1480 390040
www.nlpr.demon.co.uk
For a minimum donation of 25 pounds sterling (about $40), you can choose from a host of bird "angels" who need your help. Each adopter receives a framed photograph and an information

sheet on his or her new friend. Give a little more, and you will receive a pen, a mug, and address labels.

Ooh-Mah-Nee Farm Inc.
RD 1, Box 409
Hunker, PA 15639
724-755-2420
www.oohmahneefarm.org

Poplar Spring Animal Sanctuary
PO Box 507
Poolesville, MD 20837
301-428-8128
www.animalsanctuary.org

68.

Recycling Everything—Including Yourself!

True, you can't take it with you, but then, that's
not the place where it comes in handy.

—BRENDAN FRANCIS

But thousands die, without this or that,
Die, and endow a college, or a cat.

—ALEXANDER POPE, "EPISTLES TO SEVERAL PERSONS"

Think globally, recycle locally.

—WORLDWIDE FREECYCLE NETWORK SAYING

It's not everyone's cup of tea to leave his body to science, so that's not all that I'll talk about here, especially considering there are recycling opportunities galore—in fact, for almost every single thing—while you are still breathing.

Imagine that just about every single thing you've ever thrown away could be put to use. Also imagine that a lot of things you need or want could be found free of charge, or just for the cost of having them picked up and brought to you. Just think how much waste of resources like oil could be avoided, how many resources, like trees, could be spared, how pollution from factories would be reduced, and how many new goods and the packaging that comes with them would not have to be made.

This is not something that happens only on a faraway planet where recycling is required, but here on Earth, now.

The buzz phrase is "free, legal, and appropriate for all ages." That's what the Worldwide Freecycle Network proclaims. This recycling idea is open to all cities and to all individuals. Whether you have a chair, a fax machine, a piano, or an old door, you can post it on a Freecycle site. If you're looking to acquire something for yourself, you just might find it there too.

One constraint: Everything posted must be free. Just pick your city on the Freecycle Network Web site, sign up directly by e-mail, and you are in business. Swap away!

The network is organized by a nonprofit organization called Downtown Don't Waste It, based in Tucson, Arizona, and run by local volunteer moderators across the globe who "make each local group what it is—grassroots at its best!"

You can also start your own Freecycle Network using the simple instructions on the site.

Of course, you can reuse things yourself in creative ways. For example, Sunday comics make trendy wrapping paper. (However, buying a Sunday paper is very environmentally destructive. It is estimated that it takes seventy-five thousand trees to print a Sunday edition of the *New York Times,* so pick up someone else's or read it online!) Use other newspaper as stuffing in packages or roll it into logs for campfires. You can even use it to dry windows without streaking!

Now, on to the ultimate donation: your biggest asset, yourself.

If you would like to donate your body to science to help in the search for cures for everything from Alzheimer's to psychiatric disorders, or for use in education, it's easy enough to do by making a few arrangements in advance.

Human tissues are used in the development of improved surgical instrumentation and technique. Anatomical specimens are needed to develop and test the effectiveness of novel medical devices and new clinical procedures. Biomechanical testing using materials from cadavers allows new approaches to be tried out in clinical settings. Advance testing reduces the risk to living patients and accelerates the development of minimally invasive surgical procedures. These procedures have helped to reduce the length of hospital stays, and pain and recovery times for surgical patients have been significantly reduced in recent years.

Donating your body can help improve the quality of our medical professionals by ensuring the availability of suitable materials in medical schools. Medical educators also use donated tissues to teach human anatomy, as well as new surgical procedures and other medical techniques through continued education. The experience and education gained through the use of human tissues for education is far superior to and very different from the learning provided by animals, artificial substitutes, and textbooks. All in all, giving one's body after death is a wonderful gift.

As another benefit, treatments and medications react differently in animals than in humans. Consequently, human tissue is a better model for researchers to study human disease.

Happy recycling, in the here and now and for the hereafter!

RESOURCES

The Freecycle Network
www.freecycle.org

ScienceCare Anatomical
www.sciencecare.org
For information on body donations. Cremation is provided free of charge.

America Recycles Day
www.americarecyclesday.org

Organize a recycling event in your community through America Recycles Day.

Make-Stuff

www.make-stuff.com

Inventive ideas for reusing everything from film canisters to garden hoses.

69.

How to Donate an Unwanted Fur

There is no pillow as soft as a clear conscience.

—FRENCH PROVERB

In the parking lot at PETA, bundled up against the cold, volunteers are loading boxes of fur coats into a truck to send to refugees from Afghanistan. On the bulletin board in the kitchen upstairs are photographs of children, each one wrapped in a little fur blanket cut from coats donated to PETA by those who have had a change of heart. The children are colder than the people packing the boxes; their tiny feet are bare and they are wearing only thin pieces of cloth. Their smiles, however, are as broad as the mountain range behind them. They have been given a gift that will see them through many bitter winters.

When I was growing up, wearing fur was a mark of success. No more. To wear a fur today is widely considered a mark of ignorance about the suffering of the animals who went into it—those who were bludgeoned in steel traps or who went mad before being suffocated by having their heads stuck in jars of chloroform on a fur farm—or of pure arrogance, a lack of compassion. As Beatrice Arthur says, "Fur used to turn heads; now it turns stomachs."

Bea, whose husband bought her a fur years ago, is now a fur foe because of her love for animals, and appears in ads in opera and theater programs, asking others to have a change of heart too, and to send their furs to PETA as a tax-deductible donation. PETA, she assures them, will use them to good advantage, burying them to make a point, using them as bedding for wildlife, decorating them with soulful animal faces in education displays, and giving them to the only people on earth who can justify wearing even a used fur: those with no means and with bitterly cold days and nights to suffer through.

One person who read Bea's plea and answered the call is Marcia Hutter. When her son Larry told her that PETA was working with an organization called Life for Relief and Development and could arrange to distribute coats as blankets for the needy poor in wartorn Basra and Mosul, Iraq, she didn't hesitate. She had been wearing furs for ten years—right up until the time she made the decision to donate them.

"I wanted them to go to families and children in need. In the back of my mind, I realized that the minks and raccoons weren't being raised humanely, that they didn't have a nice but shortened life, so when Larry told me about the program, I said I'd be happy to donate my coats." Marcia wouldn't watch the video Larry offered to show her, but she didn't need to. Her heart had made her mind up for her.

"Now that I've thought about it, I wouldn't buy fur again," says Marcia. "You don't want to hurt anyone if you can avoid it, whether it's a person or an animal. My family is very proud, very happy. They think I'm terrific for doing this!"

PETA puts all donated fur items to good use and has a dozen different ways to use them. If you have a fur in your closet or attic, or if you know someone who does, this terrific program—and perhaps someone out in the cold in a faraway land—is waiting for you.

RESOURCES

Send furs with your name, address, and an appraisal if you have one to:
PETA Development Department
501 Front St.
Norfolk, VA 23510
757-622-7382

Life for Relief and Development
www.lifeusa.org

Faux Fur Coats

Fabulous Furs
www.fabulousfurs.com
Faux fur ponchos, gloves, jackets, coats, and throws.

Angie's Realm
www.angiesrealm.com
Imitation mink and other faux fur.

70.

Your Opinion Counts: Writing a Letter or Two

"Fool!" said my muse to me. "Look in thy heart and write."

—SIR PHILIP SIDNEY

In a man's letters his soul lies naked.

—SAMUEL JOHNSON

Over breakfast one Sunday, Anna Lewis had finished reading the comics and her horoscope, as she always did first, and turned her attention to the serious stuff, the editorials. On the weekends there are gobs of them, of course, with people weighing in on everything from the state of the roads to the state of the universe, from the lofty to the lightweight.

Something was bothering Anna that weekend. The fair had just left town, and this year there had been carousel ponies. After watching them turn in endless circles in the heat, the sun burning onto their heads, she had called the humane society. One of the ponies, as she told the woman who answered the complaint desk phone, seemed to favor one hind leg over the other, and having had a pony as a child, Anna suspected that he might be suffering from a strained shoulder. The carousel ride owner had refused to give the ponies water when Anna pointed out that the temperature was in the high eighties, saying that he didn't want a mess that might make people turn up their noses and turn away. The humane society officer had been too busy to get to the complaint for several hours, and by the time she arrived, the animals were dehydrated, overheated, and miserable, yet neither the children nor their parents seemed to notice in the hurly-burly of the fairground.

Anna wasn't a published writer, but she thought, "I'm part of this community and my voice should count for something." Hadn't her horoscope read, "Don't keep your feelings bottled up. Tell that special someone what's on your mind"? "Well, forget the 'special someone,'" she thought, "I'm going to tell everyone!" What she wanted was an end to that carousel ride. Anna counted the words in the editorials. Between 500 and 750. She could easily find that many to make her point.

It took Anna only minutes to write the piece because she found the words flowing from her heart and her experience, although checking and rechecking it for clarity and grammar took far longer. She wrote,

> The ponies moved in a circle, not so much animals as windup toys; trudging hour after hour on the hot ground, the sun beating down on their heads, the children pulling at the reins. Often I watched mothers hold their children's soft drinks while the kids rode. I knew the ponies could smell the sweet moisture and yet were themselves parched with thirst. Why on earth, in this wonderful county, would we allow such amusements as the carousel pony rides? Let's bring in a mechanical carousel, gaily painted, bright and impervious to what Mother Nature and our children can dish out. That way the ponies can stay at home under a shady tree, the overburdened humane society will have one less call to answer, and we can have a fair that everyone can enjoy.

The editorial appeared the next week. Anna cut it out, pasted it beneath the newspaper's masthead, and sent copies to every member of the county council and the fair committee, as well as to the head of the chamber of commerce, together with a brief appeal that they please do something to keep the pony rides out of the fair.

Anna knows victories don't always come on the heels of a polite word or two, but sometimes they do, and in this case they did! The pony rides, she has been assured, are no longer welcome at the fair.

"It feels very good to have taken those few hours to be the voice of kindness in this community," she says. "I know many people I've spoken to about the pony situation are pleased and my experience has buoyed them. I know people who, when they see something that needs correcting, now remember my letter and get a few lines in the mail pronto!"

If you wish to write a letter to the editor, may I suggest these tips:

- Keep it brief (one pithy paragraph is enough);
- give an "expert" opinion, for example, "As a theater goer/mother of two children/student/lawyer";
- type your letter if possible;
- accentuate the positive ("Take your family to a fabulous nonanimal circus" rather than "Don't go to the circus");
- be inclusive by assuming your audience will agree with you, rather than attacking them;
- be polite!

PETA credits its volunteer writers with, among many other successes, getting advertisers to take animal-unfriendly spots off the air and out of the papers and put animal-friendly ones in their place. If you would like to express your feelings, the opportunity is here!

RESOURCE

"PETA's Guide to Letter Writing" offers great tips on how to write brief but powerful letters to the editor, to businesses, and to legislators that will allow you to make your voice count and spread your message to thousands! To get your free guide, call PETA at 757-622-7382 or go to www.peta.org.

71.

Speaking Out: Using Your Voice for Social Change

I do not object to people looking at their watches when I am speaking, but I strongly object when they start shaking them to make certain that they are still working.

—LORD BIRKETT (BRITISH PARLIAMENTARIAN)

Elvis wasn't really singing about public speaking when he sang "I'm all shook up!" but the symptoms—dry mouth, jelly legs, sweaty palms, and a thumping chest—are the very same symptoms many people get when they are about to speak in front of others, or when they know they should but dare not.

I'm not just talking about people who have to give a formal speech. I'm talking about occasions when someone you're with, perhaps at work or gathered informally, says something that, in your heart, you know demands contradiction or the offer of an alternative suggestion. That's when we are called upon to overcome those butterflies, conquer our misgivings, and say something.

The fear of conflict and of sounding or looking ridiculous can be a powerful silencing force in our society, but we cannot let that happen. Imagine if Rosa Parks had sat quietly at the back of the bus! Each of us is a good person with important principles and decent values that we mustn't ever allow to be trampled just because we were a bit too jittery to put them forward. Each of us surely has something to contribute to the good of the community if we will only say so at the right moment. Yet even very powerful people admit that they break out in a cold sweat at the thought of calling in to a radio station to put in their two cents' worth or getting to their feet at a meeting. A famous actor once said that he'd rather stand in a freezing field than step onto the stage, but he went onstage every night and was applauded by an audience who had no idea of his fear that his very first line would get impossibly stuck somewhere between his wisdom teeth and his tongue.

Let me share with you some little devices and some thoughts I use to overcome this trepidation, as well as the mighty good reasons to use them.

First, never underestimate your influence! Who me? Yes, you!

Did you know that the person who speaks up first on a moral issue, stating an opinion, is the most likely to influence others? And by a mile. A sociological study on a campus proves how frightening this truth is.

A sociology professor arranged for two students to conduct an experiment. One would walk up to other students passing through the quad. He would have a clipboard in his hand and would say something along these lines: "Hi, I wonder if you'd help us by signing this petition. One of the students received a letter containing racist remarks and we want to express our interest in stopping that kind of thing on campus." The second student would walk up while this was going on and, appearing to have nothing to do with the first student, would listen in. When the first student stopped speaking, the second student, the shill, would chime in, saying either, "That sounds good. I'd like to sign too" or "Well, how do we know the student didn't do something to provoke this attack? I'd have to know more before I'd sign a petition."

What the sociologist found is both scary and enlightening. The unsuspecting students who were asked to sign the petition were far *more* likely to sign if the shill showed interest in signing and far *less* likely to sign if the shill raised a doubt about it.

What can we learn from this? That if we allow our point of view to be known, we will sway people, but if we stand quietly and let someone expressing an opposing view go unchallenged, we hurt our cause. So if we want an end to racism, sexism, speciesism, or any other exploitive practice, we must be determined not to go along with such things by supporting them with our silence, and realize that when even one person objects or puts forward a different idea, he or she is likely to influence behavior. That means we must breathe deeply, realize that only good (certainly nothing truly horrible) can happen to us as a consequence, and speak up!

Who cares if our voice shakes? At least we're using it. Who cares if we haven't formulated the best speech? All that matters is that we say, "I think that's wrong" or "Let's do something kind instead." Of course, always practice your lines if you have advance notice. That will make you more confident.

What is the worst thing that can happen to us when we speak up? People who have analyzed their fears report that they are afraid of (a) being ridiculed, (b) being drawn into an argument, or (c) their words falling on deaf ears. Let's take those one at a time.

a. *The fear of being ridiculed.* When I was a little girl, growing up in India, I once came across a dog in a drainage ditch. He was in severe distress. Someone had hobbled his legs so that he fell down when he tried to walk. Workers sitting at the top of the ditch thought it a huge joke that I untied the dog and bundled him into my arms. What if I had decided that their laughter was too great a price to pay for rescuing this poor animal? It is the same thing when we object to any injustice being spoken or planned. If everyone held their sides with laughter and called us every name in the book, that shouldn't put us off sticking up for others who need our action, whether or not they are in front of us, their pain or distress apparent, should it?

b. *The fear of being drawn into an argument.* At PETA, we devised a simple phrase to use when making a point, perhaps by saying something to a fur wearer, when we do not wish to get into an argument. If the fur wearer whirls around and shouts, "Aren't your shoes made of leather?" the only answer one needs, regardless of the composition of one's shoes, is, "There's no excuse for wearing fur." Of course, you can substitute racism or any other wrong. Try it. "There's no excuse for racism!" You see, it works. And it can be said a dozen times in a row and it's still true and keeps making your point.

c. *The fear of our words falling on deaf ears.* If your words truly fall on deaf ears, the world is no worse, and at least you know you did the right thing by trying. However, don't be so sure, even if the listeners guffaw, that nothing will come of your remarks. Human nature is such that those who heard what you said will replay the tapes in their minds. At some point what you said will resonate with what they hear again in another forum perhaps, and chances are they will never feel as comfortable saying or doing that ugly thing again. They will know that other people hold your view even if they haven't said as much.

It's not as hard as one might think to be the squeaky wheel that gets oiled to serve justice. The world will be a better place if we ask for more consideration of the earth and each other no matter what form we come in. Your voice is a very powerful tool in reducing oppression and lessening suffering. Here's to its use!

RESOURCE

Toastmasters International

www.toastmasters.org

This organization is a great confidence builder and puts you among others who have little or no public-speaking experience.

72.

Making a Library Donation

A book is the only immortality.

—RUFUS CHOATE

"What book would you most like to have with you on a desert island?" the radio announcer asked. "Ah, that would be Thomas's Guide to Practical Shipbuilding,*" replied G. K. Chesterton.*

Have you ever read a book that changed your life, in some small or large way, and thought, "I wish I could tell the world about this"? Well, you can.

By buying a copy of that book and donating it to a special reading program or a library in any number of institutions or, indeed, in your own municipal branch library, you can reach a whole community of readers and share the joy you felt. Your book will start down a path, reaching people you will never meet, much as a leaf blows up from the ground and twirls around strangers' heads, touching this one and that, linking them in its ethereal ballet.

There are all sorts of places where your favorite book would be welcome: people in retirement housing, rehabilitation homes, reading programs for new immigrants, and even prison libraries. Sometimes the book does not have to be new or from the publisher. I once dropped off a bag of books at a nursing home in New Jersey. Several weeks later I got a call from a lovely elderly woman who had found a canceled check of mine in one of the books. She had called to say how she, like me, had dreaded coming to the end of *Watership Down* and how it had given her sweet dreams of rabbits in the warrens of the English countryside.

Prison libraries are usually very short of funds, and those who use the libraries are long on time. Even if someone is in jail on a light sentence or pending trial, the clock ticks slowly, and a good book can be the closest thing someone "inside" can find to being with family and friends.

I know about the bleakness of prison libraries because I spent two stints of two weeks apiece in Pottsville Prison near Hegins, Pennsylvania. That happened because every year on Labor Day, until, thank goodness, it was finally declared illegal, the town of Hegins hosted a pigeon shoot. Bewildered little birds were trapped from bustling city centers, trucked to Hegins by the crateful, kept overnight in a shed, and then placed under boxes set out in a field. The boxes of pigeons were held tight by a series of strings, all released as the "trapper boys" were given their cue.

Shooters came from miles around, making a family affair of it. They brought beer and picnic provisions and sat on the grass or in the bleachers to watch the "fun." Cheers erupted as the birds went up, trapper boys releasing the strings to let the pigeons free. Out the birds came, some walking and looking around, dazed by the sudden light, some taking to the air, only to be blown to bits or to come spiraling back to the earth with part of a wing gone.

My colleagues and I had run onto the field to save some of the birds and had been arrested. After a quick powwow, we made the decision to stay in jail to make a point about the shoot rather than pay what we thought of as an unjust fine. We were carted off to cells in an old prison block where, in the distant past, the famous Pennsylvania coal mine strike agitators, the Molly McGuires, had been hanged just outside our barred and slatted windows.

There were slim pickings in the Pottsville Prison library, but I remember the joy of finding one book I could really lose myself in.

Of all things, it was Aleksandr Solzhenitsyn's *The Gulag Archipelago.* Reading about prison life in Siberia made me feel very privileged indeed, even if we were sleeping on mattresses on the filthy floor because of overcrowding.

Whether you choose a specialized program, such as a remedial course or one in English as a second language for immigrants, or a special institution like a battered women's shelter, or whether you decide to donate your beloved book to your town or county library or to build libraries overseas in developing countries or to those in impoverished school districts, there is a special joy in knowing you have imparted something that will stir the hearts and minds of those who love to learn and are waiting to be inspired.

RESOURCES

Ask your local public libraries and public school libraries if they will accept book donations. Many will and are grateful for them. If you don't have books lying around to give, ask what books they want, and buy one or more for them.

WBVS Book Project

A World Bank project that provides donated books to students in the developing world. Books can be delivered weekdays or sent to WBVS, 1775 G Street NW, Washington, DC 20433, but a call or e-mail is required first to 202-473-8960 or wproject@worldbank.org.

The Prison Book Project

PO Box 396
Amherst, MA 01004
info@prisonbooks.org
Keeps prisoners' minds occupied and is always in need of

thesauruses and dictionaries; books in Spanish; books about and by Africans, Latinos, and Native Americans; and art books, science fiction, and books on ethical and spiritual issues.

Amazon.com

www.amazon.com

Puts donated books into children's hands by donating a portion of your purchase price to Page Ahead. Page Ahead has a wish list too.

PETA Online Bookstore

www.petabookstore.com

A great resource for books on everything from companion-animal care to vegetarian and vegan cooking. Some great children's books are also available.

73.

Community Volunteering and Leading by Example

To transform the world we must begin with ourselves.

—JIDDU KRISHNAMURTI

The pathway to nonviolence involves the most exciting journey a person can experience.

—NATHANIEL ALTMAN, *AHIMSA*

I learned long ago that if I waited until everyone else was ready to get started, I'd never get started.

—MERCE CUNNINGHAM

Jennie Taylor Martin has a three-year-old child to care for and she runs PETA's catalog, so she is very busy. One Sunday afternoon, chores done, she felt the desire to go out and do something for her "pet" cause, the animals. What she really wanted was a list of ideas she could run her thumb down to pick something to do that weekend that would make a difference. That's how the Weekend Warrior card set came about.

Jennie created the Weekend Warrior when she envisioned fifty-two cards, one for each weekend of the year, outlining a step-by-step project that can easily be taken care of in an hour or a few. I'm going to create a list below that contains some of the ideas and adds others. What counts is that each of us is precious and so is our time.

We can put our spare hours—whether one weekend, every weekend, or even a weekday evening—to great use and make our community, our world, a better place. Whether you act alone, enlist a friend or two, or even join a group, your time and effort make a mountain of a difference.

Here are a few of Jennie's favorites:

- Cook a vegan meal to take as a treat to your coworkers and turn them on to healthy, humane cuisine. Be sure to have the recipe handy and be gentle, not pushy, in the presentation. Don't feel like cooking? Make hoagies with veggies, pickles, and Tofurky fabulous fakes in bologna, turkey, and chicken flavors.
- Sign up with a community group of people who walk AIDS patients' dogs.
- Wear a message shirt while walking or jogging or put a button on your jacket that says, "Ask Me Why I'm a Vegan."
- Organize a straw giveaway for dogs left out in winter.
- Decide how much you can give, and give it to endow a chair in ethics and animals at a university, to pay for a spay, to put an ad on a park bench.
- Use your artistic talents to paint a social message mural or to draw cards to sell for a cause.
- Give out leaflets at a church, temple, or synagogue.
- Ask your religious leader to give a sermon on kindness to animals.
- Show a video to your club, school, friends, or relatives and ask for their comments.
- Clean up a beach, riverbank, stream, or patch of ground (see chapter 33: "Preserving the Beach—Its Life and Coral Reefs," page 177, and chapter 34: "The Benefits of Beachcombing," page 181).
- Offer to clean a car for a donation.

- Ask a local eatery to feature more vegan entrées.
- Leave a tidy pile of Vegetarian Starter Kits or *Animal Times* or other useful newsletters near the StairMasters at the gym or wherever people read or gather.
- Plan a yard, garage, bake, or sidewalk sale to raise funds for a cause you care about. Make the signs and ask your friends and neighbors to give you things to sell.
- Hand out leaflets on your local campus or outside a mall.
- Go to the library and sign up to set up a display on a theme, like fur or child abuse; get materials from PETA or another social action group that can provide them.
- Volunteer to walk dogs, play with cats, or collect towels for your local animal shelter.
- Put "Free Vegetarian Starter Kit" cards on grocery store bulletin boards.
- Stack postcards by your couch, addressing them with network addresses so you are ready to write in to complain or praise as soon as you see a commercial or ad that exploits or helps animals.
- Ask permission to set up an information table in your local town center or other high-foot-traffic area.
- Write to a TV reporter, asking him or her to do a story on a local animal issue like dog and cat overpopulation (see chapter 46: "The Importance of Sterilization," page 243).
- Send someone influential a vegan cookbook.
- Write to your school newspaper with details about great alternatives to leather.
- Join a radio discussion by calling in to a station and tying in an earth or animal issue, for example, "Yes, our economy is in trouble, but one way I've found to make my dollar go further is to cross milk and meat off my shopping list."
- Ask the manager of your local coffee shop to start offering soy milk, and bring a sample.
- Order your holiday cards from a charity.

- Get your office or school cafeteria to consider a vegan option.
- Ask local restaurants to put "Veg Friendly" stickers on their window (available free from PETA for you to hand to them).
- Get your local librarian to put a request on letterhead to receive a free library pack of books from PETA and a complimentary subscription to *Animal Times.*
- Walk a chained dog or bring him treats.
- Record an educational message onto your answering machine.
- Stock your car with a rescue kit of leash, water, bandage (see chapter 32: "Being Ready for Animal Emergencies on the Road," page 173).
- Show or lend a film about alternatives to dissection to a child, parent, or teacher.
- Help out or organize a food or literature table at a street fair or concert.
- Hold a candlelight vigil.
- Write a short letter to the editor on alternatives to a cruelty.

RESOURCES

PETA Animal Rights Weekend Warrior Cards

www.petacatalog.com

The cards can be purchased for $12.95 per pack.

Also check PETA's action hotline at 757-622-7382 or Web site at peta.org for the latest letters that need writing and calls that need to be made to stop abuses.

74.

Memorializing a Loved One

I will wear him in my heart's core, ay, in my heart of heart.

—WILLIAM SHAKESPEARE, *HAMLET*

Remember!

—THE LAST INJUNCTION OF CHARLES I OF ENGLAND

Grief can take care of itself, but to get the full value of joy you must have someone to divide it with.

—MARK TWAIN

In flies a sparrow, which flutters through the hall, comes in through one door, and exits through the other. Lo, during the time the bird is within, he isn't touched by the storms of winter. But that lasts only a little while, a twinkling of any eye, before he soon returns to winter from winter. Just so this life of man appears only for a short time; what went before and what follows, we know now.

—PAULINUS TO PAGAN ENGLISH KING EADWIN, EXPLAINING THAT LIFE IS TRANSITORY

If you browse among the shelves at the public library in the little Oregon town where my father died, you will see a plaque in remembrance of Noel Ward. When he passed away, my mother made a modest donation to the library where my father had spent so many contented hours, finding books about the war, about the sea, about electronics, about computers. He knew all the staff and liked them, and my mother brought them cakes once in a while. She misses my father fearfully, but she takes comfort in, and feels right about, going into the library and seeing some mention of his presence there.

A coast away, at the PETA headquarters in Virginia, Ginger and Eddie, once rough-and-tumble kittens but now all grown up, sit patiently by the elevator in the mornings, ready to greet and be greeted by everyone coming to work on the fourth floor. The first thing anyone exiting the elevator sees, on the blue wall behind the cats and lit from above to catch the gold on the leaves, is the Tree of Life. Each leaf is inscribed with the name of an animal someone loved or someone who cared about animals and was loved in return. Each leaf is a tribute, bought in memory of that love.

A firefighter's name is there; so are those of two dogs from two different police forces, Iron and Breaker, who fell in the line of duty. Each leaf is engraved with a few words of remembrance. Some are very simple. The full meaning of some inscriptions is known only to the inscribers: "To Bud, Who Saved Us, I Act in Your Honor. From Mary, Dean, Zoe and Cookie."

Every visitor stops near the tree trunk, looks up into the bronze branches, and reads the inscriptions on the golden leaves; and those who have passed them a thousand times see them too, and are buoyed by the love they show and the lives they commemorate. One leaf on the tree is for Steve Wilkie.

Steve died in 2000, at the age of thirty-eight, together with eighty-seven other people, when the plane carrying them from Puerto Vallarta, Mexico, crashed off the coast of California. To his wife of five years, Susan, the loss was devastating. "He was the love of my life," she says. "We had plans to have children but never got to fulfill that or our other dreams."

Steve and Susan had dined and danced at a PETA Humanitarian Gala in Hollywood, California, when Paul McCartney played in concert, and Susan says, "It was such a happy night for him because Steve was a huge Beatles fan." Steve was also director of fashion and new business for Levi Strauss. When he heard that McCartney had been inducted into the Rock and Roll Hall of Fame, he picked out a Levi's jean jacket and sent it off to him in celebration of the honor. Paul wrote Steve a personal note of thanks, which he instantly framed and hung on his wall. Just before his death, Steve got in touch with Stella McCartney to discuss working with her on a new high-end line of Levi's clothes. He loved the McCartneys for their art and for their compassion; he also loved animals, loved his family, loved his and Susan's adopted Lab-greyhound mix, Rubi, and loved life.

Steve's positive attitude and compassion touched everyone he spent time with, and Susan knew that when the news of his death broke, those close to him ached for a way to keep Steve and Steve's values alive. She says, "I wanted to do something positive that Steve would like, to memorialize his life. I decided to ask everyone to donate to PETA in lieu of flowers."

Over $10,000 was raised in Steve Wilkie's name and has been used to fight the cruelties Steve always talked about and wished would end. For such a loving soul, there could hardly be a more fitting tribute. You can memorialize a lost loved one in many ways, including PETA's Tree of Life or by setting up a fund, etc., or in your own way.

RESOURCES

PETA's Tree of Life
c/o Scott VanValkenburg
757-622-1374

True Friends Memorial
www.tfmemorial.org

PART TEN

Celebrations

75.

Thanksgiving: The Harvest Festival

I used to crouch down and my beloved Gladys would rest her head on my leg and close her eyes as I tickled her neck.

—MARION EASTWOOD, WHO RESCUED GLADYS, A YOUNG TURKEY, FROM A MARKET CAGE

May our feast days be many and our fast days be few.

—MARY L. BOOTH

The history books have it that the very first Thanksgiving was really a harvest festival that Native Americans had celebrated for hundreds, perhaps thousands, of years, and that the Europeans who had arrived on North American shores were their first foreign guests.

The feast is reported to have consisted of gooseberries, strawberries, plums, cherries, cranberries (aha, we recognize a dish that has survived the turmoil that followed!), popcorn balls with maple syrup, other corn dishes, hoe cakes, pumpkin, squash, and a groundnut known by the rather unflattering name of bogg bean.

Unlike the Pilgrims in 1620, who many historians believe did not put flesh on the table, we have that option today, but many choose to make the Thanksgiving holiday something *all* can be thankful for—not only the growing number of vegetarian and vegan guests at holiday tables but even the dear turkey, the native bird Benjamin Franklin thought should beat out the bald eagle to become the national bird of the United States.

Left wild, turkeys are wonderful, smart animals who have been clocked at twenty-five miles per hour on the ground running and who can fly up to a whopping fifty-five miles per hour over short distances. Not so the poor "domesticated" or genetically engineered factory farm bird who cannot walk more than a few steps because of an unnaturally enlarged breast. As Lancaster Farming reports, "If a seven-pound human baby grew at the same rate [as today's birds] that baby would weigh 1500 pounds at eighteen weeks!"

What we do to turkeys should embarrass *us* to death, but did you know that turkeys blush? At least they change skin color to reflect changes in their feelings. They also have excellent hearing and a 270-degree field of vision. Hunters find it hard to sneak up on turkeys, hence these cowardly bullies hide in camouflaged blinds and use "turkey callers" to draw turkeys to them with a cry that mimics the sound of other turkeys.

Some people have a different kind of turkey dinner at Thanksgiving, as part of their efforts to spare a bird over the holidays. Their "turkey dinner" consists of inviting a tame rescued turkey *to* the table as the guest of honor, rather than putting him *on* it, and inviting the press to film the bird's excitement and curiosity as he watches the preparations and mingles with the other diners.

That sort of thing happened by mistake to Sam Garcia. Sam, who lives with his family in Miami, Florida, decided to get a live turkey for the holidays. He didn't think twice about the deed that would have to be done to put the bird on the table—but his children did.

According to Garcia, "I went out to pick up a meal and got a relationship instead." His family lost their stomachs for "a personable bird who likes children and gobbles back when you speak to him. At first I called him 'dinner,' but now we call him our pal."

Other celebrants, those who don't want to spend much time in the kitchen, can simply buy a veggie alternative to the roast bird, such as the national favorite, Tofurky. This incredible, turkeylike textured and flavored roast is made from wheat-bread protein, the center of which is filled with wild rice stuffing. It gets popped in a 300-degree oven for two hours and, voilà, it's ready to serve. You can buy just the yummy roast, which is the size of a bowling ball, or the whole holiday meal, including extra wild rice stuffing, faux "giblet" gravy, and Tofurky "seedpods"—light, fluffy dumplings made with Northwest potatoes and sweetly tangy cranberries and apples. Most local supermarkets carry Tofurky or will if you order early enough for the holidays, or see below for mail-order information.

In 2003 Simon Rayner of the National Farmers Union headquarters in London told the *Philadelphia Inquirer:* "We know that turkeys are very stressed when they're slaughtered and they tense up if they're afraid. If we can actually come up with a sound that improves the living conditions for turkeys, it's beneficial for farmers and turkeys alike." So the NFU sent three hundred turkey farmers a CD, asking them to help determine what types of sounds turkeys find serene and what sounds disturb them, in the hope of creating a more tranquil atmosphere and, therefore, a more tranquil turkey, before the birds "face the inevitable chop."

Before you think, "How kind!" know that frightened, tense animals release adrenaline into their bodies and that makes the meat tougher, something meat processors combat by injecting carcasses with chemicals that work to break down the adrenaline. The birds are being lulled into a false sense of calm, for the farmers' convenience and further profit.

Of course, that "chop" is "inevitable" only if we continue to eat turkeys. So let's put the Chopin on our own CD players and leave the turkeys to enjoy their lives and to join us in giving thanks for them.

Who could ask for more?

EASY VEGGIE GRAVY

1 tablespoon cornstarch
2 cups vegetable broth
2 teaspoons vegetarian "chicken" bouillon powder
1 teaspoon vegetarian "beef" bouillon powder
1 teaspoon sugar or equivalent
3 tablespoons nutritional yeast

Mix cornstarch with ½ cup cold broth. Put remainder of broth, bouillon powders, sugar, and nutritional yeast in a saucepan. Heat to boiling.

Turn heat down to medium. Stir in cornstarch mixture, stirring constantly. Cook until thick (1–3 minutes). Serve immediately.

CRANBERRY SALAD

1 pound cranberries
1½ cups sugar
1 (11-ounce) can mandarin oranges
1 small apple, finely chopped
¾ cup chopped nuts
1 (1-pound) can crushed pineapple with ¼ cup of the juice
2 stalks celery, finely chopped

Chop the cranberries in a food processor, then add the sugar and mix. Let stand for 2 hours. Cut the mandarin oranges in half. Add, along with the remaining ingredients, to the cranberries, mix well, and chill. This salad makes a refreshing alternative to canned cranberry sauce.

Serves 4–6.

RESOURCES

Tofurky

www.tofurky.com

Tofurky packaging is kept to a minimum and is made from 100 percent recycled paperboard and unbleached corrugated shipping cartons.

Books

Davis, Karen. *More than a Meal: The Turkey in Myth, Ritual, and Reality.* New York: Lantern Books, 2001. Available from www.upc.com.

76.

A Christmas Dinner Fit for Good King Wenceslas

A Christmas wish—
May you never forget
What is worth remembering
Or remember
What is best forgot

—IRISH SAYING

The discovery of a new dish does more for the happiness of man than the discovery of a new star.

—ANTHELME BRILLAT-SAVARIN, *THE PHYSIOLOGY OF TASTE*

When I was growing up in England, chances were that the ground would be white by Christmas morning. We would wake up, excited to find that Father Christmas had somehow forced his massive frame down the chimney despite the fire we needed to keep our home warm.

After the hullabaloo over opening the presents, there would be quite a production starting in the kitchen that would go on for hours, the house eventually filling with the smell of fruit pies and roasting potatoes. Our dog, Seanie, would inevitably be spoken to harshly for daring to make off with something left to cool on the counter or to keep warm on the hearth, despite having been allowed by my liberal mother to lick all the bowls of drippings and batter.

By the time we sat down to eat, wearing our paper crowns and vying to explode the crackers, we were starving. When we'd finished, after the sherry (which even little girls got to sip), everyone fought the urge to take a nap. Most of us under seventy succeeded, and off we'd tromp, in our new winter jackets, coats, hats, and scarves, seeing our breath before us, making tracks in the snow in that last crisp walk, throwing snowballs, before the early darkness sent us running back to play games around the fire.

The meal, like the roast chestnuts the night before, was traditional English fare. There was sage-and-onion-stuffed turkey or goose, gravy, roasted potatoes, Brussels sprouts, peas with mint, Yorkshire pudding, trifle, and mincemeat pies. There was also steaming hot Christmas pudding, a suet concoction with a sprig of holly on top of it and a sixpence buried inside it. Whoever bit into the sixpence and failed to chip a tooth had good luck for the next year. If you could manage to keep eating, this was followed by Christmas cake with marzipan and thick white icing, decorated with colored paper and figurines of Santa with his elves and reindeer. It's a wonder in the end that anyone could fit through the front door!

The holidays are a wonderful time to honor one's values and incorporate them into one's traditions. Passing through Heathrow Airport, I noticed that Christmas pudding can now be had without suet. In fact, Selfridges and Harrods, London's famous department stores, both carry a vegan Christmas pud. As for my mother's trifle, it is easy as pie to veganize; just see below. You can order a magnificent vegan Wellington from California to arrive frozen and ready to bake for your centerpiece dish, but I have also included a recipe for Linda McCartney's Festive Roast, just in case you want to impress your guests the old-fashioned way.

So, here, together with the details on where to recycle those

Christmas cards come January, are a few ideas for what is, as my favorite character from the English comic books, Beryl the Peril, would say, a "wowzer" of a Christmas feast—one that will bring peace on earth to all creation, including the dear birds.

Merry Christmas!

LINDA McCARTNEY'S FESTIVE ROAST WITH SAVORY STUFFING

2 tablespoons garlic powder
10-ounce package Nature's Burger
1½ tablespoons water mixed with 1½ teaspoons egg replacer
4 cups water
¾ cup textured vegetable protein (TVP)
5 Veggie Tofu brand burgers processed in food processor with ¾ cup water
4 tablespoons soy sauce
3 tablespoons oil
Savory Stuffing (see recipe below)

Start preparing this roast the day before it is needed.

Preheat oven to 350°F. Grease and flour a large casserole dish or mold. Sprinkle 1 tablespoon of the garlic powder all over the inside of this dish.

Measure the Nature's Burger, "egg," and 2 cups water into a large mixing bowl. Stir well and leave for 5 minutes for the liquid to be absorbed.

Mix the TVP and 2 cups water in a bowl. Stir well and let stand for 5 minutes.

Combine the Nature's Burger mix, pureed tofu burgers, and the soaked TVP together in a large bowl. Add the remaining garlic powder and the soy sauce. Mix well. Coat the casserole dish with the oil and pour the mixture into the dish, pressing it firmly onto the sides and bottom. Leave a large cavity in the middle for the stuffing. Firm the mixture with the back of the spoon or your knuckles.

Bake for 1½ hours. Allow to cool, then refrigerate overnight.

The next day, make the Savory Stuffing and stuff it into the roast cavity. Turn the casserole dish upside down on a cookie sheet or roasting pan without removing the dish and bake for 45 minutes at 350°F. Remove the casserole dish and continue to bake for 1 hour more.

Serve hot with gravy and extra stuffing.

Savory Stuffing

1 loaf whole wheat bread, cubed
8 tablespoons margarine
5 stalks celery, chopped
1 large onion, chopped
4 fresh sage leaves, finely chopped, or 2 teaspoons dried sage
1 teaspoon each dried rosemary, thyme, and parsley

Place the bread cubes in a large mixing bowl. Melt the margarine in a large frying pan. Add the celery and onion and, stirring frequently with a wooden spoon, sauté for 5 minutes, until lightly browned. Pour the sauté into the mixing bowl with the bread cubes. Add the herbs. Mix well. Bake any remaining after stuffing roast in a baking dish.

Serves 8.

TRIFLE

Yellow Cake Batter (see recipe below)
Vanilla Pudding (see recipe below)
½ cup cream sherry, brandy, or your favorite liqueur
¾ cup raspberry jam
1 small can peaches, drained and sliced

2 medium bananas, sliced

Tofu Whipped Cream (see recipe below) or commercial nondairy whipped topping

Toasted slivered almonds, for garnish

Preheat the oven to 325°F. Grease a 9" × 13" cake pan.

Prepare the care batter according to the recipe below, then pour the batter into the prepared pan (the batter should be less than 2 inches high in the cake pan) and bake for 25 to 30 minutes.

Prepare the Vanilla Pudding according to the recipe below. Let it cool, but do not refrigerate.

When the cake has cooled, cut it into 1-by-3-inch pieces. Line the bottom and sides of a 2½-quart glass serving bowl with the cake pieces. Moisten the cake with the sherry or liqueur and spread the raspberry jam over the cake. Add the sliced peaches and bananas. Pour the pudding over the fruit and chill in the refrigerator.

Before serving, top with the Tofu Whipped Cream or nondairy topping and decorate with toasted almonds.

Serves 8.

Yellow Cake Batter

½ cup (1 stick) soft margarine

1 cup sugar

Egg replacer equivalent of 4 eggs

1⅜ cup sifted unbleached all-purpose flour

½ teaspoon baking powder

Soy milk as needed

Cream the margarine with an electric mixer until smooth. Add the sugar gradually. Add the egg replacer and mix well. Add the sifted flour and baking powder and stir. If the mixture is too dry, add a few drops (up to ¼ cup) of soy milk.

Vanilla Pudding

⅓ cup sugar
3 tablespoons cornstarch
⅛ teaspoon salt
2 cups soy milk
1 teaspoon vanilla extract

Mix the sugar, cornstarch, and salt in a large saucepan. Gradually blend in the soy milk, stirring constantly to avoid lumps.

Cook the mixture over low heat, stirring constantly until thickened. Cook for an additional 2 to 3 minutes, stirring now and then.

Remove the pudding from the heat and add the vanilla. Let cool, stirring occasionally.

Tofu Whipped Cream

1 pound soft tofu
1 tablespoon vanilla extract and brandy if you wish
¼ cup sugar
¼ cup soy milk

Combine tofu, vanilla, and sugar in a blender or a food processor and process until smooth. With the machine running, gradually add the soy milk through the feeder cap. Refrigerate until ready to serve.

JO'S VEGAN CHRISTMAS PUDDING

8 ounces vegan suet
1 heaped teaspoon mixed spice
½ teaspoon ground nutmeg
½ teaspoon cinnamon
4 ounces flour
1 pound light brown sugar
8 ounces bread crumbs

8 ounces sultanas

4 ounces raisins

4 ounces cherries, chopped

2 ounces flaked almonds

2 ounces mixed peel

zest of 1 lemon

zest of 1 orange

1 apple, grated

10 fluid ounces stout (e.g., Samuel Smith's Imperial Stout) with 2 tablespoons malt extract

4 tablespoons brandy

2 ounces soy flour blended with 10 tablespoons water

Mix all the dry ingredients in a large bowl. In a different bowl blend all liquids and the soy flour mixture, and pour over the dry ingredients. Stir all together very thoroughly. If, after you have done this, the mixture seems a bit dry, add some more stout until you get it to a dropping consistency. Cover and leave overnight.

The next day, grease the pudding basins, fill to the top with mixture, and cover securely. Steam for 8 hours.

When ready to eat, steam for 2 hours and serve.

Serves 6 to 8.

ALMOND TORTE

¾ cup margarine

2¼ cups sugar

Egg replacer equivalent of 3 eggs

3 tablespoons fresh lemon juice

Pinch of salt

2½ cups unbleached all-purpose or all-purpose flour

2½ teaspoons baking powder

¾ cup soy milk, plain or vanilla

2 cups chopped almonds

½ cup vegan marzipan (available in gourmet and international food stores)

Preheat the oven to 400°F.

To prepare the dough, cream the margarine with ¾ cup sugar until fluffy. Add the egg replacer, lemon juice, and salt and mix well. Add the flour and baking powder, and mix until a soft dough is formed.

Place two-thirds of the dough on a sheet of plastic wrap. With a rolling pin, roll the dough into a circle about 11 inches in diameter. Invert the dough into a 9" springform pan. Peel the plastic wrap off the dough and press the dough into the bottom and up the sides of the pan. Trim the edges if needed. Roll the remaining dough into a circle about 9 inches in diameter and set aside. This will be used to top the torte.

To prepare the filling, stir 1 cup of sugar in a heavy saucepan over low heat until the sugar is dissolved. Increase the heat and boil the sugar until it turns a caramel color. Add the soy milk (which will bubble vigorously) along with the nuts and the rest of the sugar. Cook over high heat, stirring constantly, for 5 minutes. Remove from the heat and beat the marzipan into the mixture. When it is well mixed, pour it into the cake pan and put the rolled-out dough on top.

Bake the torte until golden brown, about 35 minutes. Cook completely before removing the springform.

Serves 6 to 8.

RESOURCES

Saint Jude's Ranch Card Reycling

100 St. Jude St., PO Box 60100
Boulder City, NV 89006

This nonprofit youth home gratefully receives and reuses whole Christmas cards or just the fronts to them. You can send them cheaply at library rate via the U.S. Postal Service.

Monin Organic Caramel Soy Latte

Perfect for the holidays and cozy nights by the fire. Monin has five certified organic syrups to add to coffee, hot chocolate, steamed soy milk, and even baked goods. Available in caramel, chocolate, hazelnut, raspberry, and vanilla.
727-461-3033
www.monin.com

Vegan Marshmallows

And those hot chocolate drinks are even more perfect when topped with vegan marshmallows! Conventional ones are made from gelatin, the ugly ooze that emanates from animals' hooves, but veganessentials.com (866-88-VEGAN) sells fluffy, white vegan marshmallows that you can eat straight from the bag, pop on top of warming drinks, or roast over the fire.

Ready-Made Savory Roast by Mail

Wellington Native Foods
www.nativefoods.com
An elegant puff pastry filled with savory native seitan, tangerine yams, cranberry chestnut stuffing, ruby red chard, and caramelized onions, with shallot mushroom gravy on the side. Comes frozen and you bake it. Ready in an hour. Serves six generously.

77.

A Special Passover: Celebrating Freedom with a Vegan Seder

The ancient Hebrews knew, and were perhaps the first among men to know, that animals feel pain and suffer pain.

—RABBI SIMON GLAZER

Passover (or Pesach) comes in the spring, a time when plants are in bud or bloom and the earth is renewing itself. It is a time to cherish precious Jewish values of compassion, stewardship, and family ties, when Jews contemplate the persecution of an entire people, and it is the time to retell the story of the flight from Egypt in the time of Moses and to sing joyous songs.

The Seder at Passover used to, and occasionally still does, consist of a very simple meal of a small portion of meat and a few herbs served with unleavened bread. Along with the meal are prayers, storytelling, and readings in Hebrew. The theme is freedom, and the call at table is "Let all who are hungry come and eat." It is a holiday that reminds us of a time of deprivation, but the commemoration is a time of festivity and plenty.

Philip and Hannah Schein are great cooks. They also cherish Jewish values—particularly important to them is the teaching that all suffering matters to God—and they very much want these wonderful values to be extended to cover modern-day circumstances, such as factory farming and environmental degradation. Just as the wealth of foods offered at Seder has grown and been enriched by modernity, so, they say, must the relevance of the ritual expand. In fact, there is also a special encouragement within the seder to "add to the story." Like so many others who wish their religious traditions and celebrations to be up-to-the-minute relevant, the Scheins are finding it easier each year to have their point of view accepted, and the foods they bring to the table certainly please the most discerning palate and thrill the most devoted "foodies."

Hannah points out that in Exodus we are told that Moses, Judaism's greatest prophet and teacher, was chosen by God to lead the Israelites to freedom because he had shown kindness to a lamb when he was a simple shepherd. That means, she says, that the lamb shank, which is used symbolically to represent sacrifices at the Temple, can easily be replaced with something else. Like other vegetarians, she has chosen to use a beet instead, an alternative sanctioned by the Talmud. Rabbi Huna, a Talmudic sage, stated that a beet can be used for the same purpose as the Paschal Lamb (Babylonian Talmud, Pesachim 114b). Rabbi David Rosen has pointed out that objects on the Seder plate are symbolic, hence there is no sin in improvising, and has suggested using a beet instead of a shank bone, and a mushroom to represent the festive offering instead of an egg. To add to the "authenticity," the beet, like the lamb, is red like lamb flesh, "bleeds" as a lamb would, and has a fleshy texture (eat one wearing a blindfold and you might be very surprised).

Most of the ceremonial foods on the Seder plate are vegetables: parsley, green onions, celery, romaine lettuce, and bitter herbs like raw horseradish, which symbolize the bitterness of slavery. As Roberta Kalechofsky wrote in her article, "The Four Questions and the Four Answers," one interpretation of the reason behind the tradition of dipping greens twice in salt water has vegetarian roots: "Once to remember our past in the Green of Eden and once to remember the future when we will all be vegetarians again."

Maror, the bitter herbs (often horseradish), symbolizes the mortar Jews used in building during the time of slavery. It is also vegan and is dipped in *charoset,* a mixture of apples, nuts, cinnamon, and wine.

Gourmet Jewish cook and author Judy Zeidler, who has created Seder menus that read like feasts, serves new potatoes dipped in coarse salt as part of the service and then follows up with artichokes in tomato sauce, vegetable-stuffed cabbage, and spring vegetable soup with matzo balls, and a fresh berry pudding.

Philip Schein, a born innovator, has concentrated on the Pesach egg presented on the Seder plate. A real egg makes him think not of freedom but of how today's hens are crammed five to seven into a cage offering no more floor space for the lot than an area the size of a computer screen, and he found that distracting. The olive, which is often used by animal-conscientious participants as a substitute for the egg, didn't seem to him to be quite right, although the reason for using an olive fit well: If you squeeze it, you get olive oil, and the more the Jewish people are pressed, the better they have become. It was too small and the texture was wrong. So he and Hannah hit upon the rambutan, a sweet, juicy fruit with a soft, succulent interior and a leathery, prickly outside that is available in the spring in many Asian grocery stores.

Says Philip, the rambutan "has an uncanny similarity in look and texture to a hard-boiled egg. It is a seed bringing life like an egg. The roundness symbolizes the circularity of life, and since it has no real beginning or end it symbolizes how we are deeply connected to sufferings of the past and all other beings. The rambutan also has a rough outer skin that must be peeled away (like slavery) and it carries with it that toughness/tenderness paradox that symbolizes a people who are tough on the outside because of the trials, but sweet on the inside, just like the rambutan!"

Another friend, Jayn Meinhardt—who listens with quiet amusement and deep fondness each year as her Christian husband carefully joins in reciting the story of how the Egyptians expelled the Jews from the Holy Land—has found a wealth of dishes she says youngsters seem to particularly enjoy. "Jewish kids are often told that bagels were made with holes in them so that Jews could carry them on their belts when they travel. On Passover, there are no bagels, but we tell religious stories like that and the kids adore them. We eat only unleavened bread, like matzos, which I love, to remember that when Jews fled to the Promised Land they had no time to bake their bread." Be careful to pick the kinds of matzos that contain no egg. They are always clearly marked.

Jayn likes to treat everyone to her favorite recipe of chopped "liver" spread made from mushrooms, and she usually brings Russian potato-and-mushroom croquettes and everyone's favorite: strawberries dipped in dark chocolate.

So as you can see, it's easy as pie, or should I say as strawberry-rhubarb compote, to celebrate this important Jewish holiday while helping to reinforce cherished values of freedom so that they apply to the preservation of the land and to the protection of innocent beings who are still held in bondage today. All it takes is a little creative flair.

So, welcome to the wonderful world of the vegan Seder, and "Chag Sameach" ("Happy Holidays")!

STRAWBERRY-RHUBARB COMPOTE

From *The Jewish Vegetarian Year Cookbook* by Roberta Kalechofsky and Rosa Rasiel.

2 cups ¾-inch rhubarb slices (10 ounces by weight)
2 medium apples peeled, cored, finely diced
⅓ to ½ cup sugar
½ to ¾ cup water
1 quart strawberries, hulled and halved

In a heavy-bottomed 3-quart saucepan, combine rhubarb, apples, ⅓ cup sugar, and enough water to cover. Bring to a boil, lower heat, and simmer about 10 minutes, stirring occasionally. When fruit is tender, mash apples and rhubarb into a sauce. Add berries and stir about 5 minutes over low heat. Taste, and add sugar as desired. Serve warm or cold, as a compote, or as topping for cake or tofutti. For Purim, serve as a sauce for rice.

Serves 8 as a compote, more as a topping.

PASSOVER BROCCOLI KNISHES

Recipe by Naomi Arbet from the *Wisconsin Jewish Chronicle* (www.jewishchronicle.org).

1 cup mashed potatoes
⅓ cup matzo meal
2 tablespoons potato starch
½ small onion, finely chopped
¼ cup Passover egg substitute (equivalent of 2 egg whites)
½ teaspoon black pepper
¼ teaspoon salt
1 cup steamed broccoli, finely chopped
a few drops of oil (optional)

Preheat oven to 375° F.

In a bowl, combine all ingredients except broccoli and oil. Stir well, then knead until thoroughly combined and the texture of dough. Divide in 6 portions. Flatten each portion into a 4-inch round, pressing down with waxed paper to flatten. Put one-sixth of the broccoli mixture into each circle, fold over, and press edges to seal.

Spray a cookie sheet with oil, or use a Teflon sheet. Arrange knishes on a single layer and place on bottom rack of oven. Bake 15 minutes on each side. Serve hot.

Serves 6.

MUSHROOM PÂTÉ

From *American Wholefoods Cuisine* by Nikki and David Goldbeck (www.healthyhighways.com). Copyright © Nikki and David Goldbeck.

3 cups mushrooms, diced
2 tablespoons olive oil
1½ cups chopped onion
½ cup sunflower seeds—or soy nuts—ground into meal
½ teaspoon salt
1½ teaspoons nutritional yeast

Prepare mushrooms and set aside.

Heat oil in a skillet and sauté onion until lightly browned. Add mushrooms and sauté, stirring frequently for 3 to 5 minutes until just tender.

Transfer cooked mushroom mixture to a blender or processor and puree to a coarse grind, or chop fine by hand with a heavy knife.

Stir ground sunflower seeds or nuts, salt, and yeast into mushroom paste until evenly blended. Mixture should resemble chopped liver.

Chill before serving.

Makes 1½ cups.

SEVEN VEGETABLE STEW

Adapted from the *Passover Gourmet Cookbook* by Nira Rousso.

2 onions
2 carrots
2 red peppers

2 ribs celery
1 cup mushrooms
2 zucchini
1 cup vegetable broth
2 tomatoes
Salsa to taste (2–4 tablespoons)
1 cup tomato paste
1 cup water
1 tablespoon sugar
¼ teaspoon salt

Cut onions, carrots, red peppers, celery, mushrooms, and zucchini into bite-size pieces. Sauté in veggie broth for 5 minutes until still slightly crunchy. Cut tomatoes into bite-size pieces and add the rest of the ingredients. Cover and cook for 20 minutes on simmer.

This is delicious served over roasted potatoes. Serve as a vegetarian main dish and vegetable side dish for others. Increase or substitute vegetables as desired.

Serves about 4 vegetarian entrées when served with other Seder dishes.

SPINACH AND EGGPLANT KUGEL

Adapted from *Something Different* by Dana Jacobi.

2 pounds eggplant, peeled, cut in 1-inch cubes
10 ounces frozen chopped spinach, defrosted
1 small onion, finely chopped
1 apple, peeled and shredded
½ teaspoon salt
½ cup Passover egg substitute (equivalent of 4 egg whites)
Freshly ground pepper
1 piece matzo

Preheat over to 400° F. Spray a 9-inch-square baking dish and two nonstick cookie sheets with cooking spray.

Arrange the eggplant in a single layer on the cookie sheets. Cover each one loosely with aluminum foil and bake for 10 minutes. Uncover the eggplant and turn the cubes. Recover the pan with the foil and switch the position of the pans in the oven. Bake until the eggplant is soft when pierced with a knife but still maintains its shape, 5 to 10 minutes. Place the eggplant in a large bowl.

Reduce oven temperature to 350°. Squeeze the spinach dry. Mix it with the eggplant. Add the onion, apple, and salt and stir to combine. Mix the prepared egg substitute with the pepper. Crumble in the matzo and blend well. Spread the mixture in an even layer in the prepared baking dish.

Bake at 350° until the top is browned and crispy. Let the kugel sit 10 minutes before cutting and serving hot or warm.

Serves 10.

RESOURCES

Books

Atlas, Nava. *Vegetarian Celebrations*. Boston: Little, Brown, 1990.
Contains menus for an Ashkenazic Seder and a Sephardic Seder.
Some, but not all, of the recipes contain eggs and/or dairy.

Berkoff, Nancy. *Vegan Passover Recipes*. Baltimore, Md.: Vegetarian Resource Group, 2000.
$6.00. Available from the Vegetarian Resource Group.
PO Box 1463, Dept. IN
Baltimore, MD 21203
410-366-VEGE
www.vrg.org
Contains thirty-four delicious Passover dishes, including Winter Squash with Apricot Stuffing, Apple and Herb Stuffed

Mushrooms, Zucchini/Potato Kugel, and Cinnamon Matzoh Balls.

Friedman, Rose. *Jewish Vegetarian Cooking*. Lanham, Md.: National Book Network, 1993.
Contains a Passover section with lacto-ovo recipes.
Kalechofsky, Roberta. *Haggadah for the Liberated Lamb.*
Marblehead, Mass.: Micah Publications, 1988.
225 Humphrey St.
Marblehead, MA 01945
This vegetarian, gender-neutral Haggadah is available in a number of formats from Micah Publications. The recipes it contains are lacto-ovo.

Kalechofsky, Roberta. *The Vegetarian Pesach Cookbook.*
Marblehead, Mass.: Micah Publications, 2002.
$13.00. Available from Micah Publications.
255 Humphrey St.
Marblehead, MA 01945
617-631-7601
www.micahbooks.com
This cookbook offers delicious vegetarian recipes, from soup to nuts, for the Pesach week. No animal products.

Katzen, Molly. *Still Life with Menu.* Berkeley, Calif.: Ten Speed Press, 1998.
Contains a menu for a lacto-ovo Seder.

Wasserman, Debra. *No Cholesterol Passover Recipes.* Baltimore, Md.: Vegetarian Resource Group, 1995.
$8.95. Available from the Vegetarian Resource Group
PO Box 1463, Dept IN
Baltimore, MD 21203
410-366-VEGE
www.vrg.org

Contains more than one hundred vegan Passover dishes, including eggless blintzes, carrot "cream" soup, and apples latkes.

Other

The Vegetarian Resource Group (VRG)

PO Box 1463, Dept. IN
Baltimore, Md. 21203
410-366-VEGE
www.vrg.org

The VRG is a nonprofit organization dedicated to educating the public on vegetarianism and the interrelated issues of health, nutrition, ecology, ethics, and world hunger.

Concern for Helping Animals in Israel (CHAI)

USA Office
PO Box 3341
Alexandria, VA 22302
703-658-9650
www.chai-online.org/index.htm

CHAI is an international organization committed to improving the living conditions of all animals in Israel through education, activism, and program development.

Jewish Veg

www.jewishveg.com/index.html

Jewish Veg is a comprehensive Web site with academic articles, resources, and links relating to all facets of Judaism and vegetarianism.

Jews for Animal Rights

255 Humphrey St.
Marblehead, MA 01945
www.micahbooks.com/jar.html

Jews for Animal Rights promotes vegetarianism, the insights of preventive medicine, alternatives to animal research, community action programs, discussion groups, educational programs, and speakers.

The Jewish Vegetarian and Ecological Society

853/5 Finchley Road
London, England
NW11 8LX
44 0181 455 0692
easyweb.easynet.co.uk/~bmjjhr/jvs.htm

The Jewish Vegetarian and Ecological Society (JVES) is an international group based in London that promotes vegetarianism within the Judaic tradition, and explores the relationship between Judaism, dietary laws, and vegetarianism.

JewishVegan.com

www.jewishvegan.com

JewishVegan.com has extensive resources on Judaism and vegetarianism and also provides information and links to Jewish vegetarian groups and social events.

78.

A Feast for Ramadan or Every Day

There is not an animal on earth, nor a bird that flies on its wings, but they are communities like you.

—THE PROPHET MUHAMMAD

Where there is an abundance of vegetables, a host of angels will descend on that place.

—THE PROPHET MUHAMMAD

During the ninth month of the Islamic calendar, Muslims worldwide celebrate the major holiday of their religion, Ramadan.

Ramadan marks the period when the prophet Muhammad received the holy words from Allah and put them down into the Koran, the Holy Book, in the seventh century AD.

During Ramadan, adult Muslims must fast from dawn until dusk for twenty-nine to thirty days to stir universal compassion and spiritual renewal for all. When the sun goes down each day, a meal can be taken, and after Ramadan there is a big feast.

According to religious scholars, the prophet Muhammad, while not prohibiting the consumption of meat, preferred to eat vegetarian foods and had a great love and compassion for animals. His favorite foods were vegetarian: yogurt with butter or nuts, cucumbers with dates, pomegranates, grapes, and figs.

The Holy Koran tells us that animals have souls, and the prophet

Muhammad's acts of mercy to animals are well known. The Prophet often admonished people to stop wanton cruelty, like shooting arrows at birds for fun, whipping camels and donkeys, allowing animal fighting, or slaughtering for greed, not need.

He is quoted as preaching, "Allah, the Blessed and Exalted, is kind and loves kindness. He is pleased with it and helps you with it as long as it is not misplaced." He asked people to let their camels and donkeys rest, to nourish them well, and to travel with them quicker over arid land where there was little or nothing for them to eat.

In one story, Muhammad became angry when young men stole two baby birds away from their mother who had nested in a bush, saying, "Who grieved this for its young ones? Return its young ones to it." On another occasion, he saw an ant village that had been burned and was upset.

In one of my favorite stories, a camel saw the Prophet and wept tenderly, "producing a yearning sound and its eyes flowed. The Prophet (may peace be upon him) came to it and wiped the temple of its head. So it kept silence. He then said: Whose camel is this? A young man from the Ansar came and said: This is mine, Apostle of Allah. He said: Don't you fear Allah about this beast which Allah has given in your possession? He has complained to me that you keep him hungry and load him heavily which fatigues him."

Like most of the world's religions, modern Islam does not fully support vegetarianism, although certain Muslim sects such as the Shiites and Sufis have vegetarian followers. And meat is often hard to come by in the ever-spreading desert regions, so eating dates, where they can be found, as well as porridge and camel's milk is the norm.

During Ramadan, Muslims begin the day with a predawn meal (*sehri*) of porridge, bread, or fruit. When sundown approaches, they slowly break their fast with something simple like bread or fruit, followed by a big dusk meal (*iftar*) like a hearty soup or stew. When the new moon is sighted, Ramadan ends in a huge feast for family and friends, lasting for several days, called Eid-ul-Fitr.

At this time, even while feasting, Muslims are asked to keep the poor and hungry in mind. It has become common for blood sacrifices of sheep and goats to be made. But other offerings, of money and food and, most important, of one's heart, are made by those who abhor slaughter or who think that the manner of slaughter today—when animals are cruelly treated, knives are not always sharpened, and animals may be bound by the legs—makes the meat *haram* (forbidden). There is no question that modern factory farming, in which animals are mutilated by dehorning, debeaking, and so on, raises serious questions in this regard.

Islamic law requires environmental and social justice considerations, too, including preservation of the land and the dictate that one should not eat too much while others go hungry. All these considerations make a vegetarian Eid feast a joyous choice for many, even those of us with different faiths.

JARY

This is a popular vegetarian soup from Algeria.

1½ teaspoons olive oil
1 medium onion, chopped
3–4 cloves pressed or minced garlic
¾ teaspoon paprika
Pinch cayenne or to taste
½ cup tomato puree
4 cups vegetable stock or water
½ teaspoon salt or to taste
¼ cup fine cracked wheat (or bulgur)
½ cup each of parsley, coriander leaf (cilantro), and mint leaves, coarsely chopped fresh or dried
⅔ cup cooked garbanzo beans (chickpeas)

3–4 teaspoons lemon juice or to taste
Salt to taste

Heat oil in heavy soup pot over medium heat. Sauté onion until tender. Add garlic, paprika, and cayenne; cook for 1–2 minutes, stirring constantly. Add tomato puree and stock or water. Bring to simmer and add salt and cracked wheat. Cover, reduce heat, and simmer gently, stirring occasionally, until cracked wheat is cooked, about 30 minutes (15 minutes if using bulgur).

Remove from heat and cool slightly. Transfer soup to blender or food processor (optional). Add parsley, cilantro, and mint; blend until almost smooth. Return soup to pot, stir in chickpeas and reheat. Add lemon juice and salt to taste.

Serves 4.

DEMJEDDERA

This Palestinian lentil and rice dish is truly superb.

1 cup brown lentils, sorted and rinsed, or 1 (19-ounce) can lentils
1–2 tablespoons olive oil
1 medium onion, chopped
3–4 cloves garlic, minced
Pepper to taste
1½ teaspoons cumin seeds
1 cup dried brown or white rice
½ teaspoon salt or to taste
1¾ cups water
Plain or soy yogurt (optional)

If not using canned lentils, cook dry lentils in 3 cups water until tender (about 45 minutes), then drain.

Heat oil in large skillet or pot over medium heat. Sauté onion until translucent, about 3 minutes. Add garlic, pepper, cumin seeds, and rice. Sauté for 1 to 2 minutes, stirring constantly so spices don't burn. Add salt and water, bring to a boil, and cover, cooking for 40 minutes for brown rice, 15 minutes for white.

Remove from heat, keeping cover on for 10 minutes. Stir cooked or canned lentils into rice. Add salt to taste. Serve garnished with plain or soy yogurt, if desired.

Serves 4 to 6.

SPICED POTATOES AND CAULIFLOWER

This Pakistani side dish is usually served with rice or flatbreads.

1 tablespoon clarified butter (ghee) or vegetable oil
1 medium onion, finely chopped
1–2 tablespoons minced garlic
1 teaspoon ginger, powdered or finely grated
Pepper to taste
½ teaspoon cumin powder or seeds
½ teaspoon cardamom powder or seeds
½ teaspoon ground cloves
1–2 large cooked (boiled) potatoes, peeled and diced
1 small head cooked cauliflower separated into florets
2–3 tablespoons reserved cooking water from potatoes and cauliflower
Salt to taste

Heat butter or oil in a large skillet or pot over medium heat. Sauté onion until tender. Stir garlic and spices and continue to sauté for a minute. Add potatoes and cauliflower and reserved cooking water. Cover, reduce heat to low, and cook until vegetables are very tender (about 5 minutes). Mash slightly with a fork. Salt to taste. Serve.

Serves 4 to 6.

RESOURCES

Islamic Concern

www.islamicconcern.org

Books

Rosen, Steven. *Food for the Spirit: Vegetarianism and the World Religions.* Philadelphia, Pa.: Bala Books, 1987.

A FINAL NOTE

So, that's it for this book, but I hope it is just the beginning in your own quest to find kind, positive choices in life. There are as many ways to improve the world around us from our own homes to the whole ball of wax, and from our personal, private selves to the most public of situations, as there are people on this planet.

I certainly learn more each day, not only from my own experiences but also from the letters, calls, and articles that flood into PETA. I hope to share more of them with you in the future. If you have tips, stories to share, experiences that others might enjoy and learn from, please think of sending them my way. Just pop them in an envelope with your contact details and mail them to me, c/o PETA, Norfolk, VA 23510.

Good luck to you in playing your vital part to make the music in our diverse orchestra come alive—for you, your loved ones, and all of us out here who are listening and playing too!

RESOURCES

PART ONE: HOME AND GARDEN

1. Kindness by Design: Creating and Furnishing a Humane Home

Designer Extraordinaire

Sasha Josipovicz
The Element Group, Toronto
416-921-8899

Chimpanzee Rescue

The Fauna Foundation
PO Box 33
Chambly, Quebec
Canada J3L 4B1
450-658-1844
fauna.foundation@sympatico.ca

Donations gratefully received. Paintings by Tom and other artists available for sale.

Furniture, Furnishings, and Fabrics

Original Ultrasuede

Alcantara
Italy-based, with distributors throughout Europe.
www.alcantara.it

Faux Leather and Other Fabrics

Designer Fabrics
Toronto
416-531-2810
www.designerfabrics.ca

Bamboo Rug

Nienkamper
Go online and find the distributor in your area.
www.nienkamper.com

Furniture and Upholstery

Ro-en Furniture
Can be purchased by individuals through Roots, a Canada-based home and clothing store.
877-927-6687
www.roots.com

Panda-Safe Bamboo Window Coverings

Sohjico
Montreal
514-528-4333
www.sohjico.com

Vinyl and Ultrasuede Wall Coverings

Versa
Kentucky-based.
502-458-1502
www.lsiwc.com/index.htm

No-Iron Polyester Sheets

W Hotels
New York–based.
800-453-6548
www.whotelsthestore.com

Everydaysuede

The Pottery Barn
www.potterybarn.com

Makers of Everydaysuede, a microfiber that feels like real suede but is entirely machine washable, durable, colorfast slipcover material.

2. Creating a Beautiful Garden to Attract Birds, Butterflies, and Other Natural Life

Royal Society for the Protection of Birds

UK Headquarters:
The Lodge
Sandy, Bedfordshire
SG19 2DL
United Kingdom
44 01767 680551
www.rspb.org.uk

The RSPB, Europe's largest wildlife conservation nonprofit, has been researching wildlife problems, promoting practical solutions, and working on behalf of birds and the environment since 1889.

Audubon Society

Main Office:
700 Broadway
New York, NY 10003
212-979-3000
www.audubon.org

The Audubon Society's national network of community-based nature centers and chapters works to conserve birds and other wildlife through scientific and educational programs, including "Audubon Adventures" for grade school children and camps and workshops for families, adults, and children.

National Wildlife Federation
11100 Wildlife Center Dr.
Reston, VA 20190
800-822-9919
www.nwf.org

The NWF is not animal-friendly in all matters, but it does run the Backyard Wildlife Habitat Program, through which people can have their yards certified as "backyard habitats" if they provide certain things, such as water sources and nesting sites. The NWF also puts out a handy little book called Planting an Oasis for Wildlife.

The Xerces Society
4828 SE Hawthorne Blvd.
Portland, OR 97215
503-232-6639
www.xerces.org

A nonprofit organization named after an extinct butterfly species and dedicated to conserving butterflies, bees, and other invertebrates.

Monarch Watch
University of Kansas Entomology Department
1200 Sunnyside Ave.
Lawrence, KS 66045-7534
888-TAGGING
www.monarchwatch.org

Focuses on conserving Monarch butterflies, but has valuable information about other butterfly species as well. (Drawback: Monarch Watch has a "tagging" program in which it puts a tiny sticker on butterflies 'wings so it can track their migration.)

Stokes, Donald, Lillian Stokes, and Ernest Williams. *The Butterfly Book: An Easy Guide to Butterfly Gardening, Identification, and Behavior.* New York: Little, Brown, 1991.

3. Creating an Eco- and Animal-Friendly Bathroom

For an up-to-the-minute list of which companies conduct animal tests and which do not, always carry a copy of PETA's free, wallet-size cruelty-free shopping guide, available by writing PETA at 501 Front Street, Norfork,

VA 23510, visiting peta.org, or calling 757-622-7382. Companies listed as not testing have either signed a corporate Statement of Assurance or meet the Corporate Standard of Compassion for Animals put out by the Coalition for Consumer Information on Cosmetics (CCIC), a group of seven animal-protection organizations, including PETA.

Organic Health and Beauty

www.organichealthandbeauty.com

New York's *Satya* magazine for the environmentally conscious consumer recommends this company this way: "Their name says it all—organic, wild-crafted products that are completely animal-free and don't use synthetic or petroleum ingredients."

Clear Conscience

Ten percent goes to PETA.

Cruelty-free contact lens solutions.

Tom's of Maine

PO Box 710
Kennebunk, ME 04043
800-367-8667
www.tomsofmaine.com
Toothpastes.

Gillette

www.gillette.com

Razors and shaving and oral care products, including Venus, Mach 3 Turbine, and Oral B.

The Body Shop

5036 One World Way
Wake Forest, NC 27587
919-554-4900
www.thebodyshop.com

The Drench Body Sponge is available from the Body Shop and is a thoughtful alternative to sponges removed from the sea. This one lathers very well and lasts longer than a real sea sponge.

Soap Dream

PO Box 6278
Albany, CA 94706
510-526-9668
www.soapdream.com

Natural and cruelty-free gift baskets of vegan soaps, body scrubs, body butter, lip balm, and much more; 10 percent goes to PETA.

LeapingBunny.org

www.leapingbunny.org

To learn more about why cosmetics tests on animals do not protect the consumer, and to get the answers to other questions about animal tests and alternatives.

Vegan Essentials

www.veganessentials.com

HBG aftershave for men in bay rum, sandalwood, and other scents.

4. Choosing Cleaning Products That Are Kind to More Than Your Floor

Advantage Wonder Cleaner

800-323-6444
www.wondercleaner.com

All-purpose cleaner (vegan).

Allens Naturally

800-352-8971
www.allensnaturally.com

All-purpose cleaner, dish detergent, fabric softener, laundry detergent (vegan).

America's Finest Products Corporation

800-482-6555

All-purpose cleaner, fine-washables detergent, stain remover (vegan).

BI-O-KLEEN

800-477-0188

All-purpose cleaner, bleach, carpet cleaner, dish detergent, laundry detergent, stain remover (vegan).

Citra-Solv

800-343-6588

www.citrasolv.com

Air freshener, all-purpose cleaner, dishwashing detergent, car care, carpet cleaner, drain cleaner, furniture polish, glass cleaner, oven cleaner, stain remover (vegan).

Earth Friendly Products

800-335-3267

www.ecos.com

Air freshener, all-purpose cleaner, bathroom cleaner, bleach, cream cleanser, dish detergent, drain cleaner, furniture polish, glass cleaner, laundry detergent, stain and odor remover, toilet cleaner (vegan).

Ecover

800-449-4925

www.ecover.com

All-purpose cleaner, dish detergent, cream cleanser, laundry detergent, fabric softener, stain remover.

Environmental Working Group

www.ewg.org

Information on bird deaths from household chemicals.

Huish Detergents

800-776-6702

www.huish.com

Bathroom cleaner, bleach, dish detergent, fabric softener, floor cleaner, glass cleaner, laundry detergent, stain remover.

James Austin Company

800-245-1942

www.jamesaustin.com

All-purpose cleaner, bleach, carpet cleaner, dish detergent, drain cleaner, fabric softener, glass cleaner, laundry detergent, oven cleaner.

Method Products Inc.

866-9-METHOD

www.methodhome.com

All-purpose cleaner, bathroom cleaner, dish detergent, glass cleaner, shower cleaner (vegan).

Nature Clean (Frank T. Ross and Sons Ltd.)
416-282-1107
www.franktross.com
All-purpose cleaner, automatic dishwashing detergent, bathroom cleaner, bleach, carpet cleaner, fabric softener, fine-washables detergent, glass cleaner, laundry detergent, oven cleaner, stain remover, toilet cleaner (vegan).

Orange-Mate
800-626-8685
www.orangemate.com
Air freshener, all-purpose cleaner, glass cleaner (vegan).

Planet
800-858-8449
www.planetinc.com
All-purpose cleaner, dish detergent, fine-washables detergent, laundry detergent (vegan).

Seventh Generation
802-658-3773
www.seventhgeneration.com
All-purpose cleaner, carpet cleaner, cream cleansers, dish detergent, laundry detergent, bleach, glass cleaner, toilet cleaner (vegan).

Shaklee Corporation
800-SHAKLEE
www.shaklee.com
All-purpose cleaner, dish detergent, drain cleaner, laundry detergent.

Shop Natural
www.shopnatural.com
Natumate stain and odor removers, including skunk odor remover.

Stanley Home Products

800-628-9032

www.stanleyhome.com

All-purpose cleaner, bathroom cleaner, brass/copper/silver/stainless-steel cleaner, carpet cleaner, furniture polish, glass cleaner, jewelry cleaner, laundry detergent, stain remover.

Whip-It Products

800-582-0398

All-purpose cleaner for home or industrial use, carpet cleaner, laundry detergent, oven cleaner.

5. Choices in Car Interiors

Ultrafabrics LLC (L)

400 Executive Blvd.

Elmsford, NY 10523

888-361-9216 (Sales and Marketing)

877-309-6648 (Customer Service)

Fax: 914-347-1591

email@ultrafabricsllc.com

www.ultrasuede.com

Motto is "So like leather, only better." Soft, supple, and sensuous to the touch, resistant to stains and discoloration, machine-washable and dry-cleanable.

6. Selecting the Purest Candles: Those Without Tallow, Paraffin, or Beeswax

Vegesoy Candles from Jenni Originals

480-753-5194 or toll-free 877-95-JENNI

Fax: 480-753-5196

Get the candles used by Alicia Silverstone and Brooke Shields! These are handmade with "specially formulated superior wax derived from soybeans and all natural vegetable ingredients. Environmentally safe and incredibly cleaner burners than paraffin." One hundred percent biodegradable.

Royal Products Inc.

718-417-9696

Sabbath candles can be purchased by the case; also available in kosher markets.

Ethicalwares.com

www.ethicalwares.com

Vegan pyramids, cones, and rounds.

7. Capping Your Chimney/Sealing Your Attic

The Fund for Animals

www.fundwildlife.org

Urban wildlife advice.

PETA

757-622-7382

Contact PETA for Wildlife Fact Sheet #7–"Living in Harmony."

www.helpingwildlife.com

A resource for anything and everything related to PETA's work to educate people about wildlife.

8. Dealing Kindly with Mice and Other Uninviteds

Ketch-All Company

www.ketch-all.com or www.realgoods.com/shop

Ketch All Mouse Trap ($20) uses no bait; simply wind the knob to catch mice twenty-four hours a day and release. This is a heavy-duty galvanized steel trap, with a simple goof-proof design. Each mouse should be removed as soon as s/he is caught in order to prevent injury to another mouse that enters. Measures 5½ inches H×9 inches L×7¼ inches W. Pro-Ketch Mouse Trap ($16) is made from tough galvanized steel; this trap captures multiple mice without ever resetting. Placing bait inside entices mice to enter. As they walk in, the teeter-totter-style ramp lowers to allow mice in, but snaps back once they step off so they can't exit. Clear view lid allows easy monitoring. Larger traps are available from this company.

H. B. Sherman

www.shermantraps.com

Folding and nonfolding traps. The folding one is very handy! Prices range from $11.99 to $35.00 (depending on size and material of trap).

PETA

www.petacatalog.com

With the Humane "Smart" Mousetrap ($10) you can catch mice alive and unharmed. A little dab of peanut butter is our recommended lure, and we have lots of pinprick holes in the trap.

Tomahawk Live Trap

www.livetrap.com

The Tomahawk Humane Mouse Trap ($20) is constructed of 28-gauge galvanized sheet metal for maximum resistance to rust and corrosion. This trap can be used for mice, shrews, voles, small chipmunks, or any small rodent.

9. Dealing Kindly with Insects in the Home

Holidobler, Bert, and Edward Osborne Wilson. *The Ants.* Belknap Press, 1990.

The definitive scientific study of one of the most diverse animal groups on earth. Full of amazing facts about the social behavior of these fascinating beings.

10. Saving Little Visitors Who Get Trapped in the Swimming Pool or Pond

www.petamall.com

Frog Saver Lily Pad

Frogs trapped in pools swim around the edge in search of escape. This "lily pad" gives them just the leg up they need and can be snapped onto the pool ladder or attached to the wall. Made with 100 percent recycled plastic! About $15.

11. Being Kind to Your Lawns and the Life in and on Them

www.environmentalfactor.com

Chemical-free turf care.

www.AskCarla.com

Your local library.

12. Do It Yourself: How to Avoid Commercial Cleaners

44 Things to Do with Vinegar
groups.msn.com/veggiechat/crueltyfreecleaners.msnw

PART TWO: FASHION AND BEAUTY

13. Choosing Cosmetics That Give Everyone Something to Smile About

Urban Decay

www.urbandecay.com

Products from innovative Face Case, XXX Shine Gloss, Urban Camouflage Concealer, Lip Gunk, and Eye Shadow are available in Sephora, Ultra, and select boutiques nationwide.

Aveda

www.aveda.com

Cosmetics, hair products, and spa treatments.

Avalon Organic Botanicals

www.avalonnaturalproducts.com

Facial cleanser.

M.A.C. Cosmetics

www.maccosmetics.com

Kohl eyeliner and eye shadows.

Coalition for Consumer Information on Cosmetics (CCIC)

www.leapingbunny.org

For information on the cruelty-free logo and the Corporate Standard of Compassion for Animals.

14. Some Thoughts About Wool

The Plymouth Yarn Company

PO Box 28
500 Lafayette St.
Bristol, PA 19007

215-788-0459
www.plymouthyarn.com
This company distributes hand knitting yarns to shops across the USA. Its product is 100 percent acrylic.

Yesterknits
www.yesterknits.com
Supplier of vintage British crochet and knitting patterns. The company also gives advice on pattern conversion and will send anyone a free pattern.

15. Avoiding Bits of Fur on Collars and Cuffs, and Sidestepping Shearling, the "Sheepy Fur"

Weatherproof Garment Co.
www.weatherproofgarment.com
Modern technology has made great strides in replacing animal products with humane synthetics. Weatherproof Garment Company has developed a faux "shearling" that it calls "microshearling." Microshearling is a synthetic fabric that has the feel of sheepskin but is made of polyester microfiber. This new fabric consists of a layer of specially treated polyester that is bonded to a thick layer of a synthetic pile fabric. In look and feel, microshearling is practically indistinguishable from the "real thing." Its advantages over genuine shearling are many: It is resistant to rain, wind, and snow, and because it is completely synthetic, it is animal-friendly, too.

Fur Replicas
262-790-1895
www.furreplicas.com
An assortment of faux fur capes, wraps, jackets, and muffs for rent or sale. Prices range from $18 to $82 for a four-day rental period.

16. Shoe Shopping

Moo Shoes
212-254-6512
www.mooshoes.com
Offers a wide variety of nonleather shoes, belts, and wallets.

Steve Madden

888-SMADDEN

www.stevemadden.com

Offers many nonleather women's shoes. Sells shoes in Steve Madden stores, in major department stores, and online.

Vegetarian Shoes

www.vegetarian-shoes.co.uk

This company, which Sir Paul McCartney patronizes, carries more than fifty styles of synthetic leather and synthetic suede shoes and other products, including genuine nonleather Dr. Martens bad boy boots and shoes, nonleather Birkenstocks, dress shoes, hiking boots, work boots, "pleather" jackets and belts.

Payless

877-474-6379

www.payless.com

Possibly the world's lowest-priced selection. It carries a wide variety of trendy styles of shoes and boots. So cheap, you can buy three pairs for the price of one somewhere else! And these shoes imitate many of the top designers' styles but are made of imitation leather, so you can get fashionable shoes at a fraction of the price.

For funky ultratrendy shoes, I recommend DragonFly Shoes (www.dragonflyshoes.com), and Funk e Feet (www.funkefeet.com), which, very endearingly, marks all vegan selections with a little cow symbol.

A Propos . . . Conversations (www.conversationshoes.com) offers pretty, feminine vegan fabric shoes for women.

For synthetic pumps there's Life Stride (www.browngroup.com/lifestride), which you can usually find at department stores such as Famous-Barr, Foley's, Hecht Co., Robinsons-May, Belk's, Boscov's, Rich's-Lazarus-Goldsmith's, Carson Pirie Scott, Proffitt's, and Younker's. You can call 1-800-766-6465 for a retailer near you. Delias (www.delias.com) has a wide selection of feminine faux leather and faux suede boots and shoes.

My top picks for athletic shoes are: New Balance (www.newbalance.com) for comfortable synthetic running, tennis, and basketball shoes; for hiking boots, Garmont USA (www.garmontusa.com); Airwalk (www.airwalk.com) for synthetic snow boots and skateboarding shoes; and

SiDi USA (www.sidiusa.com) for nonleather bicycling shoes. Road Runner Sports (www.roadrunnersports.com) sells nonleather running shoes including Brooks, Asics, New Balance, Saucony, Reebok, Mizuno, Adidas, and Etonic. Spalding Sports (www.spalding.com) carries synthetic leather volleyballs, basketballs, softballs, soccer balls, and footballs. You can even get vegan ballet slippers from Capezio (www.capeziodance.com); the 626 Tapette and 625 Jr. Tyette for women are both synthetic.

17. Finding the Perfect Soap

The Body Shop

www.bodyshop.com

Cocoa butter soaps, translucent glycerin ones, and rich cleansing bars.

PETA

www.peta.org

For PETA's free list of companies that test on animals and those that don't.

18. Bighearted Options to Exotic Skins

For designer faux, check out Moschino, Todd Oldham, and many of the top names in bags, wallets, and accessories.

19. Recognizing Animal Ingredients and Alternatives to Them

Buyukmihci, Nermin. *John Cardillo's List of Animal Products and Their Alternatives.* Milner, Ga.: 1988.

Cosmetic Ingredients Glossary: A Basic Guide to Natural Body Care Products. Petaluma, Calif.: Feather River, 1988.

Mason, Jim, and Peter Singer. *Animal Factories.* New York: Crown Publishers, 1980.

Ruesch, Hans. *Slaughter of the Innocent.* New York: Civitas, 1983.

Singer, Peter. *Animal Liberation.* New York: Random House, 1990.

Winter, Ruth. *A Consumer's Dictionary of Cosmetic Ingredients.* New York: Crown Publishing Group, 1994.

———. *A Consumer's Dictionary of Food Additives.* New York: Crown Publishing Group, 1994.

PART THREE: FOOD AND ENTERTAINING

20. Going Organic: Supporting Home Growers

Last Organic Outpost
www.lastorganicoutpost.com

Organic Consumers Association
www.organicconsumers.org

The Vegetable Patch
www.thevegetablepatch.com
Looking for the Web site full of organic vegetable gardening information? The Vegetable Patch offers practical information for online gardeners.

Seeds of Change
www.seedsofchange.com
Sells everything from fruit trees and flowers to herbs, and from compost starter to organic seeds for "ordinary" greens like kale and lettuce, and gourmet greens like Persian garden cress and mesclun.

Do-it-Yourself Network
www.diynetwork.com
Great source for window boxes.

Organic Bouquet
www.organicbouquet.com
Organic flowers and fruits by mail.

Books

Colement, Eliot. *Four-Season Harvest: Organic Vegetables from Your Home Garden All Year Long.* White River Junction, Vt.: Chelsea Green Publishing, 1992.

21. Putting Organic-, Worker-, and Bird-Friendly Coffee in Your Pot

PETA's Free Bird Coffee and Coffee Club

www.petamall.com

PETA offers three varieties of coffee grown without pesticides, herbicides, or chemical fertilizers: Flying Free French Roast, Morning Birdsong Breakfast Blend, and No Ruffled Feathers Decaf coffee. A percentage of proceeds from sales go to support PETA's Free Bird Campaign. PETA will send your choice of shade-grown Arabica coffee bean coffees to your home or as gifts for others. Shipping is free.

Fair Trade

For a list of traders local to you who use Fair Trade coffee retailers:
1611 Telegraph Ave., Ste. 900
Oakland, CA 94612
510-663-5260
Fax: 510-663-5264

Transfair USA

www.transfair@transfairusa.org

This is the only organization providing independent certification for fair trade products in the U.S. Look for the Fair Trade Certified label—proof that the farmers who grew your coffee or tea received a fair price.

The Roasted Bean

888-294-8886
www.theroastedbean.com

This company allows you to select coffee by "taste profile" and provides free shipping from southern Florida.

JavaSoy

www.javasoy.com

Comes in French vanilla, Swiss chocolate almond, and other flavors, and became the first soy-based Colombia Arabica coffee when it debuted at the Indiana State Fair in 2003. An eight-ounce cup of JavaSoy has half the caffeine of regular coffee, five grams of soy protein, and 2.2 milligrams of isoflavones, cancer-fighting plant chemicals.

White Wave Silk Soylattes

www.silkissoy.com

These are geared to consumers who want organic soy as part of a diet to reduce the risk of heart disease as well as customers who simply prefer a tofu taste. Available in most supermarkets.

Most coffee chains, even those that do not serve environmentally, animal-, and ecologically friendly coffees, now serve soy milk even if they do not list it on their boards, so don't forget to ask.

22. Breakfast of Eco- and Animal Champions

Fabulous soy "bacon" and "sausages" are in most supermarket freezer cases. Here are some favorites:

Gardenburger Meatless Breakfast Sausage

www.gardenburger.com

This has a satisfying meaty homemade sausage taste and is made with all-natural soy and seasoned with herbs and spices.

GimmeLean! Sausage Style

Lightlife Foods
153 Industrial Blvd.
Turners Falls, MA 01376
1-900-SOY-EASY
www.lightlife.com

A fat-free and very tasty soy replacement for breakfast or anytime sausages, this crumbles well for casseroles and lasagna too.

Yves Canadian Veggie Bacon

1638 Derwent Way
Delta (Vancouver), BC
V3M 6R9
Canada
1-800-667-9837
www.yvesveggie.com

Delicious preservative-free "bacon" made from wheat gluten and other wholesome foods, perfect with frozen waffles (vegan varieties are available in most major grocery chains).

23. Harmless Hors d'Oeuvres and Other Delights

*Cavi*Art faux cavia*

www.happycookers.com/wc.dll/products/divulge/3-4364.html

Pangea

www.veganstore.com

Organic Gourmet Pâtés, Nacho ChReese Dips, and Meditalia Roasted Eggplant Spread.

The PETA Celebrity Cookbook

www.petamall.org

Try artichoke dip, red-hot risotto, and other treats from the kitchens of Alicia Silverstone, Russell Simmons, Moby, and more.

24. The King of Barbecue

Books

Atlas, Nava. *Vegetarian Celebrations.* New York: Little, Brown, 1996.

Chelf, Vicki Rae. *The Sensuous Vegetarian Barbecue.* New York: Avery Penguin Putnam, 1994.

Chesman, Andrea. *The Vegetarian Grill.* Boston: Harvard Common Press, 1998.

Gwynn, Mary. *Vegetarian Barbecue.* North York, Ontario: Whitecap Books, North York, 2001.

People for the Ethical Treatment of Animals. *Cooking with PETA.* Nashville, Tenn.: Book Publishing Company, 1997.

25. A Lesson About Lobsters and Crabs

Tuno is available at most health food stores or through www.healthy-eating.com.

May Wah Healthy Vegetarian Food

877-668-2668

www.vegieworld.com

The PETA Mall

www.petamall.com

26. Substituting Mock Meats: Transition Foods for Macho Meat Eaters

Books

Robertson, Robin. *The Vegetarian Meat and Potatoes Cookbook.* Boston: Harvard Common Press, 2002.

Mock Meat Ideas

Chic-Ketts

www.worthingtonfoods.com

Chic-Ketts is a completely meatless, precooked, vegetable protein product, free of animal fat and preservatives. They are ideal in casseroles, soups, stir fry, and more.

Morningstar Farms Burger Crumbles

www.morningstarfarms.com

Burger Style Recipe Crumbles are a blend of vegetable and grain proteins that provide a tasty, low-fat alternative to cooked ground beef. Fully cooked and recipe ready, they can be added to your favorite recipe.

Nayonnaise

Available in most health food stores.

27. The Fun of Ethnic Eating

Holmin, Dalal A., and Maher A. Abbas. *From the Tables of Lebanon: Traditional Vegetarian Cuisine.* Nashville, Tenn: Book Publishing Company, 1997.

Le, Kim. *Asian Vegan Cooking: A High-Energy Approach to Healthy Living.* New York: Sterling Publishing, 2003.

Morse, Kitty, and Deborah Jones. *North Africa.* San Francisco, Calif: Chronicle Books, 2002.

Polemis, Aphrodite. *From a Traditional Greek Kitchen: Vegetarian Cuisine.* Book Publishing Company, 1992.

28. Bees, Honey, and Some Thoughts About Sweeteners

Sweet is as sweet does: If your taste buds are used to honey, they will need to adjust, and adjust they will, in a very short time, to another sweet flavoring. Try maple syrup or molasses, or one of the "natural sweeteners" like Sugarnot, available in almost every health food store.

Rapadura

800-207-2814

www.rapunzel.com

Quality organic care sugar.

The Ultimate Sweetener

800-THEMEAL

www.ultimatelife.com

No trees are cut down for this 100 percent birch sugar, which contains no honey, corn syrup, fructose, or animal products or artificial ingredients.

Amy Toth

amytoth@life.uiuc.edu

Book

Burke, Abbot George. *Simply Heavenly: The Monastery Vegetarian Cookbook.* New York: Hungry Minds, Inc., 1997.

29. Baking Kind Cakes: Replacing Ingredients That Hurt Animals

Ready-Made Baked Goods

If you don't feel like cooking, nip around to your local supermarket and you can find vegan baked goods galore. If you have a Dollar Store near you, you will find apple and cinnamon cookies and twists and all manner of vegan baked goods on the shelves. Here are a few other suggestions (check labels though, as ingredients can change from time to time):

- Barry's Bakery makes six varieties of French twists as well as other cookies. French twist flavors include original (cinnamon), maple French toast, chocolate chip, mocha, wild raspberry, and California almond.
- Uncle Eddie's rich cookies come in chocolate chip, oatmeal, and peanut butter flavors.
- Keebler Vienna Crème-Filled Fingers go beautifully with a hot cup of tea or coffee.
- Krispy Kreme Pies: cherry, apple, and, best of all, coconut cream—available in grocery stores and gas stations.

- Little Debbie makes a "cake doughnut" that's vegan, and available in convenience and grocery stores and gas stations.
- Newmans-O cookies are organic and made without trans fats.
- Rich Foods: Chocolate fudge stripe cookies.
- Sara Lee has several varieties of vegan pastries.

30. Preparing a Romantic Candlelight Dinner

The Lovers' Dinner

Millennium Restaurant
580 Geary St.
San Francisco, CA
415-345-3900

The Body Shop

Hundreds of retail stores around the world.
www.thebodyshop.com
usa.info@the-body-shop.com

The Body Shop offers massage oils and a series of books on body care. The books' practical and easy-to-use format provides simple solutions for everyday stresses.

Vegan Erotica

801-560-8238
www.veganerotica.com

Vegan Erotica offers everthing from cruelty-free lubricants to bondage gear custom-made from animal-friendly pleather. Its Web site also features CONDOMI condoms, which are manufactured with cocoa powder instead of casein (a milk protein), making them the only condoms to be given the seal of approval by the Vegan Society. Available in a wide range of flavors, textures, and sizes, and in packs of 6 ($3), 12 ($5.75), and 24 ($10).

Secret Garden Publishing

www.secretgardenpublishing.com

Book

Stubbs, Kenneth Ray. *Erotic Massage: The Touch of Love.*
With over one hundred illustrations, *Erotic Massage* presents detailed,

long, flowing strokes for lovers. With almost half a million copies sold, this book appears in many languages and many countries around the world.

Secret Gardens Unscented Massage Oil/Secret Gardens Scent Oil: A high-quality blend of apricot, sunflower, macadamia nut, safflower, grape-seed, and jojoba oils and vitamin E. Blend with your favorite Secret Gardens Scent Oil for a custom-scented massage aid that will relax tired muscles and delight the senses. Eight-ounce bottle.

Yo-Organic Plus
604-990-9700
Flavored lubricants with hemp oil and no animal products.

PART FOUR: RECREATION AND VACATIONS

31. Traveling Safely with Animals or Leaving Them Safely Behind

Books

Travel With or Without Pets: 25,000 Pets-R-Permitted Accommodations, Pet-sitters, Kennels, and More. Torrance, Calif.: Annenburg Communications Institute, 1997.

Ignore the boarding kennel, vet clinics, and pet-sitters, but this book does list more than twenty thousand animal-friendly hotels and motels across the USA, Canada, and Mexico from budget stops to posh resorts like the exclusive San Ysidro Ranch in Santa Barbara.

Barish, Eileen. *Vacationing With Your Pet: Eileen's Directory of Pet-Friendly Lodging: U.S. and Canada.* Gardena, Calif.: SCB Distributors, 2001.

As with all guides, it is useful to double-check to make sure hotel/motel policies haven't changed since publication. This guide lists twenty-three thousand places where animals are welcome and includes helpful travel tips and even a dog biscuit recipe.

Four Seasons Hotels Worldwide, including the Hotel Pierre in Manhattan
800-332-3442
www.fourseasons.com

Loews Hotels
www.loewshotels.com

Motel 6
www.motel6.com
Most motel 6 hotels allow one animal per room.

Super 8 Motels
www.super8.com

Vari-Kennels
www.epetpals.com
Hard plastic travel carriers, airline ready.

32. Being Ready for Animal Emergencies on the Road

The PETA Rescue Kit

The kit is available for purchase at www.peta.org. The rescue kit contains a cardboard carrier, a nylon lead, a towel, and a "Be an Angel for Animals" packet full of information on how you can help animals in your community.

33. Preserving the Beach—Its Life and Coral Reefs

Tanning Products
Banana Boat
800-723-3786
www.bananaboat.com

Eco- and Animal-Friendly Beaches
Coral Sea National Nature Reserves, Australia

Fishing is not permitted in these reserves and divers are cautioned not to disturb shells, coral, and other sea life. Nesting turtles and birds are protected.

Buck Island Reef Monument National Park, Virgin Islands

Camping is not permitted, the marine garden is closed to all fishing, and plants and animals here are protected.

National Marine Park, Had Mae Had, Thailand

Cozumel, Mexico

Reef Protection

Friends of the Reef
www.friendsofthereef.com

Project Aware

www.livingreef.org
Diving guidelines for reef excursions.

34. The Benefits of Beachcombing

The Alabama Wildlife Rehabilitation Center, Birmingham
205-663-7930
www.alawildliferehab.org

Suncoast Seabird Sanctuary, Indian Shores, Florida
727-391-6211
www.seabirdsanctuary.org

35. Making Sure Sports and Sports Equipment Are Truly Sporting

www.cowsarecool.com

For information on alternatives to leather in sports, including synthetic bicycle seats, baseball mitts, golf shoes, and ballet slippers, and to obtain a free copy of the "PETA Guide to Nonleather Products."

Balls

Spalding
www.spalding.com

Makes synthetic basketballs, volleyballs, softballs, soccer balls, and footballs.

Baseball Gloves

Heartland Products Ltd.
800-441-4692
www.trvnet.net~hrtlndp/

Biking Gloves

REI
800-426-4840
www.rei.com

Bowling Shoes

Dexter Shoes
207-924-5471
www.dextershoe.com

Ice and Hockey Skates

L. L. Bean
800-441-5713
www.llbean.com

Horseback Riding Equipment

Thorowgood
44 1922 711 676
www.thorowgood.com

Vegan Wares

44 1273 691 913
www.veganwares.com

Boots for Hiking, Work, and Play

Lacrosse Footwear
503-766-1010
www.lacrosse-outdoors.com

Motorcycle Apparel

Aerostitch/Rider Warehouse
800-222-1994
www.aerostitch.com

Alpine Stars
310-891-0222
www.alpinestars.com

Competition Accessories
800-543-8208
www.compacc.com

Cycleport
800-777-6499
www.cycleport.com

Dennis Kirk
800-328-9290
www.denniskirk.com

Draggin Jeans
828-327-2644
www.dragginjeans.com

Ethical Wares
44 (0) 1570 471 155
www.ethicalwares.com

Giali USA
866-527-6987
www.motorcycle-uk.com

Harley-Davidson
800-258-2464
www.harley-davidson.com

Heartland Products Ltd.
800-441-4692
www.trvnet.net

Joe Rocket Sports Gear
800-635-6103
www.kneedraggers.com

Marsee Products
800-293-2400
www.marseeproducts.com

MotoLiberty
800-214-RACE
www.motoliberty.com

Motonation
877-789-4940
www.motonation.com

Olympia Sports
800-521-2832
www.olympiasports.com

Road Gear
800-854-4327
www.roadgear.com

Teknic
616-866-3722
www.teknicgear.com

Tour Master
www.tourmaster.com

Vegetarian Shoes
44 (0) 1273 691 913
www.vegetarian-shoes.co.uk

Willie & Max
www.willieandmax.com

Yamaha Motor Corporation
800-962-7926
www.yamaha-motor.com

Skateboarding Shoes

Circa
www.circafootwear.com

Emerica
www.emericaskate.com

És Footwear
www.esfootwear.com

Etnies
949-460-2020
www.etnies.com

Globe
888-4GLOBES
www.globeshoes.com

Hawk Footwear
www.hawkshoes.com

IPath
www.ipath.com

Macbeth Shoes
www.macbethshoes.com

Osiris
858-874-4970
www.osirisshoes.com

Snowboarding Boots

Airwalk
www.airwalk.com

Snow Boots

Payless Shoe Source
877-474-6379
www.payless.com

Weight-Lifting Gloves

NewGrip.com
800-213-0450
www.newgrip.com

To help get the NBA to switch to a synthetic ball, write:
NBA Commissioner
c/o National Basketball Association
Olympic Tower, 645 Fifth Avenue
New York, NY 10022

36. Alternatives to Catching Fish (and Even to "Catch and Release")

NoFishing.net (PETA)

www.nofishing.net
Information on angling and handy fish facts.

Pisces

An offshoot of the Campaign for the Abolition of Angling, this organization is dedicated to fish welfare and banning fishing. Pisces is focused on youth work, education, and informing people of the welfare needs of fish in all situations.

www.pisces.demon.co.uk

The PETA Catalog

www.petacatalog.com
Bass Avenger Computer Game

Did you ever want to get back at "sports" fishers? Well, here's your chance! You're the fish and the tables are turned on the humans who normally abuse you. Works with Windows or Mac. Available from Amazon Video Games at www.amazon.com.

37. Helping Elephants and Whales by Staying Clear of Circuses and Marine Parks

Organizations

The Elephant Sanctuary, Hohenward, Tennessee
931-796-6500
www.elephants.com

You can visit and see the rescued elephants roaming free on hundreds of acres of land; you donate enough to feed a rescued elephant for a day

($30); or you can help Acres of Elephants, a fund to buy additional land to house the rescued "herd."

Captive Animals Protection Society
www.captiveanimals.org

Zoocheck
www.zoocheck.com
Works on captive animals in circuses and zoos internationally.

Book

Johnson, William. *The Rose-Tinted Menagerie.* London: Heretic Books, 1990.

This book is out of print and hard to find but worth the search.

Video

Elephant-beating video
www.circuses.com

Movies

Free Willy
Dumbo

Animal-Free Circuses

The New Pickle Family Circus, San Francisco, California
415-759-8123
laurafraenza@yahoo.com

Cirque du Soleil
www.cirquedusoleil.com

Circus Oz
www.circusoz.com.au

Circus d'Hiver
www.cirque-dhiver.nel

Cirque Eloize
www.cirque-eloize.com/en

38. Packing a Picnic

Chic-Ketts
Contain wheat and soy and is kosher.
www.kellogs.com

Recipes
Mediterranean Picnic Pie
www.pastrywiz.com
Tangy olives and hearty potatoes make this a satisfying peasant pie served cold for picnics.

Bean and Soy Cheese Stuffed Picnic Loaf
www.mexicanfood.about.com
Look under the vegetarian/vegan section and use any sharp vegan cheese to make a great spicy picnic roll.

Corn and Black Bean Salad and more
www.healthy.lifetips.com

39. Looking Out for Stolen Souvenirs

Traffic
www.traffic.org
Fighting the trade in endangered species.

Beauty Without Cruelty
http://members.tripod.com/~bwcindia/history.htm

40. Holiday Rescues: Helping Animals While Traveling

PETA
www.peta.org

World Society for the Protection of Animals
www.wspa.org

41. How Never to Be Tempted to Attend Bullfights, Rodeos, or Other "Animal Acts"

PETA

www.peta.org

For free brochures to use to educate others in your hometown or while traveling.

PART FIVE: ANIMALS IN THE HOME

42. Understanding and Dealing with Your Dog's Barking and Digging

The Sense-ation Harness

www.softouchconcepts.com

For dogs who pull on the leash, the harness doesn't hurt the neck and really works. It has the ring where you attach the leash in the front of the chest, so that if the dog lunges, he or she instantly gets turned back around to face you so that you can redirect that energy. It's pretty amazing.

Books

McConnell, Patricia B. *How to Be the Leader of the Pack . . . and Have Your Dog Love You for It*. Black Earth, Wisc.: Dog's Best Friend, Ltd., 1996.

McConnell, Patricia B., Ph.D., and Karen B. London, Ph.D. *Feisty Fido*. Black Earth, Wisc.: Dog's Best Friend Ltd., 2003. 608-767-2345; www.dogsbestfriendtraining.com.

The technique described in this book is for dogs who "freak out" at birds, other small dogs, and so on while on the leash. It involves getting the dogs, through treats and other rewards, to concentrate on the walker's face for cues as to what to do. The PETA librarian swears by it.

Miller, Pat. *Positive Perspectives: Love Your Dog, Train Your Dog*. Wenatchee, Wisc.: Dogwise Publishing, 2003.

Miller is commited to safe, effective, dog-friendly training methods that work without ever compromising the all-important relationship between dogs and their human(s). Easy to understand, with a friendly and encouraging tone.

43. Cats and Their Claws

www.petamall.com

Scratching posts and nail clippers.

Book

Newkirk, Ingrid. *250 Things You Can Do to Make Your Cat Adore You.* New York: Fireside, 1998.

Other

Letting Animals Open Your Eyes and Heart to What's Important in Life
www.helpinganimals.com

44. How Adopting Beats the Pet Shop Approach

Your Local Animal Shelter

Look for them (there is probably more than one) under "Animal Control" in your Blue Pages, the name of your city SPCA and the name of your county SPCA, and the name of your city and county animal shelter or animal control. Also look in the Yellow Pages under "Animal Shelters" and "Humane Societies." And remember, if you can provide the love, patience, attention, veterinary care, and all else that is needed for a lifetime, save two animals, not one, from death row. They will keep each other company while you are at work, not a small consideration.

American Kennel Club

Look on their Web site, www.akc.org, under "Clubs" for a national directory of breed rescue groups to find compassionate fanciers of every dog from affenpinschers to Yorkshire terriers.

Greyhound Rescue

www.greyhoundrescue.com and www.greyhoundrescue.org for two of many affiliates.

To save dogs from going from the arduous racing life at the track to laboratories for heart and other research, this organization's affiliates rescue "retired" track greyhounds and find them loving homes. The dogs are gentle companions, but do love to have room to run.

45. Why It Pays to Cook for Cats and Dogs

Supplements

Try adding small amounts (a quarter teaspoon or less) of nutritional yeast, crushed vitamin C, marmite, vegemite, alfalfa, rosehips powder, garlic, and crushed vitamins to food and check to be sure your dog or cat still finds these health-boosted dishes palatable. Use a little bit of oil like olive, high-oleic (not regular) safflower, peanut, and sunflower or sesame for dry coats.

Solid Gold Health Products
El Cajon, California
1-800-364-4863
www.solidgoldhealth.com
Seameal, a great sea vegetable powder to add to food.

Vegecat & Vegedog
Troy, Montana
1-800-884-6262
www.veggiepet.com
This company provides excellent nutritional advice as well as products and recipes for puppies and kittens as well as for adult, geriatric, and nursing dogs and cats.

Commercial Vegan Dog and Cat Food

Below is a list of companies that sell vegan dog and/or cat food.

Boss Bars
PO Box 517
Patagonia, AZ 85624
888-207-9114
100 percent certified organic dog biscuits, four flavors, including wheat- and corn-free.

Evolution
287 E. 6th St., Suite 70
St. Paul, MN 55101
800-659-0104
Dog and cat kibble and canned food, ferret kibble, fish food.

Harbingers of a New Age
717 E. Missoula Ave.
Troy, MT 59935
406-295-4944

Vegecat, Vegekit, and Vegedog supplements, recipes for homemade vegan dog, cat, and kitten food, digestive enzymes, and acidifying nutritional yeast.

Natural Life Pet Products
1601 W. McKay
Frontenac, KS 66763
800-367-2391
Canned and kibble dog food.

Nature's Recipe
341 Bonnie Circle
Corona, CA 91720
800-843-4008
Canned and kibble dog food—call for closest distributor.

Pet Guard
PO Box 728
Orange Park, FL 32067-0728
800-874-3221
Canned dog food and biscuits, digestive enzymes.

Wow-Bow Distributors
13-B Lucon Dr.
Deer Park, NY 11729
516-254-6064
Canned and kibble dog food and biscuits, nutritional supplements.

Wysong Corporation
1880 N. Eastman Rd.
Midland, MT 48642
800-748-0188
Dog and cat kibble.

Organic Dog Snacks

Diamond Organics
www.diamondorganics.com

Handmade dog biscuits that include no soy, wheat, corn byproducts, artificial flavoring, or preservatives. Oatmeal, peanut and sun crunchies cookies.

Book

Pedan, James A. *Vegetarian Cats and Dogs*. Troy, Mont.: Harbingers of a New Age, 1995.
717 E. Missoula Ave.
Troy, MT 59935
406-295-4944

46. The Importance of Sterilization

Call your veterinarian, or if you are on a limited income or need to find a low-price service, call your local humane society or SPCA and ask if there are any spay/neuter clinics available to you.

Spay U.S.A.

www.spayusa.com
Referrals to low-cost spay programs nationally.

47. Incorporating Dog- and Cat-Friendly Elements into Your (and Their) Home

The Walker Catwalk

www.thecatshouse.com

Plans for this elaborate catwalk are available, with proceeds from their sale going to the National Cat Protection Society.

Flexi-Mat Corporation

773-376-5500
www.flexi-mat.com
Orthopedic beds for dogs, cat perches to attach to your windowsill.

Coolpetstuff.com

"Canine cooler" thermoregulating bed.

Happypaw.com

Dog beds, pillows, blankets, and travel accessories.

Doggie Day Care

www.petplace.com

National Animal Poison Control Center

Run by the University of Illinois, Champaign, A twenty-four-hour-a-day emergency advice help line.

Calls billed to a credit card: 800-548-2423

Calls billed to a telephone number: 900-680-0000

48. Letting Animals Open Your Eyes and Heart to What's Important in Life

www.helpinganimals.com

PART SIX: CHILDREN AND FAMILY

49. A Most Beautiful Wedding Reflecting Beautiful Values

Vegetarian Weddings Online

Donna Zeigfinger
7 Froude Circle
Cabin John, MD 20818
301-320-2892
www.vegetarianwedding.net
For all of your vegetarian wedding needs.

Bridal Dresses

Jasmine wedding gowns are available in most major department stores.
Morilee by Madeline Garner
www.morilee.com

Caterers

Everybody's Café & Caterer
905 Main St.
Stroudsburg, PA 18360
570-424-0896
Vegetarian and vegan catering in eastern Pennsylvania and New Jersey.

Chocolates

Krön Chocolatier
5300 Wisconsin Ave. NW
Washington, DC 20015
202-966-4946
www.krondc.com
Dark chocolates in many amazing shapes and sizes.

Party Buses

Northeast Transit Inc.
Scranton, Pennsylvania
570-347-8877
Party buses without leather seats for all occasions.

Shoes

Payless
877-474-6379
www.payless.com

This store is fantastic and has outlets everywhere. A myriad of styles from hiking boots to dancing shoes, and it offers bargains and discount deals all the time.

Mudd shoes

Available at many major stores, and discount Mudd shoes can be found at www.zappo.com.

Tuxedos

Erik Lawrence Classics Polyester one-button notch
www.4atux.com

This company also sells single-breasted, 100 percent synthetic "Chaplin" tuxedos (with a satin stripe and satin-covered buttons) on the Web for $159.

sales@4atux.com

Sarno & Son Tuxedos
Scranton, Pennsylvania
800-233-1404
www.sarnotux.com

Wedding Cakes

Lotus Cake Studio
PO Box 44292
Philadelphia, PA 19144
215-848-8770
Delivers to New York, Pennsylvania, and New Jersey.

50. Why Your Vegan Baby Will Smile All the Time

The Vegan Society
www.vegansociety.com

Veg Family
www.vegfamily.com

Physicians Committee for Responsible Medicine
www.pcrm.org

Veg Source
www.vegsource.com

Books

Attwood, Charles, M.D. *Dr. Attwood's Low-Fat Prescription for Kids*. New York: Penguin USA, 1995.

Klaper, Michael, M.D. *Pregnancy, Children, and the Vegan Diet*. Gentle World, 1988.

Pavlina, Erin. *Raising Vegan Children in a Non-Vegan World*. VegFamily.com, 2003. This is a handy book that answers parents' many questions, such as "What will you say to your pediatrician when he insists you feed your child milk?" and "How will you handle family members who insist upon offering your child meat at family events?"

Physicians Committee for Responsible Medicine. *Healthy Eating for Children*. Canada: Wiley Publishing, 2002.

Spock, Benjamin, M.D., and Steven J. Parker, M.D. *Dr. Spock's Baby and Child Care*. Pocket, 1985.

51. The Perfect Baby Shower Gift

Tofutti Brands Inc.
50 Jackson Dr.
Cranford, NJ 07016
908-272-2400
www.tofutti.com

Hain Celestial
734 Franklin Ave. #444
Garden City, NY 11530
www.hain-celestial.com

The PETA Catalog
Duncan the pink pig (and his friend Simon the cow).
www.petamall.com

52. Cultivating Kind Kids

Share the World
www.sharetheworld.com

53. Retirement Income Planning with an Annuity

PETA Guide to Health Charities
www.caringconsumer.com

Dame Judi Dench introduces this guide with the words: "Instead of hurting animals, cruelty-free health charities are helping people by funding programs that focus on direct care, clinical studies, community education, and prevention. They truly deserve our support."

PETA like most charities offers a free brochure containing minimum distribution tables. You can request "Giving Through Retirement Plans," as well as other booklets on charitable remainder trusts and living trusts and life insurance from PETA's Development Department, 501 Front Street, Norfolk, VA 23510 or by calling Special Gifts at 757-622-7382, or contact the charities you favor.

54. Making a Will: Leaving a Lasting Legacy

Book

Warda, Mark. *How to Make Your Own Will* (Legal Survival Guides). Naperville, Ill.: Sphinx Publishing: 2000.

PART SEVEN: BUSINESS AND EDUCATION

55. Respecting Life's Lessons in Class: Choosing a Superior Alternative to Dissection

Guide to Animals and the Dissection Industry

www.peta.org
Patricia Trostle
patriciat@peta.org
757-622-7382

Classroom Cutups

Narrated by Alicia Silverstone.
Available from peta.org.

The Alternatives in Education Database

From the Association of Veterinarians for Animal Rights and the Norwegian Inventory of Audiovisuals (NORINA), contains thousands of alternatives to animal use in education.

American Anti-Vivisection Society

AAVS's educational division is Animalearn.
800-729-2287
www.aars.org

Humane Society of the United States

Book

Balcombe, Jonathan, Ph.D. *Animals in Higher Education: Problems, Alternatives, and Recommendations.*

An in-depth overview of the entire issue.

National Anti-Vivisection Society
800-888-6287
www.navs.org

New England Anti-Vivisection Society
The NEAVS's educational division is the Ethical Science and Education Coalition (ESEC).
617-367-9143
www.neavs.org

56. Getting Through Medical School with a Clear Conscience

Physicians Committee for Responsible Medicine
202-686-2210
www.pcrm.org
Directing medical students and medical schools to computer models, CD ROMs, videos, interactive videodiscs, and more.

57. Becoming a Kind Veterinarian

The API Primate Sanctuary
c/o Animal Protection Institute
PO Box 22505
Sacramento, CA 95822
916-447-3085
www.api4animals.org
Snow monkey sanctuary in Dilley, Texas.

Association of Veterinarians for Animal Rights
PO Box 208
Davis, CA 95617-0208
530-759-8106
www.avar.org
Publishes a useful newsletter; provides support for veterinary students and veterinarians who view animals as worthy of respect; promotes alternatives to animal experiments and practices such as declawing.

Unexpected Wildlife Refuge
PO Box 765
Newfield, NJ 08344-0765
856-697-3541
www.animalplace.org
Beaver and wildlife sanctuary of Dr. Ned's childhood. Books available, donations appreciated.

58. Investing in Green and Animal-Friendly Companies

Coop America's Socially Responsible Mutual Funds
www.coopamerica.org

Trillium Asset Management
www.trilliuminvest.com

The Calvert Fund
www.calvert.com
Calvert's environmental standards are not as stringent as some, but it bills its program as "multidimensional, covering both stated policies and actual performance." Calvert does not invest in nuclear power plant operators, owners, or contractors because of concerns that the technology is not environmentally or economically viable. It also looks for companies that have implemented innovative pollution-prevention or natural-resource-protection programs with a view to sustainable development.

Rocky Mountain Humane Investment
800-962-1980
www.greeninvestment.com

Smith Barney
Socially responsible investment section.
800-345-3050
www.smithbarney.com

59. Making Your Workplace a Healthy, Helping Place

New Leaf Paper

www.newleafpaper.com

The mission of New Leaf Paper is to be the leading national source for environmentally responsible, economically sound paper for business uses.

Roaring Spring Paper Products

800-441-1653

Distributors of Banana and Coffee Paper products.

Paper Recycling Online

www.recycle.cc/freepaper.htm

The Gold Plan

www.pcrm.org

Meals for institutions and workplace cafeterias.

Dilberto

www.dilberto.com

Healthy frozen fast "office" foods.

American Red Cross

www.pleasegiveblood.org

For help with organizing blood drives.

Meals on Wheels Inc. of Tarrant County

817-336-0912, Ext. 14

Helping the hungry of all species.

Little Orphan Angels Animal Rescue

Keller, Texas

817-741-2386

www.littleorphanangels.org

PAWS

Seattle, Washington

516-364-PAWS

60. Doing Good Business: Embracing Ethical Ideas in the Marketplace

Carol House Furniture
Valley Park, MO 63088-1698
636-225-3666 or 529-0550

PART EIGHT: HEALTH

61. Trying to Keep Our Loved Ones Alive and Healthy a Little Longer

Dr. Dean Ornish's Lifestyle Program for Heart Disease Reversal

Preventive Medicine Research Institute
900 Bridgeway
Sausalito, CA 94965
415-332-2525
www.pmri.org

Dr. Ornish uses a regimen of diet, moderate exercise, stress management, and social support that allows patients to lose weight while eating more, to reduce or discontinue their medicines, and to diminish their chest pain.

The Physicians Committee for Responsible Medicine

5100 Wisconsin Ave. NW, Suite 400
Washington, DC 20016
202-686-2210
www.pcrm.org

Providing dietary information to reduce high blood pressure and the risk of various cancers, heart attack, and stroke, as well as to prevent and treat diabetes. A wide range of books and materials available on health issues.

Books and Video

Barnard, Neal, M.D. *Breaking the Food Seduction: The Hidden Reasons Behind Food Cravings . . . and 7 steps to End Them Naturally.* New York: St. Martin's Press, 2003.

Barnard, Neal, M.D. *Eat Right, Live Longer: Using the Natural Power of Foods to Age-Proof Your Body.* New York: Harmony Books, 1995. Also available on videotape.

62. Breast Cancer: Steps to Prevent It and Finding Friends and Support

SHARE

1501 Broadway
New York, NY 10036
866-891-2392
www.sharecancersupport.org

The Cancer Project

Physicians Committee for Responsible Medicine
212-686-2210
www.pcrm.org

McDougall Wellness Center

800-941-7111
office@drmcdougall.com

A ten-day live-in program conducted at the Flamingo Hotel and Resort in Santa Rosa, California, by Dr. John McDougall and his staff.

Books

Barnard, Neal, M.D. *Healthy Eating for Life to Prevent Cancer.* Wiley Publishing, 2002. Available from the Physicians Committee for Responsible Medicine, www.pcrm.org.

Goldberg, George, J.D. *Enough Already.* Goldberg is a former Harvard Law School professor who carefully researched the literature with his wife after her diagnosis.

Heidrich, Ruth E. *A Race for Life: A Diet and Exercise Program for Superfitness and Reversing the Aging Process* and *The Race for Life Cookbook.* Honolulu: Hawaii Health Publishers, 1990. Available from Hawaii Health Publishers, 1415 Victoria St. #11, Honolulu, HI 96822.

Keon, Joseph, Ph.D. *The Truth About Cancer: A Seven-Step Prevention Plan.* Larkspur, Ca.: Parissound Publishing, 2001.

Guide to Charities

PETA's free *"Guide to Charities That Do and Don't Test on Animals"* is available from peta.org or by calling 757-622-7382.

63. Three Little Steps That Can Make All the Difference If You Are a Diabetic

Messina, Mark, and Virginia Messina. *The Dietitian's Guide to Vegetarian Diets.* Boston: Jones and Bartlett Publishers, 2004. Available through the Physicians Committee for Responsible Medicine, www.pcrm.org.

64. Dealing with Menopause Without Hormone Replacement Therapy

Books

Barnard, Neal, M.D. *Healthy Eating for Life for Women.* Hoboken, N.J.: Wiley Publications, 2002. Available from the Physicians Committee for Responsible Medicine, www.pcrm.org.

Dean, Carolyn, and Phyllis Herman. *Menopause Naturally.* New York: McGraw-Hill, 1999.

Gilbert, Monique N. *Virtues of Soy: A Practical Health Guide and Cookbook.* Boca Raton, Fla.: Universal Publishers, 2000. www.virtuesofsoy.com

Gilbert, Monique N., B.Sc. *Coping with Menopause Naturally.* Available from www.geocities.com/virtuesofsoy/book-ordering. This helpful book begins: "The first thing to remember is that menopause is not a disease," and goes on to explain exactly what is happening as hormone levels change and how to deal most comfortably with what is happening to your body.

Help Line

1-800-KNOW-PMU is a help line for women interested in menopause solutions.

Synthetic Estrogen Drugs

These drugs are widely available and FDA-approved: Duramed (Cenetrin), Estrace, Estraderm.

65. Selecting a Lifesaver Health Charity

For a handy pocket reference, "PETA's Guide to Charities that Do and Don't Test on Animals," call PETA at 757-622-7382 or go to www.peta.org.

American Association on Mental Retardation

www.aamr.org

As a strong advocate for people with intellectual disabilities, the AAMR promotes progressive policies, research, and universal human rights. Established in 1876, the AAMR is the oldest and largest organization of professionals and others concerned about mental retardation and related disabilities.

Arthritis Trust of America

www.arthritistrust.org

Arthritis Trust of America provides physician referrals and educational materials to people suffering from rheumatoid diseases, and funds alternative, holistic, nonanimal medical research.

The Cancer Project

www.cancerproject.org

An innovative approach to a medical challenge, this charity aims first to prevent cancer. When cancer has been diagnosed, it works to improve survival. The Cancer Project distributes lifesaving information on reducing cancer risk and, when cancer has been diagnosed, how diet and other factors may help improve survival.

Caring for Children and Families with AIDS

www.4ccfa.org

Caring for Children and Families with AIDS (formerly Caring for Babies with AIDS) provides services to children and families affected by HIV/AIDS and other life-threatening diseases. Established in 1987, the CCFA also promotes public education and advocacy.

Children's Burn Foundation

www.childburn.org

The Children's Burn Foundation provides educational programs and financial assistance to meet the needs of severely burned children and their families and caregivers, including therapeutic and psychological care, and specialized educational and recreational services.

Easter Seals

www.easter-seals.org

Easter Seals provides services to children and adults with disabilities and other special needs, and support to their families. They have been providing therapy, job training, day care, and other services for more than eighty years.

National Children's Cancer Society

www.children-cancer.com

The National Children's Cancer Society provides financial support to children with cancer and their families, as well as support services and education and prevention programs.

Spinal Cord Injury Network International

www.spinalcordinjury.org

The Spinal Cord Injury Network International provides referral services and information to individuals with spinal cord injuries and their families. SCINI facilitates access to quality health care by providing a vital link to organizations and agencies offering information, assistance, and services for those with spinal cord injuries.

PART NINE: VOLUNTEERING AND GETTING ACTIVE

66. Joining the Animal Savings Club

The Animal Savings Club

www.animalsavingsclub.com

67. Sponsoring the Care of a Rescued Animal

The Donkey Sanctuary

Sidmouth, Devon, EX10 0NU

United Kingdom

011 44(0) 22 48398

www.thedonkeysanctuary.org.uk

This sanctuary has several facilities that take in rescued donkeys from work situations from several countries. Donkeys have a marvelous life and extremely good care and are able to enjoy the companionship of other donkeys as well as visitors. There are many donkeys up for sponsorship.

The Elephant Sanctuary

Hohenwald, Tennessee

www.elephants.com

Farm Sanctuary

PO Box 150
Watkins Glen, NY 14891
607-583-2225
www.farmsanctuary.org

For a minimum $15 donation a year, you will receive a certificate and information on the progress and personality of your adopted cow or calf.

Humane Farming Associations—Suwanna Ranch

PO Box 3577
San Rafael, CA 94912
415-771-CALF
www.hfa.org

HFA's Suwanna Ranch is the word's largest rescue facility created for abused farm animals.

New Life Parrot Rescue

PO Box 84
St. Neots
Huntingdon, Cambridgeshire, PE19 2LB
United Kingdom
011 44(0) 1480 390040
www.nlpr.demon.co.uk

For a minimum donation of 25 pounds sterling (about $40), you can choose from a host of bird "angels" who need your help. As an adopter you will receive a framed photograph and an information sheet on your new friend. Give a little more, and you will receive a pen, a mug, and address labels.

Ooh-Mah-Nee Farm Inc.

RD 1, Box 409
Hunker, PA 15639
724-755-2420
www.oohmahneefarm.org

Poplar Spring Animal Sanctuary

PO Box 507
Poolesville, MD 20837
301-428-8128
www.animalsanctuary.org

68. Recycling Everything—Including Yourself!

The Freecycle Network
www.freecycle.org

ScienceCare Anatomical
www.sciencecare.org
For information on body donations. Cremation is provided free of charge.

America Recycles Day
www.americarecyclesday.org
Organize a recycling event in your community through America Recycles Day.

Make-Stuff
www.make-stuff.com
Inventive ideas for reusing everything from film canisters to garden hoses.

69. How to Donate an Unwanted Fur

Send furs with your name, address, and an appraisal if you have one, to:
PETA Development Department
501 Front St.
Norfolk, VA 23510
757-622-7382

Life for Relief and Development
www.lifeusa.org

Faux Fur Coats
Fabulous Furs
www.fabulousfurs.com
Faux fur panchos, gloves, jackets, coats, and throws.

Angie's Realm
www.angiesrealm.com
Imitation mink and other faux fur.

70. Your Opinion Counts: Writing a Letter or Two

PETA's Guide to Letter Writing offers great tips on how to write brief but powerful letters to the editor, to businesses, and to legislators that will allow you to make your voice count and spread your message to thousands! To get your free guide call PETA at 757-622-7382 or go to www.peta.org.

71. Speaking Out: Using Your Voice for Social Change

Toastmasters International

www.toastmasters.org

This is a great confidence builder and puts you among others who have no public speaking experience.

72. Making a Library Donation

Ask your local public libraries and public school libraries if they will accept book donations. Many will and are grateful for them. If you don't have books lying around to give, ask what books they want and buy one or more for them.

WBVS Book Project

World Bank project that provides donated books to students in the developing world. Books can be delivered weekdays or sent to WBVS, 1775 G Street NW., Washington, DC 20433, but a call or e-mail is required first to 202-473-8960 or wproject@worldbank.org.

The Prison Book Project

Keeps prisoners' minds occupied and is always in need of thesauruses and dictionaries; books in Spanish; books about and by Africans, Latinos, and Native Americans; and art books, science fiction, and books on ethical and spiritual issues.

PO Box 396
Amherst, MA 01004
info@prisonbooks.org

Amazon.com

Puts donated books into children's hands by donating a portion of your purchase price to Page Ahead. Page Ahead has a wish list, too.

www.amazon.com

PETA Online Bookstore

A great resource for books on everything from companion-animal care to vegetarian and vegan cooking. Some great children's books are also available.

www.petabookstore.com

73. Community Volunteering and Leading by Example

PETA Animal Rights Weekend Warrior Cards

www.petacatalog.com

The cards can be purchased for $12.95 per pack.

Also check PETA's action hotline at 757-622-7382 or Web site at www.peta.org for the latest letters that need writing and calls that need to be made to stop abuses.

74. Memorializing a Loved One

PETA's Tree of Life

c/o Scott Van Valkenburg 757-962-8374

True Friends Memorial

www.tfmemorial.org

PART TEN: CELEBRATIONS

75. Thanksgiving: The Harvest Festival

Tofurky

www.tofurky.com

Book

Davis, Karen. *More than a Meal: The Turkey in Myth, Ritual and Reality.* New York: Lantern Books, 2001.

Available from www.upc.com

76. A Christmas Dinner Fit for Good King Wenceslas

Saint Jude's Ranch Card Reycling

100 St. Jude S., PO Box 60100

Boulder City, NV 89006

This nonprofit youth home gratefully receives and reuses whole Christmas cards or just the fronts to them. You can send them cheaply at library rate via the U.S. Postal Service.

Monin Organic Caramel Soy Latte

Perfect for the holidays and cozy nights by the fire. Monin has five certified organic syrups to add to coffee, hot chocolate, steamed soy milk, and even baked goods. Available in caramel, chocolate, hazelnut, raspberry, and vanilla.

727-461-3033

www.monin.com

Vegan Marshmallows

And those hot chocolate drinks are even more perfect when topped with vegan marshmallows! Real ones are made from gelatin, the ugly ooze that emanates from animals' hooves, but veganessentials.com (866-88-VEGAN) sells fluffy white vegan marshmallows that you can eat straight from the bag, pop on top of warming drinks, or roast over the fire.

Ready-Made Savory Roast by Mail

Wellington Native Foods (www.nativefoods.com). An elegant puff pastry filled with savory native seitan, tangerine yams, cranberry chestnut stuffing, ruby red chard, and caramelized onions, with shallot mushroom gravy on the side. Comes frozen and you bake it. Ready in an hour. Serves six generously.

77. A Special Passover: Celebrating Freedom with a Vegan Seder

Books

Atlas, Nava. *Vegetarian Celebrations.* Boston: Little, Brown, 1990.

Contains menus for an Ashkenazic Seder and a Sephardic Seder. Some, but not all, of the recipes contain eggs and/or dairy.

Berkoff, Nancy. *Vegan Passover Recipes.* Baltimore, Md.: Vegetarian Resource Group.

$6. Available from the Vegetarian Resource Group
PO Box 1463, Dept. IN
Baltimore, MD 21203
410-366-VEGE
www.vrg.org

Contains thirty-four delicious Passover dishes including Winter Squash with Apricot Stuffing, Apple-and-Herb-Stuffed Mushrooms, Zucchini/Potato Kugel, and Cinnamon Matzo Balls.

Friedman, Rose. *Jewish Vegetarian Cooking.* Lanham, Md.: National Book Network, 1993.

Contains a Passover section with lacto-ovo recipes.

Kalechofsky, Roberta. *Haggadah for the Liberated Lamb.* Marblehead, Mass.: Micah Publications, 1988.

255 Humphrey St.
Marblehead, MA 01945

This vegetarian, gender-neutral Haggadah is available in a number of formats from Micah Publications. The recipes it contains are lacto-ovo.

Kalechofsky, Roberta. *The Vegetarian Pesach Cookbook.* Marblehead, Mass.: Micah Publications, 2002.

$13. Available from Micah Publications
255 Humphrey St.
Marblehead, MA 01945
617-631-7601
www.micahbooks.com

This cookbook offers delicious vegetarian recipes, from soup to nuts, for the Pesach week. No animal products.

Katzen, Molly. *Still Life with Menu.* Berkeley, Calif.: Ten Speed Press, 1994.

Contains a menu for a lacto-ovo seder.

Wasserman, Debra. *No Cholesterol Passover Recipes*. Baltimore, Md.: Vegetarian Resource Group, 1995.

$8.95. Available from the Vegetarian Resource Group
PO Box 1463, Dept IN
Baltimore, MD 21203
410-366-VEGE
www.vrg.org

Contains more than one hundred vegan Passover dishes, including eggless blintzes, carrot "cream" soup, and apple latkes.

Other

The Vegetarian Resource Group (VRG)

PO Box 1463, Dept. IN
Baltimore, MD 21203
410-366-VEGE
www.vrg.org

The VRG is a nonprofit organization dedicated to educating the public on vegetarianism and the interrelated issues of health, nutrition, ecology, ethics, and world hunger.

Concern for Helping Animals in Israel (CHAI)

USA Office
PO Box 3341
Alexandria, VA 22302
703-658-9650
www.chai-online.org/index.htm

CHAI is an international organization committed to improving the living conditions of all animals in Israel through education, activism, and program development.

Jewish Veg

www.jewishveg.com/index.html

Jewish Veg is a comprehensive Web site with academic articles, resources, and links relating to all facets of Judaism and vegetarianism.

Jews for Animal Rights

255 Humphrey St.
Marblehead, MA 01945
www.micahbooks.com/jar.html

Jews for Animal Rights promotes vegetarianism, the insights of preventive medicine, alternatives to animal research, community action programs, discussion groups, educational programs, and speakers.

The Jewish Vegetarian and Ecological Society

853/5 Finchley Road
London, England
NW11 8LX
44 0181 455 0692
easyweb.easynet.co.uk/~bmjjhr/jvs.htm

The Jewish Vegetarian and Ecological Society (JVS) is an international group based in London that promotes vegetarianism within the Judaic tradition, and explores the relationship between Judaism, dietary laws, and vegetarianism.

JewishVegan.com

www.jewishvegan.com

JewishVegan.com has extensive resources on Judaism and vegetarianism and also provides information and links to Jewish vegetarian groups and social events.

78. A Feast for Ramadan or Every Day

Islamic Concern

www.islamicconcern.org

Book

Rosen, Steven. *Food for the Spirit: Vegetarianism and the World Religions.* Philadelphia, PA: Bala Books, 1987.

INDEX